Gender and Child Protection

Gender and Child Protection

Jonathan Scourfield

Consultant Editor: Jo Campling

© Jonathan Scourfield 2003

All rights reserved. No reproduction, copy or transmission of this publication may be made without written permission.

No paragraph of this publication may be reproduced, copied or transmitted save with written permission or in accordance with the provisions of the Copyright, Designs and Patents Act 1988, or under the terms of any licence permitting limited copying issued by the Copyright Licensing Agency, 90 Tottenham Court Road, London W1T 4LP.

Any person who does any unauthorised act in relation to this publication may be liable to criminal prosecution and civil claims for damages.

The author has asserted his right to be identified as the author of this work in accordance with the Copyright, Designs and Patents Act 1988.

First published 2003 by
PALGRAVE MACMILLAN
Houndmills, Basingstoke, Hampshire RG21 6XS and
175 Fifth Avenue, New York, N.Y. 10010
Companies and representatives throughout the world

PALGRAVE MACMILLAN is the global academic imprint of the Palgrave Macmillan division of St. Martin's Press, LLC and of Palgrave Macmillan Ltd. Macmillan® is a registered trademark in the United States, United Kingdom and other countries. Palgrave is a registered trademark in the European Union and other countries.

ISBN 0–333–94979–X paperback

This book is printed on paper suitable for recycling and made from fully managed and sustained forest sources.

A catalogue record for this book is available from the British Library.

Library of Congress Cataloging-in-Publication Data
Scourfield, Jonathan, 1966–
   Gender and child protection / Jonathan Scourfield; consultant
   editor, Jo Campling.
      p. cm.
   Includes bibliographical references and index.
   ISBN 0–333–94979–X (pbk.)
   1. Child welfare. 2. Child abuse. 3. Children—Services for.
   4. Social work with children. 5. Family social work. I. Title.

   HV713 .S375 2002
   362.7—dc21
                                                      2002072308

10   9   8   7   6   5   4   3   2   1
12 11 10 09 08 07 06 05 04 03

Printed in China

Contents

v

Acknowledgements

My first acknowledgement has to be to the social workers who let me eavesdrop on their work. They were always welcoming and gave generously of their time. Throughout the research process I relied on the intellectual guidance of Amanda Coffey and Ian Welsh as PhD supervisors. Thanks to them for their brave attempts to turn me into a sociologist. I also relied on Sally Holland for ongoing advice and consultation on the research. I am grateful to Joanna Wilkes for transcribing interviews. Ian Shaw gave helpful comments on Chapter 7 and has more generally supported my career development as a mentor. Ian Butler and Andy Pithouse helped me with research access. Andy, along with Nigel Parton, went on to make me think hard about what I was doing by examining the PhD that this book draws on. Thanks also to Jo Campling and Catherine Gray for their encouragement and support.

In terms of friends and family, I should mention Peter Shiner who forced me to think hard about how to justify what I was doing. Sally has always been supportive in so many ways, as have my parents. My parallel life has been with Annie and Gareth, and thanks to them for taking my mind off academic work.

Some of the material in the book has already appeared in the following places: *Sociological Review*, *British Journal of Social Work*, *Child and Family Social Work*, *Men and Masculinities*, *Qualitative Social Work* and 'Interviewing interviewers and knowing about knowledge' in Shaw, I. and Gould, N. (2001) *Qualitative Research in Social Work* (London, Sage). I should like to thank the editorial boards of these journals and the editors of the book for their permission to reproduce the material here.

1

Introduction

I find the men, er, a lot of macho about the men – the men are arrogant, very opinionated. . . . I don't deal with the men in a lot of cases, mainly with the wives, but that's often the case in any area, as men are less susceptible to social work. (a social worker quoted in Pithouse, 1998: 134)

I had no worries about the difficulties of translating theory into practice; I was not suffering from overload or burn-out common to social workers who had been any length of time in the work; and I received excellent support from the team and allied agencies . . . It was with some confidence, therefore, that I began retrospective analysis into the outcomes of my investigations and interventions for these families. This confidence quickly gave way to dismay as I discovered that the progress of the families through the child protection system was depressingly familiar and predictable. Despite all the favourable circumstances in which I was practising, I had unconsciously operated all the filters which serve to legitimate male authority over women. (Milner, 1993: 56–7)

The author of the second of these excerpts, Judith Milner, is describing her experience of doing child protection social work as a feminist with a well-developed knowledge base in the relevant research and social scientific theory. She found that despite her feminist perspective on her job, she had persisted in working in such a way as to make mothers responsible for protecting children, even where it was clearly men (as fathers or as mothers' partners) who were the original cause for concern. She asks 'how . . . is it that I spent most of my time . . . working with mothers, particularly single mothers and ignoring fathers?' (Milner, 1993: 48–9). She seems genuinely surprised that a feminist consciousness did not change her practice. It is this persistence of gender bias in child protection social work, despite the increasing

1

influence of anti-oppressive rhetoric in the profession, which this book sets out to explore.

The book is about how the work of child protection gets done, and should therefore, I hope, be relevant to practitioners as well as to students of gender relations on a variety of social science courses. A crude attempt to offer a simplistic, naive or idealised checklist of action would not be relevant to social work practice in this complex area. I believe, however, that reflections rooted in observation of the everyday dilemmas and challenges of actual practitioners in an actual social work office will be more relevant and helpful for people who have to do the job of child protection in the real world. The term 'evidence-based practice' tends to be used with reference to approaches whose effectiveness has been tested in quantitative research studies: the 'empirical practice movement' (Reid and Zettergren, 1999). The evidence presented in this book is of a very different kind. It is qualitative, and does not aim to prescribe effective practice. The book is, however, based on evidence of social work practice. The discussions throughout the book, and in the concluding chapter in particular, which draw out the potential implications of this qualitative research for practitioners, could therefore be described as dealing with 'evidence for practice' (Shaw, 1999).

Social work qualifications at all levels demand linkage of theory with examples from practice. Social workers often find this difficult to do, and this book is intended to aid the process of linking theory with practice. It refers to relevant theories, and is *all about practice* in a way that 'how to' textbooks tend not to be. It describes in detail the daily talk and recording of childcare social workers. It is grounded in the everyday life of a typical social work office. Admittedly this grounding was gained from research rather than practice, but the advantage the researcher has over the practitioner is that of time and distance for reflection. Cheetham and Deakin (1997: 440) have commented that published work on anti-oppressive social work practice has a tendency to be 'assertive rather than analytical, and lacking robust theoretical and conceptual underpinning'. This book attempts to respond to these words, in recording what social workers say and write in everyday practice, and analysing these in relation to some relevant aspects of social theory. Whilst reflecting on gender issues is the book's rationale, inevitably this requires attention to other issues of power and oppression – class, ethnicity, sexuality, the construction of children – and a wide range of social science research and theory.

I believe the research featured in this book can claim relevance to practice, not in the crude sense that it will conclude with a checklist for good practice, but in the sense that the reflections are rooted in observation of practitioners at work. I equally believe that an emphasis on the construction of gender in the culture of the social work office is justified. As Pithouse and Williamson argue:

> engaging users in contemporary welfare cannot be grasped analytically without recourse to the ways in which welfare workers routinely 'construct' users through formal theory, policy, practice wisdom, practice evaluation, and their own values. (Pithouse and Williamson, 1997: xii–xiii)

Parton (1996) makes a similar argument about child protection specifically. In discussing the limitations of the Department of Health commissioned studies (Dartington Social Research Unit, 1995), he has called for qualitative research into child protection as *work*: how decisions take the form they do and how practitioners make sense of child abuse in the day-to-day routines of practice.

Social work and the scrutiny of mothering

> I felt that they were accusing me and I wasn't the abuser, my husband was. (a mother interviewed by Thoburn et al., 1995: 54)

Social work services are responsible for helping children in need and protecting children who are likely to suffer significant harm. They work both with families who have requested help and with those who have not. As noted above, many commentators have discussed the tendency for social workers to focus almost exclusively on engaging with women in situations where there are also men around in the home. Farmer and Owen's study of child protection practice (1995, 1998) has showed that in two-parent families, the focus of intervention tended to switch from the abusing father-figure to the mother and to general childcare and support. O'Hagan and Dillenburger (1995) label this process 'the abuse of women by avoiding men'. They observe that this process is documented, either explicitly or implicitly, in the large majority of the high-profile child death inquiries, including those into the deaths of Maria Colwell (Department of Health and Social Security, 1974), Jasmine Beckford (Brent, 1985), Kimberly

Carlile (Greenwich, 1987), Tyra Henry (Lambeth, 1987) and Sukina Hammond (Bridge Child Care Consultancy, 1991). The process is also evident from the research studies that were summarised by the UK Department of Health's *Messages from Research* document (Dartington Social Research Unit, 1995). Ryan (2000) has published a retrospective analysis of these research projects which focuses on questions of gender.

Various reasons for this process of attention switching from men to women are discussed in the social work literature. A dominant idea is that abusive men aggressively resist any intervention, and social workers avoid confronting them out of fear (Milner, 1993). My research sets aside questions of parental behaviour, and instead examines what social workers believe about their men and women clients, and how they respond to them. There does not seem to have been any qualitative study of this aspect of gender in child protection. This is a gap that this research hopes to fill. I conducted an ethnographic study of a childcare social work team in the UK. The research focused on the ways in which social workers construct their adult clients as gendered, in relation to child protection cases in particular.

This failure to engage men is not usually seen in the social work literature as an issue of injustice to men, but rather as an injustice to women. It is not usually claimed that men are missing out on a supportive service (social work as empowerment, or even as welfare provision), but rather that women are bearing the brunt of state scrutiny of parenting. This emphasis perhaps reflects the current investigative climate of child and family social work (Dartington Social Research Unit, 1995) and the critiques of social casework as based on social control (for example, Bailey and Brake, 1974).

Gendered practice in child protection work has been the subject of a great deal of published commentary. Much of this commentary is grounded in the authors' practice experience and review of relevant literature (for example, Parton and Parton, 1989; Milner, 1993; O'Hagan and Dillenberger, 1995; Featherstone and Trinder, 1997; Daniel and Taylor, 1999; Krane and Davies, 2000; Ryan, 2000; Turney, 2000). Where commentary is rooted in the authors' empirical research in social service organisations, discussion of gender issues often arises in the course of some more general study of the child protection process (for example, Farmer and Owen, 1995; Parton et al., 1997). This inevitably limits the extent to which gender dimensions can be explored in depth. Of the published empirical research that sets out specifically to tackle gender issues in child protection work, two are historical (Gordon, 1988; Tice, 1998) and two others based on the views of mothers who have been clients of social workers (Hooper, 1992a; Croghan and Miell, 1998). Edwards's research (1998) is concerned with how professionals construct clients as gendered, but in the context of more general services for families rather than child protection services specifically. All this published work is very interesting in different respects. However, there is arguably a gap in this literature for a detailed study of the construction of gender in the occupational culture of a social work team engaged in the child protection process. The nearest thing to this in existing literature is Swift's work (1995), which concentrated on gender issues but with specific reference to the construction of the category of 'child neglect', rather than also including institutional categories of 'abuse' to allow consideration of child protection more generally. The aim of this book is to build on this work, by presenting a qualitative study of one social work team, in order to explore the construction of gender in all categories of child protection work, the analysis of which may generate some helpful ideas about the problem.

There are various aspects of gender in child protection work that the book does not concentrate on. There is no first-hand evidence of the views or behaviour of men, women or children who receive services – 'clients', as they are called by the social workers I studied. There will be no discussion of any distinction between men and women social workers in the book. In general I found that occupational culture overrides differences in the gender identities of the workers. Where a gender discourse has power in the workplace culture, it seems to affect the work of men and women alike. Neither is there much discussion of the construction of boys and girls by social workers because, as Chapter 3 explains, I found boys and girls to be constructed as equally vulnerable, whereas adult men and women clients are strongly differentiated by social workers. These aspects that the book does not focus on strongly will nonetheless appear at various points, and some relevant existing research is summarised in the next chapter.

My starting point

My interest in the topic stems from an ongoing interest in social work with men (Scourfield, 1998; Scourfield and Dobash, 1999) and from my encounters with childcare social workers during my time as a practitioner (albeit not in a childcare job), as well as from the experience of friends and family who have worked in child protection roles. In researching this topic, I am motivated by the belief that the failure to engage men should be seen as a problem. An assumption on the part of social workers that women will do most of the caring for children might be expected within a society that is structured according to this assumption. It might also be a realistic reflection of the division of labour in client families. The failure to engage men perhaps goes beyond this, though, since even where men are identified as abusers, it is often women whose parenting is scrutinised.

The relevance of the study to considerations of justice perhaps needs further explanation. The research set out to deconstruct the occupational culture of social work and explore the gendering of the child protection process. This exploration was not intended to be an evaluation in the sense of commenting on whether or not the social workers were constructing gender 'correctly'. I took for granted that organisational life is suffused with gender (Witz and Savage, 1992), and aimed to study the detail of this in the social work office through ethnography. The outcome of the research will not be a crude list of things that social workers need to change. At the same time, such research cannot be value-free. Inevitably the researcher brings assumptions which frame the design and the process, and a reflexive approach demands that these should be made explicit. In the case of this research, there are inherent assumptions about both gender and statutory childcare.

Fox Harding (1997) has outlined the main paradigms in considerations of childcare policy: laissez-faire and patriarchy, state paternalism and child protection, the modern defence of the birth family and parents' rights, and children's rights and child liberation. Inevitably, researchers position themselves somewhere on this continuum. The issue that inspired my research was the concentration of child protection investigation and intervention on women, as an issue of justice to women in that they bear the brunt of scrutiny, rather than as an injustice to men because they are left out. In fact, as the material that follows will show, the picture is a little more complex than that. This is, though, a concern about parents' rights. That is not to say, of course, that children's rights have not been an issue in the research. It is to choose to study aspects of the system that put pressure on women as parents or carers rather than on men.

All those who comment on the child protection system should be open about their family ideology. It simply begs too many questions to claim to be child-centred. Not all children express a clear view on the question of with whom they want to live. Even when they do, we know from existing research (for example, Butler and Williamson, 1994) that social workers do not necessarily follow children's stated wishes, taking the view that children do not always know what is best for their welfare. Therefore we have to decide whether we are inclined towards the view that children are basically better off with birth parents or whether we think families of origin are often so damaging to children that they will be better off, at least in the long term, with trained carers who have a commitment to child-rearing and experience of vulnerable children.

As well as acknowledging my own value base, I have to accept that, realistically, some of the findings may be read by some people as implying criticism because these issues are politically highly charged in the context of the anti-discriminatory discourse of the last couple of decades. However, the research is not, to repeat the assertion above, a straightforward evaluation of social work practice. Rather, the aim is to explore how social workers understand men and women as parents, partners, carers or abusers.

The broad research question, then, is how and why is child protection work gendered? More specifically, I have chosen to look for the answer in the occupational culture of the social work office. This warrants detailed examination because, despite the occupational culture being influenced by anti-discriminatory social work discourse (see, for example, Thompson, 1997), there still seems to be a concentration on women and little work with men.

The prime focus is on parent clients as gendered through the occupational discourses of child protection social work. I will examine the various gendered discourses that impact on child protection work: discourses of family law, childhood, class and respectability, child abuse and neglect, and social work. Inevitably, a qualitative study of this kind feeds into major theoretical debates, and raises bigger questions than those it immediately set out to answer. This topic raises questions about current constructions of family life: childhood and child abuse; gender, class and sexuality; the transmission of knowledge; and the nature of the gender order.

The ethnographic research that informs the book was conducted during 1997 in a local authority children and families team in the UK, 'the Uplands'. The population covered by the Uplands team, their 'patch', was founded in the last century around a specific industry that barely now exists, except in its cultural significance. It is an area of social deprivation according to all the standard indices. I spent three months based in the social work team's office. Because of sensitivity of access I did not observe worker–client interaction, but instead observed collegial talk around the office, conducted an in-depth interview with each team member and analysed in detail the files on all cases on the child protection register. Opportunities for observation included routine case discussion between colleagues in the office, more formal case discussion in individual supervisions with the team manager, telephone conversations with clients and other professionals, and regular team meetings. The data were analysed according to the principles of grounded theory (Strauss, 1987), and the validity of emerging themes was checked through constant comparisons across the data. A computer software package, NUD*IST 4.0, was used to facilitate the coding of data. When presenting data, from Chapter 3 onwards, I use pseudonyms throughout for all social workers, clients and locations.

The social work team comprised six women and three men social workers, and a woman team manager, all of whom were white. The population of the Uplands is 99 per cent white, and, during the fieldwork, all the child protection cases I studied were white, poor, working-class families. The picture of the construction of clients is, therefore, a partial one. A clientele of poor working-class families is typical of child protection practice (Lindsay, 1994), but an all-white research setting is only typical of this geographical region. In such a setting, research cannot explore constructions of people of colour which are a crucial dimension to the processing of child abuse in multi-ethnic districts. Neither are there any data on representations of lesbians, gay men or disabled people, because all the clients referred to during the fieldwork were able-bodied and ostensibly heterosexual.

Research findings from a case study can obviously not be generalised in the crude sense that the social phenomena observed would be straightforwardly replicated in a similar setting elsewhere. Rather, I would hope that my ethnographic research might highlight dominant discourses of gender and clienthood in a specific social work setting. It is likely that these findings will reflect the dominant discourses in the occupational culture of childcare work, particularly since there is a common professional training, legislation and increasing central government guidance. Wattam, in discussing research on child protection decision-making, writes that practitioners ... do not begin from a standpoint of knowing that only a few (local) people will understand what it is they are saying and will see it in the same way. Rather, they utilise 'rules' that are shared in common in much the same way as the rules of language are. That the 'rules' or methods are generalisable, is their rationale for use. (Wattam, 1992: 13–14)

It has been claimed, for example in the inquiry into the death of the child Tyra Henry (Lambeth, 1987), that there can be idiosyncratic local office cultures in social services. However, Gordon and Gibbons' recent survey (1998) of 1,752 referrals in eight English authorities found that indicators of child and family vulnerability were more important than local area in explaining selection for initial child protection conference and placement on registers, which suggests a certain common culture of constructing child abuse. To make some defence against the possibility of a partial perspective from an unusual local office culture, I conducted 'pilot' interviews in another local authority, which I have also drawn on in the analysis presented in the chapters that follow. Considerably more detail on methodology and the research process can be found in Scourfield (1999).

Social work is a broad field, informed by several disciplines, including sociology, psychology, philosophy and politics. I should also acknowledge where the book fits within this broad spectrum. It is largely based on sociological insights. A sociological understanding of gender relations and organisational culture underpins much of the material and the empirical research that is discussed is sociological research.

The book's structure

Before describing in the next chapter the current policy and theory context that needs to be understood when considering gender issues in child protection work, I will outline the structure of the rest of the book:

● *Chapter 2* will outline the contemporary policy context of child protection and summarise key debates about gender, in particular looking at gender in social work practice. This chapter will also explain my use of the concepts of social construction and occupational culture and summarise ideas about the family and social control.

- *Chapter 3* provides further context for the discussion on the construction of gender by highlighting some of the concepts that are central to the construction of 'clienthood' in child protection work. These are the dominant constructions of childhood, class, respectability and the social work 'patch', and the coercive tone of interventions.
- *Chapters 4 and 5* in some respects form a central axis to the book. They offer overviews of the gendered discourse of child protection work, Chapter 4 focusing on constructions of women and Chapter 5 on constructions of men.
- *Chapter 6* offers a specific example of gendered practice by looking at how particular child protection problems are given priority in social services departments. The example discussed is that of child neglect.
- *Chapter 7* looks at the connection between gendered discourse in child protection and the knowledge and value base of social work. As well as introducing new data, this chapter begins a process of reflecting back on previous chapters.
- This process of reflection on research findings is continued in *Chapter 8*, which attempts to draw some theoretical conclusions from the study.
- This is followed by some concluding comments (*Chapter 9*) on the relevance of the study to social work practitioners. There will be some general comment on the relevance of qualitative research to social work practice, and a summary of messages for practice, both practical and theoretical.

2

Child protection, gender and social work

The aim of this chapter is to prepare the ground for the rest of the book by outlining the policy context and the theoretical perspectives that are drawn upon in what follows. The first section of the chapter briefly explains how the social control of the family has developed, with reference to the work of Foucault and Donzelot. The next section then deals with the policy context of contemporary child protection practice, including an overview of the commentary in the social work literature on gender issues in child protection. The rest of the chapter then sets out the book's central theoretical assumptions, through discussion of gender relations, social constructionism and occupational culture. I begin by locating child protection work in its historical and sociological context.

The family and social control

It is important to understand the contemporary child protection system in the light of the broader conceptualising of the state control of family life in the sociological literature; theorising that has not centred on gender, although encompassing important gender dimensions. This involves considering the development, at the end of the last century, of professional intervention in families, with particular reference to the important work of Foucault and Donzelot.

Foucault's *Discipline and Punish* (1977) charts the transition in penal practice in the last century from the tortures, executions and public confessions of the Classical Age to the modern system of imprisonment and surveillance. He describes how the burgeoning population of industrialising societies provoked fears about the social order, resulting in new measures of social control that he refers to as 'bio-politics';

regulation of the health, welfare and productivity of individual bodies. New forms of knowledge provided discourses for technologies of intervention. Foucault describes the combined forces of these new human sciences (medicine, psychiatry, psychology, criminology) as the 'psy' complex. This powerful discourse created a regulatory framework of 'normalisation'; the spread of specific norms of living.

Donzelot's *The Policing of Families* (1980) relates more specifically to the development of social work. He writes of the birth, in the last century, of the 'social', a discourse that developed in the space between the family (the private sphere) and the state (the public sphere). The development of the 'social' saw philanthropists, later succeeded by social workers, becoming involved in the judicial process in relation to children. These social workers' contact with families was based on moralisation, normalisation and coercive intervention (the 'tutelary complex'). Moralisation is the use of material resources to enable people to overcome moral failure. Normalisation can take place following entry to the family via complaints, which are usually made by women about men. All these elements, moralisation, normalisation and coercive intervention, are alive and well in contemporary child welfare work.

Parton (1998), drawing on Donzelot and Foucault, reminds us that child welfare both interrelates with and is dependent upon a number of other more established discourses, particularly law, health, psychiatry and education. It is inherently ambiguous, filling the gap between civil society, with its allegiance to families, and the state's responsibilities. He writes that social work is

> a compromise between the early liberal ideas of unhindered private philanthropy and the vision of the all-pervasive and all-encompassing police or socialist state which would take responsibility for everyone's needs and hence undermine the responsibility and role of the family. (Parton, 1998: 10)

Philp (1979), writing of social work's origins in the late nineteenth century, observes that it emerged in the space between poverty and wealth. Charity work represented the humanity of the privileged to the poor and the essential 'goodness' of the poor to the privileged. Social work came to occupy 'the space between the respectable and deviant' (p. 96).

There are some explicitly gendered dimensions to the work of Foucault and Donzelot. Donzelot (1980) describes a process of 'government through the family'. In the last century the medical profession enlisted women as accomplices in the disciplining of the family: 'the woman was brought out of the convent so that she would bring the man out of the cabaret' (p. 40). As Stenson (1993) points out, this focus on the mother was embarked upon in the hope that she would restrain and civilise poor boys and men – still the most recalcitrant and troublesome threats to a liberal social order. Foucault (1984) has described a process he calls the hysterisation of women's bodies, beginning in the last century, which included the giving to women of the biologico-moral responsibility of motherhood. This process saw the 'creation' of the 'Mother'.

It is important to understand the historical origins of the social welfare systems we see today, and of course theoretical insights from historical research can have contemporary relevance. However, it is also the case that much has changed since the days of the early penal and welfare systems described by Foucault and Donzelot. The next section of the chapter therefore brings us up to date by mapping some of the most crucial influences on contemporary child protection work.

Child protection policy and practice

Child protection is one of the most contested areas of social policy. The state sets out to intervene in some families to protect vulnerable children, whilst giving due regard to the privacy of families in general. This task is an inherently controversial one, and social services departments are often accused of failure and held up to public scrutiny through well-publicised inquiries (Parton, 1991). This has happened both because social workers are seen to have not intervened enough (the inquiries into the deaths of Jasmine Beckford, Kimberley Carlile and Ricky Neave, for example) and because they are seen to have intervened too much (the inquiries into child abuse investigations in Cleveland, Rochdale and Orkney).

In this part of the chapter I outline some key aspects of the social and political configuration of contemporary child protection work. I begin with mention of the increasing recognition that child abuse is socially constructed. I then move on to map the late twentieth-century shift from child welfare to child protection, whilst emphasising that there is still disagreement among researchers (depending on their perspectives) as to whether intervention should be characterised as coercive or supportive. Next I highlight the preoccupation with risk across the personal social services, but in work with children and families in particular. Finally I make the connection between the current state of child protection and the dominance of New Right ideology.

Not surprisingly, child protection has attracted a great deal of comment and research from the academic world. Much of this has been an evaluation of the effectiveness of the system (for example, DHSS, 1985; DH, 1991; Dartington Social Research Unit, 1995). There has also been some attention given to the social construction of child abuse. Wattam (1996) points out that this perspective gained official recognition in the influential Department of Health document *Messages from Research*. This document asserts that 'Society continually reconstructs definitions of maltreatment which sanction intervention' (Dartington Social Research Unit, 1995: 15). Definitions of child abuse are so contested that Corby (2000) claims the only definition possible is that of a decision reached by a group of professionals after considering the circumstances of a child. Attention to the social construction of child abuse has included some very interesting qualitative research into the culture of the social work office and the organisational processes through which cases are constructed and decisions made about children (Wattam, 1992; Dingwall et al., 1995; Hall, 1997; Parton et al., 1997; White, 1997a; Pithouse, 1998). The chapters that follow will make reference to some of these studies.

It is generally agreed that there has been a shift in emphasis from child welfare to child protection in the UK over the last twenty-five or so years (Parker, 1995; Otway, 1996). By the time the Department of Health research studies were published in 1995 (Dartington Social Research Unit, 1995), the predominant concern was 'dangerous families'. In particular, sexual abuse had become a major target of investigation (Parton et al., 1997). The conclusion of the Department of Health, in their summary of twenty research studies, was that 'too much of the work undertaken comes under the banner of child protection' (Dartington Social Research Unit, 1995: 54). This view was based strongly on Gibbons et al.'s research (1995) which found that six out of seven children referred to the child protection system were filtered out of it without needing to be placed on a child protection register, and that a high proportion of cases received neither protection nor any other family support service.

There are different trends in some European countries. Pringle (1998a) characterises the French and German child welfare systems as much less focused on investigation of child abuse, and more on family support. However, an emphasis on investigation of families, at the expense of family support, in response to a mushrooming of referrals alleging abuse, has also been recorded in North America and Australia (Lindsay, 1994; Parton et al., 1997). It seems there has been an explosion of child abuse referrals, with very many being unfounded or unsubstantiated, or found to be concerns about parenting style rather than harm to children (Parton et al., 1997). It is also generally agreed that the child protection system in these countries has become more legalistic and bureaucratic (Parton, 1991; Howe, 1992; Otway, 1996). Most commentators agree that the current emphasis is more on the gathering of evidence than on finding ways to help people change, as in traditional social work (Howe, 1996). Parton (1996) summarises the message of the Department of Health studies:

> What the research seems to demonstrate is that while there is little evidence that children are being missed and suffer harm unnecessarily at the hands of their parents, as implied by most child abuse inquiries, and [intervention] is thus 'successful' according to a narrow definition of child protection, this is at a cost. Many children and parents feel alienated and angry, and there is an over-emphasis on forensic concerns, with far too much time spent on investigations, and a failure to develop longer-term co-ordinated treatment, counselling and preventative strategies. (Parton, 1996: 5)

Certainly, consumer studies of childcare social work in general, those amongst the *Messages from Research* studies included (Cleaver and Freeman, 1995; Thoburn et al., 1995), show parents to be extremely fearful of the consequences of child protection investigations and to feel violated by the process. Cleaver and Freeman argue that

> preoccupation with the putative damage done to the young can elbow aside the violation experienced by parents, siblings and the wide family. In terms of outcome, the voicing of suspicion may be more abusive and long term in its consequence than the bruise which prompted investigation. (Cleaver and Freeman, 1995: 155)

And neither does research on children's views of the child protection system make comfortable reading for social services staff. Butler and Williamson (1994), for example, spoke to a number of children who felt they were not consulted or listened to, and did not have their views taken into account when decisions were being made about their future. However, there are some indications that the culture of child-care social workers' orientations towards children is changing, at least in some parts of the system. Thomas and O'Kane's (1999) study of looked-after children found that between a half and two-thirds of the children they spoke to were invited to reviews and planning meetings. They concluded, however, that considerable progress is still needed, and that the current involvement of children could not be described as a 'partnership'.

Not all commentators are in agreement about the tone that contemporary child protection services take in relation to their clients. Whilst Parton is generally of the view that social work has become more authoritarian rather than more liberal, Dingwall et al.'s (1983) ethnographic research in the early 1980s described a 'rule of optimism' in operation: the organisational culture was disposed towards expecting families to improve. This research was very influential, being cited by the Jasmine Beckford report (Brent, 1985). White's ethnography (1997a), a decade and a half later, found social workers employing routine scepticism about parental accounts. We could conclude that the tone of child protection changed substantially through the 1980s and 90s. However, Dingwall et al. (1995), in their postscript to the second edition of their book, maintain that the rule of optimism is still operating, albeit in different ways. Corby (1987, 1991) steers a middle way here, arguing that social workers are authoritative for the most part, but that the substance of intervention in the long term is fairly liberal. His research found that generally a psycho-social view holds sway with social workers, which emphasises the effects on parents of emotional deprivation and a stressful environment, and that social workers believe that friendly, supportive surveillance is the best they can offer. The discussion in Chapter 3 on state control and family life will return to this question of liberalism and authoritarianism in child protection work, as will the final chapter.

To follow on from Corby's point about supportive surveillance, Howe (1992, 1996) has argued that mainstream social work is currently focused on the act, rather than the actor, that is, monitoring of observable behaviour rather than therapeutic interventions has become the principle task. Parton et al.'s research (1997) describes a child protection system based on monitoring of parental (which most often means maternal) behaviour, rather than of children, although it is the well-being of children that is officially the *raison d'être* of the system.

Several commentators have argued that a preoccupation with risk lies at the heart of child protection practice. Kemshall et al. (1997) argue that a categorisation process of risk has emerged as a central organising principle across the personal social services. Parton et al. (1997) draw on the work of Mary Douglas (1986, 1992) to demonstrate that the concept of risk has become increasingly associated with negative outcomes: hazard, danger, exposure, harm and loss. Douglas points out that the term 'risk' has overtaken 'danger', because danger does not have risk's aura of science and does not conjure the possibility of accurate prediction. She also comments that the major significance of the current emphasis on risk is its forensic functions, which are particularly important in the development of blaming systems. In the light of this risk–blame connection, Parton (1998) argues that audit becomes a key element in responding to the inherent uncertainty of risk. Social workers have to make themselves auditable. In this climate it is not the right decision that is important, but the defensible one. Ferguson's ideas (1997) on child protection in the risk society disagree with this emphasis on constraint and control. He argues that such writings are one-dimensional, and ignore how people actively make themselves the subjects and not just the objects of social processes. He draws heavily on various writings of Giddens (1990, 1991) and Beck (1992) on risk and reflexive modernisation, and sees subjects of social regulation as increasingly critical and reflexive with reference to these systems (see also Ferguson, 2001).

UK child protection policy and practice also need to be understood in terms of the hegemony of the New Right in the late twentieth century. The combination of economic liberalism and a strong state (Gamble, 1988) with attempts to strengthen the nuclear family and enforce individual responsibilities have inevitably impacted on the poorest people who are the clients of social workers and on child welfare professionals. Parton (1998) describes a range of new strategies of government, which he terms 'advanced liberalism', that have had a particular impact on the field of child welfare. These are the extension of market rationalities to domains where social, bureaucratic or professional logic previously reigned; governing at a distance by formally separating the activities of welfare professionals from the local state and the courts; governing welfare professionals by new systems of audit, devolved budgets, codes of practice and citizen's charters; and giving individuals new freedoms by making them responsible for their own present and future welfare and the relations they have with experts and institutions.

Clearly the New Labour era in the UK has seen both continuity and change (Jordan, 2000). The Blair government has far from rejected neo-liberalism, but the Comprehensive Spending Review of 2000 saw major increases in spending on some public services. Devolution has meant the beginnings of social policy variation between the different nations of the UK. It can be argued that social authoritarianism has continued from the Thatcher/Major era (Butler and Drakeford, 2001). In terms of the welfare professionals, there is yet more regulation in the Care Standards Act 2000 and, despite changes in the NHS internal market, there is no sign of retreat from the marketisation of welfare. Chris Jones's (2001) recent research with state social workers found everyday working practices to be profoundly affected by the enduring legacy of New Right social policy.

UK government policy on the child welfare system has in fact shifted in response to *Messages from Research*. The Assessment Framework for children (DH, 2000) and Quality Protects (Children First in Wales) are important steps towards the 'refocusing' of services from child protection to family support. It is too early to say whether or not these measures have been successful in shifting the efforts of local authorities away from investigation and monitoring, although anecdotal evidence from practitioners in South Wales would suggest that front-line child and family social work in the state sector is, if anything, even more focused on protectionism than ever before. The president of the British Association of Directors of Social Services has described child protection services as on the brink of collapse under a 'bombardment' of new referrals (McVeigh, 2001). The national shortage of qualified staff in the UK would make it more likely that social work teams will continue to concentrate on risk management. On a slightly more optimistic note, Parton and Mathews (2001) have reported that efforts to refocus services in Western Australia towards family support show some encouraging outcomes. Their evidence suggests that the energies of practitioners are still focused on high-risk cases, but that the numbers of substantiated cases of child maltreatment have reduced without any observable increased risk to children or loss of services. For families who are considered low risk, there still seems to be a deficit in services, however, and for these families there is a high rate of re-referral.

This section has attempted to introduce some of the issues that will be important in any consideration of contemporary child protection.

These surface throughout the rest of the book, but particularly in Chapters 3 and 6. Having raised some issues of general relevance, next I shall devote some space to the critiques of the child protection system that are the main concern of this book: the feminist critiques.

Gender and other inequalities in child protection

This next section will firstly give an overview of the feminist critiques of the child protection system. I then mention the different explanations for gendered practice in the existing literature and very briefly summarise existing knowledge about men and women as abusers of children, whilst explaining my position in relation to this issue.

Few commentators would dissent that contemporary child protection work maintains a long tradition of focusing on mothering. Tice's historical work (1998) on case recording in child welfare organisations in early twentieth-century USA shows the highly gendered history of social work as the policing of the morality of poor families. The excerpt below is her summary of the portrayal of 'malignant clients':

> In these menacing accounts, social workers constructed a vast array of portentous signifiers to denote moral and sexual disorder, writing tales replete with signs of women's conduct disorders: vermilion lips and arched eyebrows, ruptured hymens, dirty kitchens, unsupervised children on city streets, liquor bottles, and mysterious men hanging about. (Tice, 1998: 15)

The current preoccupation with child abuse as a social problem is often dated back to Kempe et al.'s work (1962) on battered child syndrome. It is telling that this research used a women-only research sample. Times have changed, and second-wave feminism has had a profound impact on the culture of social work and, to a lesser extent, on the family welfare professions in general. The scrutiny of mothering remains, however, a feature of professional interventions, as can be seen in research such as that by Swift (1995), Farmer and Owen (1995, 1998), Parton et al. (1997) and Edwards (1998).

In terms of the history of child protection in the UK, the NSPCC's Rochdale Child Protection Unit was highly influential in the late 1980s. For example, their ideas were a formative influence on the official guidelines on comprehensive child protection assessments that were used until 2000 (DH, 1988). Their *Dangerous Families* text (Dale et al.,

1986) recommends that social workers see their relationship to parents as a 'transference of mothering'. Featherstone (1997b, 1999) has written that this and similar rhetoric in the child welfare field rest on a misplaced optimism about mothers' natural affinity with child-rearing. Hearn (1990) takes up Dale et al.'s metaphor and points out that an increasingly investigative and interventionist culture in child protection work could be seen as a move towards social work as the transference of fathering, that is, a traditional, patriarchal model of the distant, disciplinarian father.

Contemporary studies of the culture of child protection work show that gendered constructions of women are mainstream organising principles. Parton et al.'s (1997) analysis of Australian data concluded that maternal response was more influential than harm to children in deciding whether or not cases moved into a 'child protection' category. The key process was one of moral categorisation of the mother. Hall et al. (1997a) show how routine social work case talk appropriates and reinforces cultural formations of motherhood and family life. These formations will also be rooted in class-based assumptions. As Jones (1983), amongst others, asserts, clients of social workers do not represent a broad socio-economic spectrum, but are, in the main, the poorest of the poor working class.

As Lewis's (2000) analysis demonstrates, the everyday practice of social workers, and indeed the social welfare system of which they are part, also need to be understood as thoroughly racialised as well as gendered. Black and minority ethnic families tend to be overrepresented in child protection caseloads. This is demonstrated in research by Thorpe (1994) and Swift (1995) amongst others. Corby (2000) observes that the overrepresentation of black and minority ethnic children in the child protection system is not surprising in the context of higher levels of surveillance and racist constructs of non-white cultures. He also observes that some black and minority ethnic families will experience more surveillance because of social class factors – higher levels of social deprivation compared to the white population – as well as because of racism. He makes the point that black families are unlikely to be overrepresented in terms of reported sexual abuse because cultural ignorance in this area might lead to less intervention rather than more. Discrimination takes place at a structural and institutional level as well as at the level of front-line practice. Research by Humphries et al. (1999) into the experiences of Asian families in child protection case conferences in a local authority in the UK found that, in spite of the good intentions of many individual workers, the families experienced a discriminatory service, because discriminatory policies and practices were perpetuated at an organisational level.

Constructions of gender in child protection are in many ways inseparable from constructions of sexuality. The binary opposition of men and women that we see throughout this book is in part a reflection of a heterosexual paradigm. It was noted earlier that there is no discussion of the construction of gay or black clients in this book's empirical material because of the caseload I was presented with. We can see, however, from researchers such as Hardman (1997) and Hicks (2000) that various forms of heterosexism are to be found in social work culture. Hicks applies queer theory to an analysis of fostering and adoption assessments and finds that lesbian applicants pose a challenge to the heterosexual premise which structures these assessments. Lesbians who apply to foster or adopt are constructed as a 'threat', 'militant' or 'automatically safe' and only certain versions of the lesbian subject are likely to be approved to foster or adopt.

It is often claimed that mainstream child protection practice fails to engage men. O'Hagan's overview article on this issue (1997) asserts that a particular problem is the failure to engage the male partners of women who are ostensibly 'single' parents. Lupton and Barclay (1997) observe that the family welfare literature assumes that fathering will be problematic. Child protection intervention in relation to men has been profoundly affected by the relatively recent discovery of sexual abuse as a social problem. Stainton Rogers and Stainton Rogers (1992) describe the dominant view that equates child sexual abuse with masculinity as 'whole gender blaming'.

There is also research on what women clients say about their experience of the child protection process (Hooper, 1992a; Croghan and Miell, 1998). The mothers whose children had been sexually abused who talked to Hooper often wanted help from social services, and even legal action. However, they also often contested the degree of responsibility expected of them, and they resented the stigma and loss of control that could follow intervention, especially where no effective control was exercised against the abuser (Hooper, 1992a: 132). Croghan and Miell interviewed women who had effectively been labelled 'bad mothers' in the course of childcare proceedings. They found that attempts to foreground social and economic factors were a consistent feature of mothers' accounts of their dealings with welfare professionals. The women tended to emphasise the need for practical support rather than personal change. One described her attempt to flee a violent man and the interpretation put on her behaviour by social workers:

> I was scared of him. I used to run and grab the baby and move on somewhere else but he'd always find me. That's why they took her away from me. They said it was an unstable life for her just moving from bed-sit to bed-sit. I stood up in court when she was 18 months old and I said, 'Look, it ain't me. He just keeps following me around.' (Croghan and Miell, 1998: 451)

Chapter 7 returns to this issue of how social workers understand the role of social and economic factors. The topic of gender in the child protection process is, of course, not without controversy. Gordon's historical research (1988) argues for a more complex understanding both of the nature of family violence and the role of child protection services than some feminist accounts have allowed. She stresses the fact that the case records she analysed showed many women asking the authorities to intervene, and that these authorities could be humane and helpful.

Understanding gendered practice

Various explanations have been given for gender bias in child protection work. There is the general critique that the organisations that co-ordinate the work are 'masculinist' (Harlow, 1996; Otway, 1996). Others have concentrated on specific elements of the system that screen out men (Milner, 1993; O'Hagan and Dillenburger, 1995; Farmer and Owen, 1998). On this theme, O'Hagan (1997: 28) writes that 'the structure, guidelines and procedures of the organisation may in fact make it extremely difficult for the worker *not* to avoid men'. Examples of gender bias in specific operations are women attending case conferences and not men, and fewer men attending court and, when they do so, not automatically being called to give evidence (King and Trowell, 1992; Thoburn et al., 1995).

It is often assumed that social workers have traditional expectations of men and women and a functionalist approach to the family. For example, Maynard's research (1985) found social workers encouraging women to stay with violent men because the nuclear family was thought to be a good thing in itself. Dicks et al.'s research (1998) on service providers in ex-mining communities found there was an exclusive concern with male unemployment, although 50 per cent of women were also unemployed. The Western ideology of motherhood has certainly been a dominant influence in the construction of women by professionals. The child welfare industry has historically focused on mothering rather than parenting. O'Hagan and Dillenburger (1995) summarise the ideas, including those from social work theory, that have contributed to the concentration on women in childcare social work. Particularly prominent have been the enduring legacies of Freud (for example, 1924) and Bowlby (for example, 1953). Their writings on, respectively, the psychodynamics of the mother–infant dyad and the quality of maternal attachment have been interpreted as an argument for the necessity of women being primary carers.

Legal discourse is central to the construction of child protection clients. Child protection work has become increasingly dominated by a legal paradigm (Howe, 1992; White, 1998a). Both family law and criminal law constitute this discursive field. It could be argued that family law constructs ideal motherhood and criminal law the deviant woman. A consideration of the criminal justice field can illuminate the construction of deviant women within legal discourse. Worrall (1990) outlines how women law-breakers are constructed by the criminal justice system within the ideologies of domesticity, sexuality and pathology: they are represented as family members, sexual objects, or sick. As Carabine (1992) has observed, women are also constructed as heterosexual within social policy.

What do we know about child abuse and gender?

Whilst this book has not set out to establish any 'truth' about child abuse, the question of who is responsible for the maltreatment of children is a key gender controversy that has to be considered as part of the context for researching gender discourse in child protection work. Different research studies reach different conclusions, and the weight of evidence has to be carefully assessed. Pringle (1995: 40), citing Finkelhor (1984) and Kelly et al. (1991), claims that 'the most methodologically sophisticated' of prevalence surveys in the UK and the USA have found that about 90 per cent of child sexual abuse is perpetrated by men. Some commentators have claimed that too much emphasis on men's sexual abuse can make us blinkered to the possibility of women sexually abusing children (Elliott, 1993). There is relatively little dissent, however, from the general picture of sexual abuse being far more often perpetrated by men than by women. The evidence on physical abuse is mixed, but indicates less of a marked divergence between the frequency of assaults by men and by women (Martin, 1983). With reference to emotional abuse, Parton (1990) cites Creighton's research (1987) on UK child protection registers to show that more women than men are found to be responsible in this category. She goes on to argue that this can be related to the concentration of services on mothers and the gendered division of labour in the family. Mullender and Morley (1994) have drawn attention to the adverse emotional affects on children of witnessing violence against their mothers from male partners. Although it cannot be taken for granted that this is a straightforward problem of men's behaviour, the field of partner violence research being a very contested one (Gelles and Loseke, 1993), I have chosen to side with what I regard to be the majority view on this issue, supported by the most convincing research methodology (Dobash et al., 1992), namely that men are responsible for initiating the majority of domestic violence.

Child neglect, as Swift (1995) has shown from her study of social work practice in Canada, is essentially a construction of bad mothering. It is overwhelmingly women who are found to have neglected children, because neglect is constructed as a lack of care, and women do most of the work of caring for children (Turney, 2000). Chapter 6 discusses this category in detail. Whilst the simplistic equation of child abuse with masculinity has been rightly challenged (Carter, 1993; Featherstone, 1997b), and I would not seek to construct an idealised, essential womanhood which is all-caring, there is certainly a great deal of abusive behaviour by men that has a negative impact on children's quality of life. In the light of contested definitions of what is meant by 'abuse', and contested research findings, it is not possible to assert with confidence whether or not men are *more* likely to cause harm to children than women, except perhaps in relation to sexual abuse. But in the context of men being responsible for a significant amount of abuse, it does seem that the weighting of child protection intervention towards mothers is unjust.

As for children as victims of abuse, Corby's (2000) overview of research in this area shows that overall boys and girls are equally likely to be placed on child protection registers in the UK. The picture is more varied when these figures are broken down, however. Boys are more likely to be registered for reasons of physical abuse, neglect and emotional abuse. Corby mentions a possible reason for the gender difference in one of these categories, namely that physical punishment is more sanctioned against boys than against girls. Indeed, there are widespread beliefs about the virtue of 'toughening up' boys and the comparative 'frailty' of girls. In contrast, prevalence studies tend to show that girls are much more likely to be sexually abused than boys. This difference is perhaps unsurprising since most of those who sexually abuse children are men, and a dominant construction of heterosexuality in most societies has arguably been the sexual possession of women (and therefore girls in the context of child sexual abuse) by men.

Having focused specifically on the existing commentary on gender in child protection, and the existing knowledge on gender and child abuse, I now introduce some of the key debates about gender relations more generally and will attempt to position myself within these.

What is meant by 'gender'?

Social science perspectives on men and women have developed rapidly over the twentieth century. It is not necessary to attempt a thorough overview here (see Beasley, 1999, for an attempt at one), but rather to point up the central debates that form the background to the material in this book. I begin by briefly summarising key developments in theorising gender, before going on to make connections between these debates and the feminist social work literature.

Biological explanations of the differences between men and women were challenged earlier in the century by the idea of sex role socialisation (usually credited to Mead, 1935). This perspective has in turn been challenged on the basis that it is overly rigid and does not take account of non-traditional identities and behaviours that resist the dominant sex role (see, for example, Connell, 1995). An emphasis on gender construction has attempted to provide a more flexible framework, but that too has been challenged by theorists who want to collapse the sex–gender distinction of Ann Oakley (1972), arguing that sex is also constructed, and can be seen to 'precede' gender (Delphy, 1993). Feminist studies of gender have arguably reached their most radically deconstructive in the work of Judith Butler (1990, 1993), who conceptualises gender as 'performance'.

These feminist writings, informed by post-structuralism and post-modernism, have been a challenge to the notion of patriarchy. This concept refers to men's domination of women in society. Walby's (1989, 1990) account of patriarchy is a relatively nuanced version, although it raised debate at the time of publication (Acker, 1989; Walby, 1989; Waters, 1989). She describes six structures of patriarchy: the patriarchal (household) mode of production; patriarchal relations in paid work; the patriarchal state; male violence; patriarchal relations in sexuality; and patriarchal culture. She argues there has been a shift from private patriarchy based on the household to public patriarchy based in sites such as the labour market and the state. The patriarchy idea has been criticised for not taking account of the power that women can wield against each other. Some authors have stressed the heterogeneity of women, and the importance of other power relations along the lines of class, race and sexuality (Brittan and Maynard, 1984; Williams, 1989; Hill Collins, 1990). Connell's (1987, 1995) framework of gender relations is a sophisticated and multi-faceted one, which uses the notion of patriarchy whilst also allowing for other aspects of power within the sexes as well as between them. He uses the idea of a hierarchy of masculinities, for example. He also allows for the dimension of subjectivity in identity formation.

The concept of patriarchy has to be an important one to consider when studying the regulation of women by a state agency. It may be difficult, however, to maintain any simple notion of male power and dominance when most child protection social workers are themselves women and there are significant class differences between them and their clients. The chapters that follow use a post-structuralist emphasis on gender discourse. The theoretical basis of the term 'discourse' will be explained in the section on occupational culture below. The writers who argue that sexed bodies are socially constructed (Gatens, 1995; Daly, 1997; Collier, 1998) will influence the analysis in the book in as much as the construction of gendered others will involve the 'imagining' (Young, 1996) of poor men and women clients as embodied. Theorists such as Butler (1990, 1993) emphasise the fluidity of gender construction. As Bristow (1997) observes, Butler has been accused of voluntarism, that is, suggesting genders can be made and unmade at will. Bristow himself disputes this criticism, arguing that Butler does not see the performer as standing outside discursive structures. The analysis of my research will not assume that individual social workers are free to construct their clients as gendered in an infinite variety of ways. I am choosing to research occupational culture, so am necessarily exploring the constraints on knowledge about gender that are imposed by that culture.

If I were to define my use of the term 'gender' in the book in one sentence, the definition would be: the differences between men and women as understood by the research participants. This research project is about the occupational construction of gendered others ('clients') rather than social workers' own gender identities (although clearly these topics overlap, to an extent). It is this dimension of the debates about theorising gender that is central to the research. I use the term 'gendered' often in the book (for example gendered practice, gendered discourse). It is important to note that this does not refer to differences between men and women social workers. It will be mentioned several times in the chapters to follow that I did not find there to be significant differences in the social work team I studied. When I write that something is gendered I mean it has very different implications for men and women clients.

Gender relations involve power relations, but gender is not, of course, the only power dimension at work in child protection social work. As many commentators have observed, there are also significant dimensions of class, sexuality and 'race' (Jones, 1983; Dominelli, 1997; Brown, 1998). Chapter 3 will discuss some of these other power relations as an introduction to the chapters that are centred on the construction of gender. But just as these other power relations are gendered, so also the reverse is true – constructions of gender inevitably have a class and 'race' dimension (Brittan and Maynard, 1984; Skeggs, 1997). So, although gender is not everything, it could be said to be *in* everything. As Morgan (1996a: 71) expresses it, 'all social situations are gendered although few, if any, are purely a matter of gender'. Gender does not stand alone, but is affected by other social forces and in turn affects these others. Many of the observations made in the book are general ones about child protection work; aspects of the organisation of the child protection system that have implications for both men and women. But as soon as we start to think about implications for men and women we encounter ways in which the organisational construction of these clients is gendered. Similarly, observations are made about the theoretical basis of social work, which are not *solely* about gender, but do affect the picture of how men and women are worked with by social workers, and how they are worked with as *men* and *women*, not as sexless or genderless clients. The book sets out to correct the tendency in some social work and social policy literature, noted by Oakley and Rigby (1998), of constructing the users of welfare as non-gendered.

Up to a point the debates on sex/gender mentioned above are reflected in the social work literature, although, as Graham (1992) observes, the social work discipline has been rather slow to consider the implications of later developments in feminist thought. Early texts, such as Hanmer and Statham (1988) and Dominelli and MacLeod (1989), emphasised women's common experience of being oppressed by men. Since the 1990s, some authors have analysed the differences between women within a feminist framework (Sands and Nuccio, 1992; Fawcett et al., 2000).

Not surprisingly, considering the breadth of theoretical influences, there are some very different emphases to be found in the literature on social work with women in relation to child protection. The perspective of many of those who have commented on the tendency to scrutinise mothering is that women are unfairly targeted and that many of the 'problems' attributed to them are not real but are the product of social work bias (for example, O'Hagan and Dillenburger, 1995). In opposition to this argument, Wise (1990, 1995) argues that there are often genuine conflicts between the interests of the mother and those of children in child protection work and that social work is rightly about social control, because vulnerable children often need protection from the adults they are living with. Alanen (1994) has similarly argued that feminism tends to be adult-centric, marginalising the legitimate, separate interests of children.

In the last few years, feminist thinking about social work has extended to consider work with men, and similar tensions and outright disagreements can be found in this field (Pringle, 1998b). There has been rather more discussion of work with offenders in the criminal justice system (for example, Newburn and Mair, 1996) than with men across the personal social services (although Christie, 2001, is a recent exception). Arguably the key tension in these writings is between a perspective which incorporates some kind of focus on the difficulties for men themselves of gender identity and one which concentrates on changing behaviour which causes problems for others (women, children and other men). Advocates of the former perspective have been accused of 'letting men off the hook', and advocates of the latter of 'giving men a hard time' (Scourfield and Dobash, 1999).

This book does not of course make reference to the whole spectrum of topics within gender studies, but the literature drawn upon is oriented towards the family and state intervention. The key sociological observation on the gendered family worth noting at the outset is that, despite some evidence of change in gender relations (Walby, 1997) at the start of the twenty-first century, we are nonetheless inheriting sharply contrasted discourses of fatherhood and motherhood. Glenn neatly summarises the dominant construction of motherhood in the West:

> responsibility for mothering rests almost exclusively on one woman (the biological mother), for whom it constitutes the primary if not sole mission during the child's formative years. The corollary view of children is that they require constant care and attention from one caretaker (the biological mother). (Glenn, 1994: 3)

Similarly, Collier (1995), in his work on masculinity in family law, has observed that the father as breadwinner is the enduring version of men in families in British society. Connell (1987) emphasises the importance to gender relations of assumed heterosexuality and the reproductive division of people into male and female, both of which are central to the dominant discourse of family life (I also accept that there exist alternative but subordinated discourses; of gay families for example). Crucially, it must not be forgotten that the domestic division of labour in the West is as unequal as ever. As McMahon's (1999) research review clearly demonstrates, the work of feeding, cleaning and clothing children still most often falls to women, despite popular discourse which claims that men are changing in this respect.

The terms 'constructing' and 'construction' and 'occupational culture' have already been used many times in the book. It has been explained that the main concern of the book is the construction of gender in the occupational culture of child protection work. These terms do not feature largely in the everyday talk of social workers. They are academic sociological terms. In order to make clearer the ideas at the heart of the book, I will briefly summarise the concepts of social constructionism and occupational culture at this point.

Social constructionism

The term 'social construction' is generally credited to Berger and Luckmann (1967), but, since their influential book *The Social Construction of Reality* was published, the field has greatly expanded. The ideas of social constructionism have been specifically applied to the field of social work practice (see, for example, Jokinen et al., 1999; Parton and O'Byrne, 2000). The terms 'constructionist' and 'constructivist' are often used interchangeably, although Payne (1999) argues that constructionism tends to imply a sociological approach and constructivism a social psychological one. Burr (1995) outlines four key assumptions of social constructionism: a critical stance towards taken-for-granted knowledge; a belief in the historical and cultural specificity of knowledge; a belief that knowledge is sustained by social processes; and a belief that knowledge and social action go together. As Craib (1997) points out, these assumptions would appropriate the whole of sociology to social constructionism. More distinctive, Craib argues, are anti-essentialism and anti-realism: the assumption that there is no essence of people that can be objectively known.

One of Craib's critiques of social constructionism is that it denies subjective agency to those it studies. The researcher who studies people around her or him, and claims that they are social constructs, is claiming subjectivity for herself or himself in being able to deconstruct those she or he studies. This is an interesting challenge to constructionist research. In this case, I, a social worker by training and recent experience, am claiming to be able to deconstruct the occupational culture of the social workers I study, whilst simultaneously claiming that their beliefs and their decisions are, to an extent, trapped within that culture. It is possible to sustain this divide on the basis that I am now based in a university, and am therefore able to spend considerable time reflecting on the culture of the social work office at a distance. I also have time to read the reflective writing of others on the topic. Some researchers working full time as social workers (for example, White, 1998b) have nonetheless been able to learn critical reflection on their own workplace culture again. Arguably the crucial factor here is, again, connection to external academic support. It is perhaps more difficult for the practitioner researcher who does not have this support to attain a critical distance on occupational constructions.

However, the term 'social construction' will not be used in the book to suggest that social workers' beliefs and practices are completely socially determined. I would seek a balanced stance on occupational discourse, as explained further in the section on occupational culture below. Equally, the book does not argue that any version of social reality is an equally valid one, without any recourse to material reality and the actual behaviour of clients. The term 'social construction' remains a useful one because there is considerable scope for different ways of understanding and responding to men and women in relation to child welfare and child abuse. It is these interpretations and responses that the research focuses on. If social problems are socially constructed (Kitsuse and Spector, 1973), and social work is 'social problems work' (Holstein and Miller, 1993), then constructionism is an appropriate research perspective for the study of social work. I am working within what Best (1989) has called 'contextual social constructionism', focusing on the making of claims about social problems, but accepting that knowledge about social context and objective information can help to explain how claims arise. So throughout the book there will be reference to material reality as well as to social construction.

The research is concerned with knowledge about men and women, with the production of that knowledge in the culture of the social work office, and also with the practical interventions that follow. So the concern is with both cognitive and practical construction; the beliefs about clients that are permitted within the occupational discourse, and the consequent interventions.

So far I have attempted to explain what is meant in the book by the often-used terminology of gender and social constructionism. Two other major sociological concepts remain whose use in the book needs to be clarified: occupational culture and discourse. The following section will outline the use of each of these, starting with occupational culture.

Occupational culture

Studying occupational culture means putting the emphasis on social work as *work* (Parton, 1996). This emphasis means paying close attention to the effects of what social workers do, the beliefs they profess, and the organisation of social services departments, their routines and bureaucracies. It means considering the influence of both the formal and informal occupational knowledge base, as well as the workplace interactions that translate this knowledge into practice. Workplace interaction is an essential element in the construction of gender in the social work office. Ideas about cases are tested out and developed through both formal supervision with managers and informal discussion with colleagues. Various meetings – core groups, case conferences, reviews, team meetings – form the context for decision-making, so interaction is a focus. The aims of this book are similar to those of Pithouse:

> The aim is to display as fully as possible the ways that the social workers themselves perceive and create their occupational arena...the study focuses on the orderly and mundane way that social workers make sense of their daily tasks and problems. (Pithouse, 1998: 7)

The concept of 'tacit knowledge' is an important one for under-standing occupational culture. It refers to the taken-for-granted, 'common-sense' notions about the job and the clients that are rarely articulated but which are understood by all. Collins (2000), writing from within the sociology of scientific knowledge, outlines three ver-sions of tacit knowledge: the motor-skills metaphor; the rules regress model; and the forms of life approach. He states the case for using the third of these, seeing tacit knowledge as rooted in specific social settings: common socialisation will lead to common solutions to problems. He writes:

> If it is the case that the true sources of our beliefs are in large part the social contexts we inhabit, yet we think the sources of our beliefs (including beliefs about the natural world) are something else, then the sources of our beliefs are hidden from us. Our beliefs, then, are based on tacit knowledge. (Collins, 2000: 111)

The question of how social workers think about cases has been dis-cussed by several authors. Howitt (1992) has described a threefold model of social workers' thinking about cases: 'templating'; 'justifica-tory theorising'; and 'ratcheting'. Templating he describes as checking individual cases against a social template to see if they fit a particular pattern. Justificatory theorising refers to the ideas that make it diffi-cult to question decisions already taken. An example would be the central importance of contrition; clients having to accept the social workers' line on an incident, which will often mean accepting responsibility for harm caused to a child (see also Holland, 2000). Ratcheting refers to the tendency of the protection process to move in a single direction, and the difficulty of altering a previous decision. Sheppard (1995) argues that when thinking about their assessments of cases, social workers should use techniques for analysing qualitative research. In particular, he recommends analytic induction, and he implies an optimistic view that this kind of approach is already main-stream practice. Dorothy Scott's research (1998) found the opposite, that the social workers she studied were 'verificationist' in their approach to cases, looking for evidence to support decisions already taken. There are, of course, organisational limits to what knowledge can be produced about a client. Handelman (1983: 3) has written that social workers build 'a case that "makes sense" within the context of a bureaucratic life world'. The routines and conventions of case talk (Pithouse and Atkinson, 1988) and case recording (Askeland and Payne, 1999) will limit the scope of knowledge production.

Harlow and Hearn's summary of theories of organisational culture (1995) outlines the breadth of different theoretical perspectives that have been applied to the topic. This book will use the perspective that Harlow and Hearn label 'culture as discourse'. The concept of 'discourse' was somewhat overused in the social sciences in the 1990s. A proliferation of meanings are attached to it, and very different emphases can be found within and between different academic disciplines. This book will draw on a Foucauldian interpretation of discourse. Whilst narrowing the field of potential interpretations, referencing Foucault does not provide immediate clarity, because of the wide range of interpretations of his work. I will attempt to explain how I understand the application of a Foucauldian notion of discourse to child protection social work, whilst accepting that there are other possible interpretations.

The contribution of the Foucauldian idea of discourse to the study of social work has been neatly summarised by White:

> Foucault's assertion is that through the medium of language (or discourse) 'regimes of truth' become constructed, which when harnessed to professional power, can function as apparently neutral 'knowledge' and as such are able to circumscribe the activities and formulations of health and welfare agencies. (White, 1996: 69–70)

So the activities of social workers are circumscribed by discourse, which defines what can be spoken about and how client problems can be understood. But should we think in terms of one discourse, or many? Philp (1979), analysing social work knowledge as a structural-ist, argues that there is *one* fundamental discourse underlying the profession; that of the production of knowledge about people as subjects. Some commentators on Foucault (for example, Turner, 1996) have described him as a structuralist, drawing on his writings which emphasise the ways in which discourse constrains and limits knowledge. Foucault is more often, however, given the label 'post-structuralist' (for example, Craib, 1992) because of his recognition of the interplay of multiple discursive elements:

> We must not imagine a world of discourse divided between accepted dis-course and excluded discourse, or between the dominant discourse and the dominated one; but as a multiplicity of discursive elements that can come into play in various strategies... Discourse transmits and produces power; it reinforces it, but also undermines and exposes it, renders it fragile and makes it possible to thwart it. (Foucault, 1984: 100)

Foucault certainly does not lead us towards a view of social workers as trapped within a single discourse. Instead we ought perhaps to think in terms of occupational discour*s*es, and discour*s*es of child pro-tection. Social work knowledge is less a coherent body of knowledge than other professional discourses, medicine for example, but there are nonetheless important discursive elements, some of which might be seen to be in tension with each other (for example, sociology and psychology). The position of this book will be that social workers' con-structions of clients are to a large extent limited by the discourses of their workplace. This is not to argue that the social work profession is homogeneous in its construction of gender or that there is one coher-ent set of 'official' professional discourses. Clearly social work has a diverse knowledge base and lay knowledge is an important element of occupational discourse.

My use of 'discourse' is not restricted to what social workers say and write. It is not the intention to separate 'knowledge' from 'practice'. As Haraway (1992: 111) writes, 'discourse is a material practice'. Where I have heard social workers talking to clients on the telephone, read case recording of actions taken, or observed the forming of deci-sions in the office, I have reflected on this practice as occupational culture, from the perspective of understanding occupational culture as discourse.

Conclusion

In this chapter I have attempted to outline what I see as the key policy developments that frame this research, as well as explaining my theoretical base in the writing of the book. This has meant drawing out relevant themes in child protection policy. Particularly important were the shift from child welfare to child protection, the preoccupation with risk and the concentration on mothers. I went on to explain which aspect of gender relations the research is to focus on. Since the book is about the *work* of child protection, this chapter also introduced the concepts of social constructionism and occupational culture, and, more specifically, occupational culture as discourse. The next chapter will conclude the context-setting for the book. It is not primarily about the construction of gender, but focuses on the other crucial categorisations of clients that form the context of gendered practice.

3

Who are the clients?

This chapter introduces two main questions: who are the clients in child protection work, and what is the nature of the social worker–client relationship? It is especially concerned with the way that the potential client population is divided according to criteria *other than gender*. In that sense, it serves as an essential introduction to the substantive discussions on working with men and women clients that follow in Chapters 4 and 5. It will outline the *context* of gendered clienthood in child protection work.

Gender is, of course, not the only concept used to categorise and differentiate clients. Other concepts are employed to make sense of the mass of allegations and evidence of child abuse that workers encounter on a daily basis, and the previous chapter reviewed some of the literature on ethnicity, class and sexuality in childcare social work. This chapter will focus on the construction of childhood, the significance of class and community, and social control in the social work role. None of these will be examined as a major theme for analysis, but it is necessary to acknowledge the importance of each as the context of gender construction. The chapter will explore what it means to be a client, what is involved in ascribing to someone the status of 'clienthood' (Payne, 1991). Central to the argument is that some people become clients in a stronger sense than others.

Pithouse's (1987) interactionist account of a social work team in the early 1980s tackled the question of the occupational construction of clients in a childcare team. He found that clients were simultaneously revered as the object of service and morally judged: 'both worthy and unworthy; a supernal abstraction and simultaneously a morally defunct and discredited species' (Pithouse, 1987: 85). His analysis does not particularly distinguish constructions of men, women, boys and girls as clients in social work talk. He returned more than ten years later to interview social workers in the same team about the observations in his earlier book, and found changes in how clients were perceived (Pithouse, 1998). Parents were still seen as problematic, but were also thought to deserve an open and honest approach. This openness was also seen, however, as leading to more conflict. The social workers were very clear that the principal client was now the child and not the family. The communities they worked in were seen as hostile to their essential task of investigating harm to children. He summarises the nature of childcare work in the late 1990s:

> It appeared far more embattled, more stressful, more interventionist, yet far more conscious of ethical imperatives around anti-discriminatory practice and partnership working. Clients – parents and children – enjoyed a more open relationship but one that sought to gather facts in order to satisfy concern over safety rather than a relationship that might, if time allowed, seek more lasting solutions to family needs. (Pithouse, 1998: 155)

I cite Pithouse's follow-up research at some length because its findings are close to those I describe below. The first issue to be discussed is the matter of who counts as the client: family, parents or children? This next section covers four aspects of the construction of children within the family and in relation to welfare services: the occupational rhetoric of child-centredness; the preoccupation with the child's vulnerable body; the idea that it is children who make the job worthwhile; and the requirement for parents to put their children's needs before their own.

Families, children or parents?

'We are child-centred'

If asked 'who is the client?', social workers will clearly state that it is, of course, the child:

> I think also something to remember is that the child is our client, we are child-centred. You know, first and foremost we are looking at the child's needs. (interview with Margaret)

They claim their child-centredness differentiates them from other professions, including those in the wider world of social work:

We have an overall responsibility to the overall well being of the children. There are other agencies involved with the children. There is education and people like health visitors. In both cases I suppose their role is quite specific. I mean health visitors visit up to a certain age and most teachers do take an interest in the wider welfare issues, but I really see that in the context of attendance and non-attendance of school. We have an overall sort of role. We can be involved in families where there are problems with education, problems with health care. Other agencies might be involved with families like, say, probation, but they are going to be involved primarily with the adults, you know they will co-operate with us but I mean their essential duty is towards the adults, who have maybe offended in some way. I think quite what the task of social work is is quite an enormous question, in that it varies so much from case to case, but certainly a child and family social worker has to be linked with the welfare of the children in some way, protection from significant harm and promotion of well being you know. (interview with Mike)

As far as the police are concerned, and we have got a very good working relationship with the child protection unit, they work from a totally different angle to us. They are there to convict and to get evidence and to get a conviction for the main perpetrator that has been involved with the child. Obviously we are more concerned with the welfare of the child. (Sarah from Docktown)

In the first excerpt, Mike is identifying the social work role as necessarily generalist and, unlike other professions, centred on the child's overall functioning. Whilst he is not criticising other professions, he is speaking with some pride of the childcare team's philosophy in contrast to these others. Sarah, in the second excerpt, identifies the police role as forensic and implies that the concerns of social workers are broader and, again, focused on what is best for the child. In both excerpts there is a sense in which other professions are respected as having their own niche and their own specific responsibility, whereas it is only childcare social workers who see the whole picture of what is needed to secure a child's welfare.

This rhetorical emphasis on the 'welfare of the child' is to be expected in the light of British government guidance since the Children Act 1989. The definition of client does not stop there, however. Much of the time social workers use the term 'client' in an ostensibly generic sense and very often this usage in fact refers to parents, unsurprisingly, because most of their contact is with adult caregivers. As Parton et al.'s research (1997) shows, in routine child protection work the assessment and monitoring of parental behaviour is more important to decision-making than the views of children, who are often 'silent' in case records. The Uplands social workers' use of 'clients' to mean parents is interesting. It often refers to women *and* men, although it is women who social workers spend a good deal more time working with. This is likely to be an example of the rhetoric of equal treatment – both men and women should be involved. Williams (1998) has commented that the language of 'parental' involvement with children in the Children Act 1989 obscures gender inequalities.

Fundamental to the argument of this book is that 'child' tends to be a unified concept in child protection practice (boys and girls are equally vulnerable), whereas 'parent' is not, because women and men are in fact strongly differentiated (see Chapters 4 and 5). There are gendered constructions of boys and girls that my research could have explored, but I made an early decision to limit its scope to examining the construction of *parents* as gendered. This strategy was vindicated by finding that there were considerably more common factors in the construction of boys and girls than between constructions of men and women. The construction of children will, however, be explained briefly at this point, since adult male and female clients are constructed in relation to children in the social work office.

Fernandez (1996) suggests that phrases such as 'child-centred', 'the child's needs', 'risk to the child' and 'in the best interests of child' are important rhetoric in social work talk, and are used as if they are universally understood terms, without any analysis of who decides the meanings of such phrases for an individual child. Research on children's experiences of the child welfare system has shown that a child-centred doctrine does not necessarily lead to children's wishes being followed. The following examples show children clearly challenging social workers' practice of interpreting 'best interests' without reference to the child's own views:

How can they know your 'best interest' when they don't even know you? What kind of contact do social workers have with their kids? One visit in two or three months? Nothing at all. (girl aged 14 in Butler and Williamson, 1996: 94)

Basically the review meeting was about them – it was about what they thought was best for me. I could say what's best for me as well, like you could say what's best for you. I don't need – well I do sometimes, but most of the time I don't need people to say what's best for me. (child, quoted in Thomas, 2001: 111)

There were instances in the Uplands team of children's wishes being ignored when social workers had decided these wishes were clearly in opposition to the safest option for the children. On one occasion, Lisa reported in a light-hearted manner how there had been considerable 'weeping and wailing' the previous evening when she had taken seven children from one family into the temporary care of foster parents against the children's will. She was not of course at all callous about their welfare. She felt utterly justified because she thought the children's strong desire to stay with their stepfather was against their best interests.

Assertion of the primacy of the child's needs often has the effect of setting the interests of children against the interests of birth families. Being primarily concerned with the welfare of children could lead to a strategy of supporting birth parents as the people with whom the children would ideally most likely to live. In practice, it is often employed to contrast an idealised notion of the child's welfare with that currently on offer from birth parents. This is an important aspect of the construction of families, and will be returned to at the end of the chapter, in the sub-section about putting children's needs before your own. Next I consider the importance of the child's vulnerability within the culture of childcare social work.

The child's vulnerable body

Children are constructed in social work as everywhere else. Stainton Rogers and Stainton Rogers (1992: 8) write that 'all children are "manufactured" ... via a process of representational labour'. In contemporary culture, children are seen as both vulnerable and dangerous. Collier (1998) has observed that the child of postmodernity has come to symbolise both nostalgia for lost innocence and also, particularly in the form of the criminality of boys and young men, social breakdown and moral dislocation. Also, as Scott et al. (1998: 695) tell us, 'children are often characterised in everyday talk as little devils in one breath and little angels in the next'. In professional child welfare services, however, it is the discourse of children as innocent and vulnerable that predominates. This reflects legal discourse. King and Piper (1995) have summarised how the law 'thinks about children'. They identify the child as victim, the child as witness, the child as a bundle of needs, and the child as a bearer of rights.

In child protection work, the child as a vulnerable body (Christensen, 2000) is a powerful discourse. White's study of social workers' case talk describes the affirmation of occupational identity through the 'invocation of the child's wounded, damaged or precariously endangered body' (White, 1997b: 7–8). Ferguson (1997), writing on child protection, has commented on the symbolic importance of the death of children, connecting this with Giddens' notion (1991) of the sequestration of death in late modern society. He also cites Shilling's idea (1993) that the inability to confront the reality of the death of our own bodies makes us anxious about the presence of death in the bodies of others. Scott et al. (1998) use the concept of 'risk anxiety' to describe contemporary fears about children and childhood. For child protection workers, risk anxiety is particularly powerful, because they have responsibility for the safety of their child clients. A child client dying is a social worker's greatest fear. Newspaper clippings about the Rikki Neave case pinned up next to the kettle remind the Uplands social workers of this everpresent fear (as if they needed reminding). The fieldnote below illustrates how child death can be invoked in routine office talk, usually to argue for intervention.

> Janet, a social worker from another child protection team, was talking to Mary about a case they both seemed familiar with. Janet said 'I reckon someone's going to go out of that house in a box. I've told them that. I just hope it's not the kids.' (from fieldnotes, 3 July)

The ethnographic data from the Uplands team suggest that certain constructions of embodied children have particular power in the organisational culture of the social work office. In the Uplands team, an interest had developed in the neglected child. The neglected child is dirty, smelly, hungry and inadequately clothed. This construction is, in part, a local phenomenon arising from their reaction to a child death, and is discussed in more detail in Chapter 6. Also evident was an abiding interest in the sexualised child. Other research (for example, Parton et al., 1997) would suggest that the attention to child sexual abuse is not just a local phenomenon. The statistics quoted by Corby (2000: 89) show us that there was a 54-fold increase in the number of cases registered for sexual abuse in the UK between 1978 and 1999. I return to the issue of sexual abuse in Chapters 4 and 5.

Despite the rhetorical and symbolic importance of the child's body, however, Parton et al.'s analysis (1997) of case recording in Australia and the UK shows that social workers' attention is focused on parents, and most often mothers, whose behaviour is assessed according to expected moral standards. Also, Kähkönen (1999) has observed from child welfare case records in Finland that parents' problems were the focus of practice rather than problems in parenting or the qualities of the parent–child relationship. The work of the Uplands team gives qualified support to these findings. Attention is indeed focused on parents, but the child's body is often used as a means of judging parents (see Chapter 6).

The dominance of a discourse of children as vulnerable was vividly illustrated by a conversation with Debbie on the last day of my fieldwork. She had just begun extra work as an out-of-hours 'duty' social worker, being called on for crisis work during the night. She recounted being called out to see a 16-year-old boy who was being remanded in custody. She did not mention the offence he was charged with, although it must have been seen as a serious offence for the police to keep him in the cells overnight. She said she was angry with the police because 'he was just a child'. Whereas much popular discourse on youth crime in the 1990s has emphasised the danger of young men, and argued for treating teenage offenders like adults, Debbie saw this offender as a boy who could be psychologically damaged by the experience of being locked in a cell during part of the night.

Children are nearly always to be believed in the course of child protection work. There is a recognition that children will sometimes say things that are untrue, but when it comes to the most controversial and difficult area of competing truths, sexual abuse against children, it is a matter of faith that children do not lie. It is often asserted about very young children that they could not make up sexual stories because they would not know how to unless something had happened to give them that knowledge.

I think where a child makes a disclosure we start on the premise that we believe the child and then look at what the child is saying ... often there are clear disclosures which a child of a young age couldn't possibly know but it would have happened to them. (interview with Margaret) conference needs to mindful that two year olds do not generally make things up. (from case conference minutes, Richards family)

So children are generally regarded as vulnerable and child protection concern tends to be focused on the child's body, although, as the chapters that follow will show, it is the behaviour of parents that comes under scrutiny. I shall now discuss working with children in terms of job satisfaction.

Children make the job worthwhile

The rewards in the job are good outcomes for children. Successful adoptions are often cited as rewarding, but so too are birth families that make major changes and so allow children to stay at home and flourish. The passage below from an interview with Lorraine sees her talk about why she thinks the job is worthwhile. Although she is referring to a client who is a mother, she sees her as the child she has known for several years, through the care system.

> I suppose I could overestimate my importance to them, but the fact that you have been there for six or seven years, you know. For one girl I was dealing with this morning who has a baby, I am the longest established person in her life really, because she has changed placements, foster placements and she has little contact with family. So you take on that role and that then brings difficulties because as a good trade unionist or whatever you should be working your hours, you shouldn't be working extra hours, you shouldn't be expected to work at weekends. That brings a dilemma because I still feel that for children particularly on a care order, in long-term care, children who are in that system, we should be available you know, within reason. The emergency team should be able to contact you first and say... 'tell us a bit about what is going on'. (interview with Lorraine)

So children deserve commitment, even above and beyond contracted hours, even as a trade unionist that believes staff should not exceed their contracts.

'Direct work with children' is a highlight of the job. During the fieldwork, a glass-fronted cupboard next to the team manager's desk was cleared out and rearranged. I was told it would be divided into 'direct work with children stuff' and 'general stuff' on separate shelves. Several social workers said that direct work with children was the most rewarding part of the job. The specification that this is 'direct work' illustrates how the social work role has moved away from the workers using their own therapeutic interventions in families, towards something of a case manager role. Whilst some authorities have a formal purchaser–provider split in child and family services (Hood, 1997), the Uplands team is perhaps more typical in operating a less formal case management system. Social workers in the Uplands team assess risk and need and then tend to arrange for relevant services to be provided by other agencies. Having the opportunity to do 'direct work' is a therapeutic treat for the worker.

Work with parents for its own sake is not considered to be part of the social work task. Even work with parents that might impact on the children is arguably seen as secondary in import and status to direct work with children. Hall et al. (1999) cite a data extract where a social worker sees counselling for a father as within the domain of other professions, and not social work, whereas talking to a child *is* social work. This division existed in the Uplands team too. There exists a form of parent–child dichotomy.

Putting the children's needs before your own

The requirement for parents to put the children's needs before their own is a constant reference point in case talk and case recording. As Twigg and Atkin (1994), amongst others, have argued, need is an irredeemably contested concept. It can be invoked in defence of ideological or pragmatic positions. Within child welfare discourse, as King and Piper (1995) have pointed out, the child is constructed as a 'bundle of needs'. The background to this is what Zelizer (1985) has called the 'sacralisation' of the child in the West. As Lawler's (1999) research on 'needs talk' describes, the dominant idea seems to be that 'children need, mothers only want'. As stated above, the rhetoric of 'the child's needs' and 'the welfare of the child' is often employed to contrast an idealised notion of the child's welfare with that currently on offer from birth parents. The ideal of putting your children's needs before anything else is used as a standard against which parental behaviour can be matched.

> Quite often it (neglect) is about adults with emotional needs which tend to take precedence over the children. (interview with Mike)

Helen Warren seems unable to put Cathy's needs and welfare before her own. It has been suggested to me that she appears jealous of Cathy at times. Mrs Warren has shown a lack of interest in Cathy's health needs, e.g., preferring to stay in bed rather than attend a hospital appointment with her daughter. Her reluctance to visit Cathy on a regular basis and to take an active role in her care has identified her inability to put Cathy's needs and welfare before her own. (case conference report, Warren family file)

Occupational rhetoric would suggest that this principle is applied to both men and women as parents or carers. In practice, however, the concept is frequently invoked in relation to mothers. In particular, it is invoked in relation to mothers who choose bad men. The excerpt below, from a social worker and team manager supervision, concerns a woman, Nicola, who is seen as putting her children at risk by continuing to live with a violent partner, Jason.

Lisa: And plus the fact that Nicola is putting Jason's needs first.
Margaret: Yeah.
Lisa: And not able to protect the children.
Margaret: She's putting Jason's needs, but she is also putting her own needs first as well, isn't she? Because she needs to have a partner, doesn't she? I don't know whether I go as far as saying that she needs Jason in particular.
Lisa: Well she needs a partner.
Margaret: Because she has got seven kids I suppose to share the burden.
Lisa: Yeah, I mean saying that I think she, I think the situation as it stands now is that she, she really wants him to stay around because she is pregnant with his child.

The social workers see the ideal response for a woman in this situation as freeing herself of such a man. That is seen to be the natural response and one that would demonstrate the prioritising of the children's needs. This theme of women freeing themselves from violent men is discussed at some length in the next chapter.

Although the book's topic is gender, it has been noted above that this is of course not the only social division that affects the culture of the social work office. Although ethnicity has been found to be an important factor influencing the construction of child abuse and neglect, there were no significant ethnic divisions represented in the work of the Uplands team. As was noted in Chapter 1, the local population is overwhelmingly white, and those clients whose files I studied were all white. They were all ostensibly heterosexual, and gender constructions are in many ways founded on an assumption of heterosexuality. The client population is also living in poverty, and class is an important issue in the Uplands team. It is almost a truism of much contemporary feminist writing to state that gender relations cannot be considered separately from questions of class (see, for example, Brittan and Maynard, 1984; Skeggs, 1997). The next two chapters will go on to consider constructions of men and women, and will include a class dimension. Firstly, however, this next section will more generally introduce the issue of class and clienthood in child protection work.

Social class and community

In the 1970s and 80s, class was a major issue in academic social work discourse. A widely articulated perspective held that class structure was the key determinant of the nature of social work; it shaped the social 'problems' that social work was meant to solve, and determined the power relation of workers and clients (see, for example, Jones, 1983). This emphasis on class has been replaced by a concentration on discrimination and oppression, with particular attention paid to racism and sexism. Whilst many have been keen to maintain a focus on structural disadvantage, which would include an appreciation of economic factors, the centrality of class has undoubtedly faded. There is still some mention of poverty, but class, however defined, does not feature strongly in contemporary social work literature (an example of an exception is Kennedy, 1999).

Most of the clients of social workers are amongst the poorest in society (Becker and Macpherson, 1986). Child welfare work is no different. Parton writes that this work takes place at:

> the junction of the self-managed world of the affiliated and the twilight world of the socially and economically marginalized and excluded, particularly those sections of the poor who make up the biggest proportion of the 'clients' of child welfare services, such as single parent households, substance misusers, homeless families and certain ethnic groups. (Parton, 1998: 20)

As well as operating at the junction that Parton describes, Philp (1979) has also observed that social work occupies the space between the respectable and the deviant. This position is crucial to understanding how clients are constructed. There is recognition from all the Uplands social workers of the socio-economic status of most clients. At my very first meeting with the team, Brian told me that they only really work with poor working-class clients. Another colleague interjected that child protection can involve middle-class clients too, particularly with sexual abuse cases, but Brian maintained his argument, saying that they only really encountered middle-class people through adoption work. Both Brian and Margaret, the team leader, told me in interviews that an important part of their motivation to become social workers was wanting to be of use to working-class people.

> I came through in a working-class area and when I came of age I wanted to put something back into the area. (interview with Brian)

In a loose sense, the culture of the social work office is politicised. There is certainly a belief that, somewhere along the line, political decisions in the last couple of decades have adversely affected their clients. In the excerpt below, Lynne is referring to the social effects of Conservative Party policies from 1979 to 1997.

> I also believe that in the last 18 years we have had a government in power that has created an underclass if you like, and that we have got families out there that their children have now grown up and know nothing different to being on income support, don't know the work culture. It is the norm to be at home, it is the norm to apply to the DSS to buy a fridge or whatever. (Lynne, Docktown)

There is a general consensus in the Uplands team that they are working with people from an 'underclass'. The underclass idea has been articulated in many different ways in academic discourse (see Morris's summary, 1994). Gallie (1994) has summarised these different perspectives as 'conservative' and 'radical'. The conservative approach concentrates on the moral deficit of poor communities, and poor people's own responsibility for social problems. This discourse finds support in much of the popular press in the UK, with the use of censorious labels such as 'teenage mum' and 'feckless father'. In academic writings there is, for example, Murray's work (1990). Bagguley and Mann (1992) caricature such work as portraying poor working-class people as 'idle thieving bastards'. The other discourse, that Gallie calls the 'radical' approach, speaks of economic marginalisation, claiming that a distinction should be made between the quality of life of working-class people in general and the poorest group within the working class. People in this poorest group are seen as victims of the development of the labour market in advanced capitalism. The Uplands social workers make reference to both discourses in their talk about their patch.

As stated above, there is an appreciation of the structural and economic roots of poverty. Pete, in a passage from an interview that is both too long to reproduce and also difficult to quote without the risk of identifying the region, lists the deprivation factors which he identifies, many of which were cited at various times by other colleagues. He took me on an oral tour of the Uplands patch, which is summarised below:

- One estate has an 'award-winning' design with mid-floor entry to houses. There was initially no central heating, and downstairs bedrooms are damp. Forty per cent of houses are boarded up. Only people with problems end up living there. There is a transient population.
- On another estate, police only enter in twos and threes, or in cars. On one occasion some workers cut through an electricity cable and extinguished the streetlights, and left them not working because they decided it looked better in the dark. A while ago people were setting fire to their houses to get moved out. Now a tenants' association has been formed, social services have less work to do.
- Another estate is in two sections – new rebuilt red brick houses and other non-brick ones – most childcare referrals come from the latter.
- Other estates have no facilities (except a Spar shop and a social club in one case) and poor transport to local towns. In the case of one estate only, this is because most people live in private housing and have cars. In the others there are few cars. Geographical isolation and expensive shops lead to a poverty trap.

The deprivation outlined here is not seen as of the residents' own making. These are clearly seen as problems with a political and economic cause, but there is also a belief in the Uplands team that deprivation creates a distinctive patch culture, a cycle of poverty, a power deficit that leads to damaging behaviour:

You can get a patch culture, low incomes, poor housing, people out of work, school not seen as important and children out in the street all day. (county child protection officer, from fieldnotes 21 August)

Poverty...I think in many respects it is cyclic as well in that I am a great believer in expectations and aspirations and children having parental role models. Some children break out of it, but a lot of children just get caught up in the same sort of spiral, the same spiral that their parents have been caught up in. This is the bit about not a particularly high value on school and of education, leading to not a particular effort, leading to few qualifications, leading to lack of employment, leading to benefits, leading to the same sort of cycle of deprivation and poverty really. And a lot of our clients are clients that have been around for a while and we are seeing children of clients and children of children of clients. (interview with Pete)

Disciplining. I try to talk about making bedtime a pleasurable time, but they can't read stories to them because they can't read. Discipline is the only way they've got of having power over someone, I suppose. (interview with Debbie)

This power deficit Debbie alludes to is a concept employed to explain Uplands men in particular. They do not have access to opportunities for conventional male power (job, house, property) so they seek power in other ways which can be damaging to those around them, particularly women and children. Chapter 5 will return to this issue. The culture bred from deprivation is not regarded as vibrant and resilient, as working-class communities are often described in popular discourse. Rather, the effects of deprivation are seen to include cruelty, as shown by this example cited by Lisa of cruel humour in a local community:

she's victimised, mind...she hung herself and her little girl found her. They call her Nicola Choker up there. (Lisa, from fieldnotes)

Vibrancy and resilience do not form part of the construction of clients precisely because these are not regarded as people from the traditional working class. The excerpts above illustrate that both discourses of the underclass are present in the Uplands team. The New Right extreme of the moral failure discourse is not represented, but there is a belief that politically created deprivation does affect people's moral framework.

The language of community is very important in the social workers' talk about class and locality. Dicks (1999) describes two important academic and popular discourses of community, the 'good community' and the community as a 'vanishing other'. The former is a political usage entailing the potential for communal resistance or self-reliance. The latter is a nostalgia for a way of life found only in 'tightknit' communities, and typically in the past. In the Uplands there are thought to be traditional communities with relatively few social problems and newer ones that provide the raw material for most of the child protection work.

> I suppose there are areas of rural deprivation in many ways ... stuck in a bit of a time warp, but also meeting, particularly some of the areas north of Markettown, meeting the 20th century with, sort of, picking up all the wrong bits. The kids are getting into car crime, there is a tremendous drug problem in the estates. There is very little for young people to do, very little in terms of employment unless you come out of the valley. Um ... pretty hopeless actually, but within the Uplands still, in a way it is two separate lots of people. There are still very close-knit families and communities who have been there for generations and who social services have never heard of and probably never will and who never want to move outside the Uplands, totally self-sufficient, it is quite a mixture. (interview with Margaret)

This represents a crucial discursive distinction between the respectable traditional working class and the unrespectables, albeit a distinction described here in socio-political terms. It is a distinction that affects which cases are referred to the team and influences all professionals working in the field. As Skeggs (1997) has shown from her research into the intersection of class and gender identities, respectability is a central factor of identity formation, especially for working-class women. Many of the professionals involved in the wider child protection process, such as health visitors, family carers and social workers, are women from lower middle or working-class backgrounds. In the context of my research, many of this wider group will have been brought up in the Uplands area.

The office is not situated in the Uplands, but in the county town of River County. The 'patch' is therefore geographically distant. The social workers studied by Pithouse spoke of:

> the need for physical and social space between themselves and the twilight world of families on run-down council estates and the tightly packed terraced homes of the dock and sea-front areas they visit. (Pithouse, 1987: 87)

The Uplands social workers did not particularly speak of the need to keep a distance between themselves and their clients, but in fact a definite physical distance is created by the position of their office. The distance may, in part, contribute to the attribution of particular characteristics to the region of which the Uplands is part. The attribution of particular qualities to clients on the basis of their local identity is a fascinating feature, but not one that can be analysed in any depth without abandoning the anonymity of the region. It is important, however, to note that the ascription of class status and regional culture intersect in the construction of clients (see also Callaghan, 1998).

There is a general feeling that the parts of the Uplands where most clients live, the estates, are a very unpleasant environment. There is genuine sympathy for people who have no choice but to live on such estates. Debbie declares that she could not live there herself:

> The houses are damp, I wouldn't want to live there. I suppose if I had to I could, but I can't imagine it. I definitely wouldn't want to live there. (interview with Debbie)

In the face of this unpleasant environment, in which social workers spend a good deal of their day, one of the coping strategies is humour. This is a shared humour of those who know the area, know the stories that are told about different estates and different villages, and, in some cases, either live in the Uplands themselves or were brought up there. Lisa, the team member most likely to use humour in this way, gives a typical example below. She sets a client's inflated talk against the reality of his poverty and the poverty of the general area:

> he [a client] keeps talking about a plot of land he's inherited. It's probably an allotment or something. (Lisa, from fieldnotes)

So clients are the underclass. It is fully expected that clients will come from certain districts and share an experience of poverty, with associated factors such as unemployment, little education and poor housing. The roots of this are seen as economic, but the resulting problems are thought to be moral and emotional as well as material. Newer areas are much more likely to provide clientele than traditional working-class areas.

Many of those who have commented on gender and class in child protection have done so on the basis of an assumption that social work in general, and child protection work in particular, can be characterised as social control, or at least that family welfare professionals have considerable potential for control and coercion of families. For the final section of this chapter on the context of achieving clienthood, the discussion will move on to the relationship between worker and client in child protection work, specifically considering the issue of coercion and social control.

Social control

Whereas concern about the scrutiny of mothering in feminist literature has stemmed from the critique of child protection as social control, Gordon (1988) disagrees that child protection work is simply controlling, in that her historical research found many women choosing to seek help from protective agencies. She also argues that social control is not necessarily a bad thing anyway because protecting children some-times means going against the wishes of parents, and that means mothers too (Gordon, 1986). Wise (1990, 1995) argues a similar point from her own experience of working in child protection. As mentioned in the previous chapter, Ferguson (1997, 2001) has argued that much of the existing commentary on child protection is overly negative, focusing too much on its controlling aspects and downplaying the potential for child protection professionals to be genuinely enabling and empowering.

My fieldwork in the Uplands team suggests that there is in fact overt control in much routine practice. That is not to argue that there is no support or help for clients. It may well be that many clients regard their social worker very positively, but clients' accounts of their experiences are beyond the scope of the research design. As noted in the previous chapter, existing consumer research provides a fairly bleak picture. Parents found investigations and case conferences particularly distressing in Cleaver and Freeman's (1995) research, and the researchers concluded that social workers tend to be unaware of the extent of parental anxiety (see also Scott, 1996). In the next section, I intend to draw out some of the important aspects of social control in the child protection role, because these fundamentally affect how clients are constructed.

The relationship between worker and client in child protection social work is inherently problematic, and the difficulties in the relationship form the context of the construction of clients in the office culture. Local authority children's services in the 1990s became increasingly preoccupied with responding to allegations of child abuse (Dartington Social Research Unit, 1995). Not all abuse investigated is familial. Allegations are made against other parties, including family friends, neighbours, strangers, and people with professional contact with children, such as teachers. The Uplands team cases that I read about in files or discussed with social workers were, however, all cases of alleged familial abuse, using that term in its broadest sense to include, for example, the boyfriend of a child's mother who does not live in the home full time. Investigating familial abuse and neglect cannot be done in the context of a straightforwardly warm and trusting relationship between social worker and all family members. Some parties may well have asked for social services intervention: perhaps a child directly asking for help, or confiding in someone who then contacts the social services department, or one parent making an allegation against another. Also some parties may already have an established bond with a social worker. But conflict, on one level or another, is inevitable. There is an atmosphere of coercion surrounding the child protection role. Social control is very explicit. Lorraine acknowledges the trend by labelling child protection as authoritarian:

> *Lorraine*: You know there is less of this sort of welfare work I suppose.
> *Jonathan*: Right, right.
> *Lorraine*: And it is more sort of child protection and authoritarian if you like. (interview with Lorraine)

The authority role does not mean that all adult clients are seen as equally difficult. I found the picture to be more complex than that, as would be expected from my stated emphasis on multiple discourses. Chapters 4 and 5 will discuss the various different ways in which men and women are regarded by the social workers. But the possibility of coercion is inherent in a relationship with such a power differential. Client self-determination has been an important element of traditional social work values, although more recent statements of the ethical base of the profession have incorporated an acknowledgement that the use of authority to override client's wishes can be necessary (see, for example, British Association of Social Workers, 1996). The Uplands team staff manage the challenge that overt social control poses to their social work identity by deciding that in order to be fair to their clients they must be overt about the power differential. They speak of the importance of being clear with clients, that this is good social work and thoroughly compatible with their occupational identity.

> I spell it out... if we don't do ABC we'll be going back to court. If things don't change there'll be consequences... spelling it out – this is the situation. (interview with Claire)

> I think that from what Graham was saying, it was very much presented to her as 'this is your last chance, you know, if we find the kid's are still not going to the school and that you're still leading the same sort of lifestyle as before we're going to start looking at care'. (Mike's supervision with Margaret)

> This is very concerning as I thought you were doing much better than before. I am worried that this may mean that your standards have slipped and that you are returning to the way things used to be when living in Woodlands. As you know I do not like making threats or giving people ultimatums but I have to consider the children's needs. The children are still subject to care orders (except Leanne of course) and as such we still have shared parental responsibility and the right to remove them to a safe place if necessary. (letter from Pete to the Brown family, in their case file)

Making power overt seems to acquire the status of a social work intervention. As Howe (1992, 1996), amongst others, has observed, traditional therapeutic social work intervention does not form a very significant part of the contemporary social work role, and child protection workers have become care managers, as was noted above. The traditional idea of helping clients to learn strategies that will lead to change in their lives has faded. It has not disappeared. There are referrals made to specialist agencies for this traditional social work help, and some workers try some strategies with some clients. There is a great deal of support in the form of daycare for children, to ease stress on parents. But many of the 'redeemable' clients are, in the last analysis, expected to change solely in response to the threat of losing the care of their children. In practice, for the Uplands team social workers, 'working with' clients usually means monitoring the quality of their parenting and telling them what they have to change. As Howe puts it:

Clients are expected to comply and conform; they are not diagnosed, treated or cured. If they know the rules, it's up to them to decide whether or not to abide by them. (Howe, 1996: 88)

It was noted in the previous chapter that one of the most important rules is to agree a plausible explanation for abuse or neglect that fits with that of the social workers (Holland, 2000). Some clients understand the importance of compliance very well; Thoburn et al. quote a mother and father comparing the child protection process to getting parole:

It's a bit like a guy getting out of Broadmoor. What he has to do is say 'I'm terribly, terribly sorry about the whole thing. I'll never ever do it again.' And he's got to convince everyone of that, because if he doesn't, he's never going to get out. What he can't do is say 'No, it wasn't like that, that's not how it actually happened. What's happened to me has been wrong or unfair' or anything like that. Because if he says that, he's going to get another four or five years in Broadmoor, and it's very much the same kind of feeling. (Thoburn et al., 1995: 56)

The extent to which 'being clear about concerns' has achieved the status of a social work intervention is illustrated by the two pilot interviews in Docktown. The respondents were asked: 'What do you think helps people change? What kinds of things that social workers do are more likely to help?' The responses are reproduced below:

I think it very much depends on the family themselves and how they see the problem. The family, as I was saying earlier, the family need to recognise that there has been a difficulty or a problem and that that difficulty needs to be overcome, and that they want to change, to move forward. And unless the family recognise that, then change will not happen and obviously then that is where we start going down the road of care proceedings or whatever. I mean that is the last resort. You usually try all sorts of family support systems first to try and get change going as soon as possible, but we can only allow so long for that to happen, and if there isn't any movement towards making improvements and I think as long as you are open and honest with the family all the way through, that makes life easier for the social worker to say 'right, this is the cut-off point, you haven't done this, that and the other as expected and which you agreed to do, therefore we go along the lines of care proceedings and will work against your wishes if necessary, to gain what we think is best for this child'. (interview with Sarah, Docktown)

I think that the best policy is to be open with them and not to have a hidden agenda. If you put your cards on the table and not hold things back and say 'look, these are the concerns, these are the choices we have got, this is what we would like to do, this is how we think we can achieve that' and involve them in that process, they may think that it is a totally different problem, you know. I have always worked in a way that I have never hidden issues. I have always been completely honest with the clients and I think they respond to that. I don't know what else to say really. (interview with Lynne, Docktown)

These two social workers are, in effect, choosing this approach as their favoured social work intervention: the thing we do which most helps people to change is telling them they have to. I wonder whether Lynne's 'I don't know what else to say really' is effectively an admission that this is all that is on offer; that traditional social work helping strategies are just not part of the job. There are many accounts of cases which suggest that most, if not all, clients are aware of the social worker's ultimate authority:

You can't get hold of him because he thinks that we are to do with the police, you see. (Lisa's supervision with Margaret)

Mike mentioned a visit he had just done to an 11-year-old boy with learning difficulties. Mike said, 'I'm no expert but I think he was functioning as a 5-year-old.' On a previous visit, the boy had hidden under the table because he thought Mike had come to take him away. Mike said that because he is in local authority care he associated social workers arriving with him having to move to another placement. (from fieldnotes, 8 July)

It could be argued, of course, that clients are well aware of the power differential anyway. It should be stressed that making power overt does not necessarily lead to a uniformly conflictual situation. Many worker–client relationships continue to be very warm and, arguably, a generally positive experience. An example of where power is potentially subverted through humour is that of the Brown family. This was the only family I met during my fieldwork. As previously explained, the decision was taken to study only the social work office, but I took the chance when it was offered to accompany Pete on a visit to their home. The Browns received an overtly threatening letter from Pete, their social worker (see above), but continued to have a relationship with him that seemed genuinely warm. During a formal meeting in their home that the team manager also attended, the story was told (not for the first time, I gathered) of how Dean Brown had previously joked that Tracey, his wife, needed a diary for meetings like this since all the social workers had one. He had gone the next day to buy her one for 35p in Poundstretcher, a local budget shop. The price and the chosen shop contrasted sharply with the origins of the social workers' thick institutional diaries, serving to illustrate the difference of class and income, as well as poking fun at the trappings of authority.

Protecting children is the highest status role in the Uplands team. Although other work goes on, such as general family support and contact with children in long-term care, child protection will always take priority. In particular, a child protection emergency overrides everything. Although it is the most used phrase in this book, and therefore becomes somewhat mundane, in fact the words 'child protection' have a great deal of power in the social work office culture. That was one of the reasons I decided to focus on this aspect of the work of the childcare team. An example of its power is the sheet of paper pinned to the office noticeboard that explains the idea of 'prime time'. This is protected time for written work – two hours each week away from the office – that can be interrupted 'for child protection or personal emergency only'. On one occasion during the fieldwork I arrived in the office to find a fully fledged child protection emergency. A young child on Lisa's caseload, from the Jones family, had sustained a broken leg, and a doctor thought it may have been caused by the man in the house, Jason, the mother's boyfriend and father of the youngest child. Lisa and Margaret were spending all their time on the case that day, and there was a palpable air of excitement in the office. There was a sense in which this kind of crisis work was as important as it gets in the team. The metaphors used for child protection further illustrate its special status. In supervision, Joan talks of a case 'teetering on the brink of child protection'. The category 'child protection' is a distinct place that family problems move into. Joan also illustrates the emergency nature of child protection status when she talks of the same case 'ringing alarm bells'.

There is also some awareness in the team of the idea that child and family services should be 'refocused' away from child protection and towards more emphasis on children in need (Little, 1997). Brian shows his familiarity with the 'refocusing' debate when he says:

Jonathan: Interesting that unlike the others you didn't mention child protection.

Brian: I think of it in terms of the family, not just a child with a bruise. To see child protection as a child with a bruise doesn't get you very far. They're a child in need really. I know different social workers have different perspectives. (interview with Brian)

It was somewhat surprising to me that I did not encounter more talk of refocusing, given its prominence in policy debates in the late 1990s. In general it seemed that for most social workers the caseload of the team was relatively unquestioned.

Conclusion

The purpose of this chapter has been to complete the context of gender construction in child protection. Not every aspect of child protection work is *explicitly* gendered. There are other important divisions of the potential consumer population which fundamentally affect the construction of the client and will overlap with the gendered aspects covered in the next few chapters. Firstly, the local population is divided into likely potential clients and those who are unlikely to require a service because of social class and location, which are inseparable from the notion of respectability. It will be seen in Chapters 4 and 5 that constructions of men and women clients are fundamentally constructions of marginal class status. It was also shown above that family members do not have equal client status. Children are the rhetorical object of concern, they are claimed to be the principal (or only) client, but in fact everyday reference to 'clients' tends to mean parents because it is parents the workers focus on in day-to-day practice. The separation of children's clienthood from that of parents is a recurring theme, especially in the next chapter.

It was argued above that the parent–worker relationship is an inherently difficult one, where the power differential is deliberately made explicit, this openness itself achieving the status of a social work intervention. It will be seen in the chapters that follow that making authority explicit, in the shape of the giving of ultimatums, is, again, gender-specific. Men and women can both be given ultimatums, but of very different kinds. Although most of this chapter dealt with aspects of child protection work that are not explicitly gendered, a consistent theme of the book is that even ostensibly gender-neutral aspects of the construction of child protection work impact more on women because women are there with the children. The next chapter goes on to explore the issue of women as clients in detail.

4

Working with women

This chapter begins to explore the process of gender construction in the social work office, by focusing on working with women. Chapter 5 addresses working with men. There are many dimensions of gender construction in occupational culture that could be explored, including ethnomethodological study of talk about men and women, and detailed analysis of how accounts of clients are constructed for particular audiences. In this chapter I present an overview of social workers' expressed opinions about women in collegial talk, research interviews and case records. At the end of the chapter I identify some defining discourses of femininity.

Whilst the chapter focuses in particular on constructions of women, it is clear that, as previously asserted, these cannot be considered in isolation from constructions of men and children. There is a sense in which this chapter and the one that follows are not separate discussions. The construction of clients in the culture of the social work office assumes a framework of gender relations, and this assumed framework is predicated on heterosexuality. Clienthood is thoroughly gendered, and men and women clients are understood in direct relation to constructions of the other sex. As Connell (1987), amongst others, has observed, the concept of gender is inherently relational. Men and women clients are also constructed as distinct categories, with often strikingly different attitudes and behaviour. Because child abuse is the primary concern of the child protection system and more of this abuse is committed by men, constructions of men influence how women are constructed. Equally, the dominant construction of family life in the West is based on women's work as primary carers (Glenn, 1994; Dalley, 1996; Turney, 2000). There is, inevitably, an underlying dichotomy of men as abusers, and women as carers. Interestingly, there is also simultaneously a notion of equality that sees all clients as deserving to be regarded and responded to in the same way (see Chapter 7).

Women as mothers, women as social workers

The previous chapter noted some historically dominant family ideologies, namely the mother as primary carer and father as breadwinner. It is as mothers or grandmothers in the main that women clients feature in child protection work in the Uplands team. There are foster carers who are women, but they are not regarded as clients. I shall introduce this chapter with some mention of the historical construction of mother-hood, and of women in social work. As Chapter 2 noted, Foucault (1984) describes the creation of the modern mother in the last century through the hysterisation of women's bodies. Oakley (cited in Glenn, 1994: 186) has written that the contemporary 'myth of motherhood' rests on three beliefs: 'that all women need to be mothers, that all mothers need their children and that all children need their mothers'. Women are assumed to know what to do with children because they are seen as more embodied and emotional (Lupton and Barclay, 1997). Women have historically been subordinated in families to the extent that men's violence against their wives was regarded as legitimate until relatively recently (Dobash and Dobash, 1979). In the later twentieth century there have clearly been shifts in mothering, with more women employed outside the home (Walby, 1997) and alternative family formations such as lesbians bringing up children (Sullivan, 1996).

As Hallett (1989), amongst others, has reminded us, the majority of both clients and staff of social services departments are women. So 'social work is an activity carried out in the main by women with women' (Featherstone, 1997a: 175). Day's ethnographic research (1997) found that the staff themselves perceived childcare social work to be a woman's culture. Bella (1995) argues that social work is, to use Witz's term (1992), a 'successful female professional project', although her case is somewhat undermined by the continuing pre-dominance of men in the senior management of social services departments (Christie, 1998a). Social work is also, however, an arena in which the commonality of women is lost through categorisations of child welfare where poor and minority women become clients (Swift, 1995).

Mothering is central to occupational constructions of women in child protection work. The focus on the child as client described in the previous chapter has resulted in a tendency for social workers to respond to mothers only in relation to their impact on children, not as complex subjects in their own right (Featherstone, 1999). Parton et al.'s research (1997) found that maternal response as classified by the social worker was one of the most influential factors in deciding whether family situations would be classified as child protection cases warranting further action, including substitute care. Decisions about children's futures were made with reference to moral statements about maternal identity. In relation to sexual abuse cases, the necessary maternal attributes that social workers looked for were as follows:

> that they did not know about the abuse, and that when they were informed they responded in a way which was wholly maternal. That is, they made themselves available (to the child, and others in relation to the child such as the investigators, the courts, education and health professionals), their actions could always be interpreted as supportive of the child, providing for and nurturing the child, and their insight or knowledge was articulated to show that they knew they must do this. (Parton et al., 1997: 215)

In the material that follows, I attempt to trace the process of social workers' construction of women clients. Firstly I deal with the social workers' perceptions of the reality of women clients' lives, and then move on to discuss how women come to be seen as responsible for protection. The issue of worker empathy with clients is discussed, and the chapter ends with some initial ideas about messages from this research for practitioners.

The reality of women clients' lives

In the Uplands team, the tension that Pithouse (1987) describes between the abstract notion of the client as the object of service and the experience of encountering actual clients can also be found. It is hardly surprising, given the emphasis in contemporary child and family social work on investigation of alleged abuse, that the experience of the social workers is that the reality of women clients' lives does not usually conform to the ideal of family life outlined in the last chapter. Women often 'fail' as mothers. This section will describe the perceptions in the Uplands team of the reality of women clients' lives: the reality of family structures; the effects of oppression; women who choose to transgress; and the capacity for change.

The perceived reality of local family structures

Some sociological work by eminent scholars on current developments in gender relations and intimate relationships is optimistic about the extent to which change is underway (Giddens, 1992; Beck and Beck-Gernsheim, 1995). Ferguson summarises the change in the gender order outlined by this work: 'a reconstruction of family morality, gender destinies and taboos relating to marriage, parenthood, childhood and sexuality that were at the core of the triumph of simple modernity' (Ferguson, 1997: 229–30). The Uplands team social workers are not so upbeat about the reality of gender relations on their patch:

> The children tend to be with the women. Where there are men around they tend not to have the caring role. It's a cultural thing round here ... I think there's a feeling around that it's worse if a woman doesn't look after the kids than if a man doesn't. (interview with Brian)

> There is a macho culture in the Uplands particularly, I don't know whether it is as strong in other areas but it is noticeable in the Uplands. (interview with Lorraine)

> I suppose this is the Uplands, and I would think probably that the majority of day-to-day physical caring of children still falls upon the woman. I don't think the new man has reached the Uplands yet. (interview with Margaret)

There is a shared assumption in the team that the gender inequalities in the patch are severe; that women reluctantly bear all the domestic responsibility and men both dominate women and opt out of childcare work. It is also assumed, as all three excerpts above illustrate, that in the Uplands area, gender roles are more traditional than elsewhere (see also Callaghan, 1998).

The effects of oppression on women clients

In contrast with some research, for example Swift's (1995) encounter with social work practice in Canada, the Uplands social workers are, to an extent, influenced by some of the messages of second-wave feminism. This traditional family set-up is seen to be oppressive for women and often to have profoundly negative effects on them. So, for example, women's 'not coping' is often connected with the absence of help from the men in their lives. This failure to cope can be in relation to the practical demands of childcare and housework, or failure to manage children's behaviour. Pete, in the excerpt below, sees responsibility for mothers' difficulties as being located with partners and those who live nearby:

> A lot of women feel as if they are on their own, as if they can't cope anymore because there is no help, they are not getting enough help. Well that is not a matter of social work help. It is a matter of community help, partner etc. Some have their husbands as the disciplinarians and they are kept to one side and then wheeled in as and when necessary to administer punishment to the children. But over so much of the problems that the women are presenting is the fact of just not being able to cope anymore with the behaviour of the children. (interview with Pete)

The experience of having been abused is seen as leaving women with very low expectations of quality of life. Debbie, in an interview, told me 'our women clients don't expect anything'. In the following interview extract, Mike makes the general point that he is struck by how much his women clients put up with. He describes a particular case where the woman finally asserted herself with her partner over something Mike considered to be a fairly minor offence in comparison with the physical abuse she has suffered. There is a cultural gulf here. Mike is sympathetic to the woman's oppressive situation, but cannot understand her at all:

> Certainly there is a fair number of women on my caseload who aren't even really able to meet their own needs in terms of relationships, putting themselves first occasionally. A fairly common experience is women who for instance won't go to the doctor when they are feeling ill, or won't go to the doctor when they are obviously under an awful lot of stress and perhaps do need to go and see the doctor about that. I suppose another example of that kind of behaviour is women whose expectations from their partners seem kind of surprisingly low in terms of putting up with an awful lot, right up to physical abuse from their partners on a fairly frequent kind of basis. The most surprising thing that I ever encountered was someone who put up with years of really quite bad beatings from her partner and I went around there one day and she said 'I have chucked him out.' And the reason why she had finally chucked him out was because he had bought this car and

there were an awful lot of difficulties with it because it wasn't taxed or MOT'd. It was sitting outside and the police came around and happened to pick that one up and they ended up going to court and having a load of fines and things like that. She chucked him out then. She got cross about that and chucked him out, but she hadn't got cross at all about having to hide black eyes and bruises around the neck and things for years and years. That surprised me, but I think there certainly are quite a large number of women who will put up with an awful lot in terms of what happens to them. (interview with Mike)

Social workers talk of patterns that women get into. Swift's research (1995) found frequent reference to the idea of cycles of abuse: the abused becoming the abuser. In the Uplands team, the notion of a cycle was much more often invoked in relation to men and child sexual abuse (see the next chapter). The pattern the social workers described in relation to some women involves abuse begetting abuse, but in the sense that being a victim of one form of abuse will make it more likely that you will be a victim again in a different situation, not that it will necessarily turn you into an abuser. In particular, the pattern concept is invoked in relation to living with bad men:

The mother has low self-esteem, a poor self-image. She's grown up with a father who's violent, got herself into that kind of relationship. (interview with Claire)

The same pattern. All the women hooked up with men at a young age. Her sister is with a dominating man. (Mary to Mike, from fieldnotes)

The reality of the lives of many of the women clients is understood to involve living with bad men. The priority of the social workers, however, as is constantly repeated, is 'the welfare of the child' (see Chapter 3). So, although there is an appreciation of how an experience of oppression has negative outcomes for women, there is more practical concern about the effects of this on the children than on women themselves. The following excerpt illustrates how a social worker sees the effects on the children of living with a man who is violent towards their mother:

That can sometimes have two different effects on childcare. One is that partners who are abusive towards them are more likely to be abusive towards the children as well, and their own abilities to cope with the kids obviously get knocked back if they are being abused themselves or if they are not looking after themselves. To look after your kids you have got to look after yourself. (interview with Mike)

The Uplands social workers are aware of the potential for gender bias in service provision. Most recounted anecdotes about men clients being offered help with ironing or babysitting (see also Edwards, 1998), providing these as illustrations of unfairness to women, for whom such 'non-essentials' would not be considered.

Choosing to transgress

There are also women who are clearly judged to have chosen to transgress expected standards of motherhood. It has been claimed that women's failures as mothers are punished by the authorities in a way that men's are not. For example, Swift's research (1995) in Canada found that virtually any childcare performed by a man produced a positive view of him, whereas for mothers who are under scrutiny, much of the routine work of caring for children disappeared in social work accounts, while failures were highlighted. Tice's historical analysis of social work case files in the USA found that:

> Women's transgressions were . . . typically treated more harshly than men's because of the serious consequences thought to ensue when women neglected what were perceived as their primary obligations: scrubbing their homes and shielding their children. (Tice, 1998: 111)

I now discuss several examples of women being seen to transgress in the Uplands team. These are broadly grouped as choosing not to put children first and being an abuser.

Choosing not to put children first

Under this heading I discuss women choosing bad men, choosing drink or drugs, and being aggressive to social workers rather than co-operating. Howe (1992, 1996) has claimed that contemporary social work practice, purged of psychodynamic influences, views clients as making free rational choices to act in the ways they do. I deliberately use the word 'choose' because a traditional social work emphasis on the social and economic context of client's problems seems to be balanced by an ethic of ultimate individual responsibility (see also Chapter 7 on this). This balance is to be expected in a policy climate that has prioritised the targeting of dangerous families over broader social interventions (Parton, 1991). The following excerpt illustrates this. It is Mary's view that social policy can help many but not all:

> I think there is a hell of a lot that can be done in wider social policy, like housing, education, community services like play schemes, after school clubs, there are loads and loads of things. Benefits as well is the other thing. If a lot of those things were changed, a lot of the work that we do wouldn't be necessary. But that is not to say, I mean there was one point where I thought that would be the whole answer but I don't think that now. I think there are people who have got deeper problems and would always need some sort of social services. (interview with Mary)

The most overt way in which women choose not to put their children first is in choosing a bad man. This is an aspect that this chapter returns to more than once. It is a very interesting and important aspect of the construction of gender because it illustrates the process (highlighted by Farmer and Owen, 1995, 1998) of attention moving from abusive men onto the women who 'allow them' to stay around and abuse them or their children. This 'choice' will be discussed in more depth later in the chapter.

Another example of women choosing to prioritise something other than their children is through use of alcohol and drugs. As Ettorre (1992: 139) writes, women substance users are seen as 'unfit mothers' and 'polluted women'. Brian gives an example of such a case here:

> We couldn't get the mum to see the risks. Drugs take over. You give up your independence. You become dependent on how the drugs react in your system. It's difficult. You've got to put the welfare of the child first. There's nothing to be gained if the child is injured or killed, you've got to protect them. The mother accepted the child should go into care. She signed the forms. She recognised that what she could offer wasn't enough. (interview with Brian)

Some women are experienced as aggressive. Margaret makes reference to such women in the course of arguing that not only men clients are aggressive:

> I can think of a bloke who had me pinned up against the door once, but I can also think of a 17-year-old-girl who had me pinned up against a wall once, so I don't automatically look at blokes as being the aggressive ones. I can think of very aggressive women, screaming down the phone. In fact I think women are probably more aggressive down the phone than men actually, but then again there are more of them. (interview with Margaret)

This aggression is, in a sense, seen as a choice too. Although one possible interpretation of aggression is as an attempt to ward off interfering professionals and protect your custody of your children, it is more likely to be seen as damaging a mother's case because she is choosing to fight rather than co-operate with social services. Putting your children first means co-operating. Behind this is the assumption that if your own relationship with your children was threatened you would do anything that would work in getting them back. Allowances are not made for clients' lack of pragmatism and inability to read the professionals' etiquette.

When children are separated from their mothers, through enforced accommodation in the care of the local authority, there are still judgements made about the extent to which the women put their children's needs first. The appropriate response to separation is, again, one of total co-operation with the social services plans. Parents need to conform to the plans for contact that the authority has dictated in order to meet their children's needs The excerpts below concern women who failed to conform, either, in the case of Janice, by demanding more contact than was on offer or, in the case of the mother Mike describes, by not attending enough contact sessions.

Pete: Even despite the fact that Sian has said, and Janice knows, that Sian doesn't want overnight stays.

Margaret: That is certainly putting pressure. Why is she doing that? You know I can imagine the scenario on a Sunday, taking her to the bedroom and saying 'look this is the bedroom that you could have if you stay here'. (Pete's supervision with Margaret)

They went into care. They were one and a half and two, and the mum never really built up a satisfactory pattern of contact. Seeing mum was always on the cards but it had never actually happened. She would disappear for months on end and so she didn't appear in these children's lives. She would begin to sort of build up expectations, start visiting regularly, and it is 'oh you know you are coming back to live with me', and then she would disappear. This happened a number of times and eventually to get the kids out of this pattern, the build up of hopes and then dashing the hopes, we decided we would place them for adoption. (interview with Mike)

Because the children's welfare is the only real consideration, there seems to be relatively little concern about the potential emotional impact of separation on mothers. Thoburn et al. have reported the overwhelming fear of losing children that is engendered by a procedure such as a case conference. One mother they spoke to said she experienced 'sheer panic. I just thought I wouldn't have my son anymore, that they'd take him away. I was just all over the place' (Thoburn et al., 1995: 53). There did not seem to be any overt consideration in the Uplands team of the possible emotional implications for mothers in seeing the children at all, or in seeing them as little as social services allow. Mothers have to follow the rules, and wanting too much contact or not wanting enough are both regarded as transgressions. It is perhaps a necessary mechanism for coping with an inherently uncertain role that social workers who have decided children are best off away from their mothers do not give much consideration to the effects of this on the mothers.

Being an abuser

As Coward (1997) has observed in her commentary on the popular media, maternal abuse tends to be portrayed as particularly horrifying. It violates the image of the nurturing mother. An example of this from the social work office is the case file on a family in which the father was convicted of attempting to murder the mother. The original referral related to his complaint to the police that his wife had tried to 'drown' his son. Although it was seemingly accepted by all professionals that the incident involved holding the boy's head under the bath water for a few seconds in exasperation, and did not constitute an ongoing risk to the boy's safety, the 'drowning' reappeared in documents for many years, even though awareness of the father's violence had overtaken it as perceived risk to the child.

The mother was reconstructed as victim of the father's violence, but the horror of the 'drowning' was evident from the ongoing reference to the event.

There are also cases where the woman is not seen as sole abuser, but as contributing to an abusive family situation. These are cases where she is 'as bad as he is'. This construction of family violence and abuse is also mentioned in the next chapter, but the following extracts give a flavour of the construction of such cases. Mike recounts his experience of working with couples who are in the process of separating. He regards these as a 'type of case' where the problems are interactive and intractable. Sarah, although from a different social work office, shows a similar tendency to cast doubt on a woman's assertion that she is straightforwardly a victim of violence, as I found in relation to some cases in the Uplands.

> It's matrimonial stuff – horrible! They have their own agendas. There are two very plausible people and who the hell do you believe? I hated it. Somebody is lying. It could be both. If you do a few, you get to know who's lying. (Mike, from fieldnotes, 8 July)

> It is perceived by the partner, the female partner that is, that the male partner is the one causing the problems. How sure that is I don't know. I mean there are certainly difficulties with both female and male partners but certainly the arguments in the household have increased. (interview with Sarah, Docktown)

The capacity to change

The Uplands social workers are generally not very optimistic about their success rate in helping parents to change. There is an expectation that family situations will remain much the same, any improvements being gradual and fairly subtle.

> Often with cases on the child protection register there's drift, and no change, and you wonder 'why bother?' (interview with Claire)

There is, however, the 'exceptional client' (Pithouse, 1987). In the Uplands team this is someone who shows dramatic change. This is much more likely to be a woman than a man:

What stood out was the dramatic change. Often there's no progress at all. Quite quickly there was change in the children's behaviour, her self-esteem, the home conditions, the school noticed a change in the children, her commitment to working with us changed. There was a real threat the children would be removed. Often it's fight or flight, but often people don't change...I don't think he will ever change. I was impressed by her. (interview with Claire)

I don't know what keeps you in it [the job]. I suppose it is the individual, just if you feel that, not your personal intervention, but that the interaction with this person has made a positive difference, and the long-term difference probably does keep you going. (interview with Lorraine)

It is this exceptional client who tips the balance towards the job being a rewarding one for Lorraine. The case Claire described was out of the ordinary precisely because there was observable change in the woman, although not in the man. There is perhaps an underlying assumption in the team that men are unlikely to change, whereas women can. This leads to the expectation that when there is a problematic man around, it is the woman's responsibility to act to change the situation. This responsibility is discussed in the next section.

Women's responsibility for protection

Hooper (1992b) has written that the child protection system has always sought to enforce rather than replace parental responsibility for children, and in doing so has reflected and perpetuated gendered definitions of proper parenting. She argues that child protection discourse is preoccupied not with causality but with parental responsibility, so rather than looking to intervene with abusers, officials look to strengthen the protection of the child by non-abusing parents. Since it is men who are more often responsible for abuse, mothers are the main alternative source of child protection. It is they who are bodily present in families. Some of the Uplands social workers were overt about this:

More of my work has been with children in long-term care, and also with trying to keep children out of the care system, so there is a lot of intensive work with families and families generally means mothers. (interview with Lorraine)

I think also something to remember is that the child is our client. We are child-centred. First and foremost we are looking at the child's needs, and radiating out from the child's needs are the primary carers and the people involved, and invariably the woman is the primary carer. (interview with Margaret)

Working with women is also so deep-rooted in the culture of child protection social work as to be unquestioned, to an extent. Despite my stated interest in working with men, Claire, in the more lengthy extract below, only seems to be able to conceive of women as the parental clients when men are violent in the home:

Claire: I've got strong views on domestic violence. My feeling is that with domestic violence on all levels, children are affected. Even if not physically abused it stays with them for life. I think it should become a child protection issue. In the first case domestic violence and drinking was the main issue. Families, mothers, sometimes don't realise how serious it is. We should never ignore or play down violence.

Jonathan: What do you think social workers should do about it?

Claire: Educating people, perhaps in groups, mothers' groups, play groups, parenting classes. It becomes the norm – 'he hits me but only when he has a drink'. There are two classic myths, the other is 'he hits me, but that's OK because he never touches the kids'. Quite often children are caught up in it, intentionally or not. Apart from education, liaising with family support. It should be high on the agenda, there should be more training for social workers. I've been on courses, things like how women get into a cycle of violence, how it becomes a way of life – they have a violent father, then a violent partner. It's never acceptable, there are never any excuses. Not all social workers think it should be that high profile. I do. Often neighbours, extended family, friends know it's going on. They say 'well it's nothing to do with me', or 'he can be nice'.

Claire starts by using the rhetoric of 'domestic violence is bad for children' that is relatively new to childcare social work (Mullender, 1996).

She immediately gives away that she believes this is an issue for mothers by slipping from 'families' to 'mothers', and then goes on after my question to reveal that she can only encompass the possibility of working with women on the issue of violence. She implies that by 'parenting classes' she in fact means the previously stated 'mothers' groups' when she describes the content of such a group as addressed to women who believe myths about violent men. It is the *women* who are caught in a cycle of violence, and it is women who you engage on the topic. It seems that the possibility of addressing a violent man about his behaviour is not on the agenda.

Failure to protect

Women's responsibility for protecting children against men is a recurring theme in the ethnographic data. Working with abusive men in any way is not an option. The response is to put pressure on her to get him out. This is the case with both sexual abusers and men who violently abuse their women partners (Hooper, 1992a; Mullender, 1997; Humphries, 1999). Women are held responsible for protecting their children from men's bodily excesses. The key concept that reinforces women's responsibility for men is the 'failure to protect'. It is explicitly used in the following:

> Well, failing to protect is usually around where there is another in the household. The mother is not putting the child's needs before her own basically. She wants a relationship; she therefore is blinkered to the fact that the man in the relationship could pose a threat. (interview with Margaret)

> *Jonathan*: What's the issue with the six children?
> *Lisa*: Escalating violence in the home. Mother's failure to protect the children. (from fieldnotes, 24 July)

> The mother was supporting the father and saying he couldn't have done it, so we were in a situation where we had to look at the possibility of the mother protecting these children, and she wasn't. (interview with Lynne, Docktown)

In cases where the woman is expected to protect the children by getting the man out of the house, there does tend to be a clear understanding that the violence is coming from him. She is a victim, but to maintain an untainted position of the innocent victim she needs to act immediately. If she does not, she can be tainted in some way, either as unable to escape because abuse is all she has ever known or, less often, as attracted to bad men. As mentioned above, there are other cases where the woman is constructed as 'as bad as he is'. The excerpt below relates to one such case. Here the woman is expected to do the protecting, but with the man still present in the house. The statement effectively asserts that she has a role in the violence:

> It was agreed that Ms Faulkner would, for the sake of the children, try to diffuse any altercations before they lead to violence. (child protection plan, Faulkner family file)

As Hooper (1992a), amongst others, has shown, there is a tradition within academic and professional commentary on sexual abuse of viewing some women as colluding with sexual abuse. As Parton and Parton (1989) point out, this tradition is reflected in the most high-profile official document on sexual abuse in the UK, the Cleveland Report (Secretary of State, 1988). Brian conveys this theory about some situations of sexual abuse when he recounts the content of his Faithfull Foundation course to colleagues:

> Sometimes the man is authoritarian, but sometimes the mother is matriarchal and still allows the man to carry on his tricks underneath. (Brian, from fieldnotes, 28 August)

Outside the criminal justice process, there is no provision in the law for the enforced removal of a perpetrator. In Britain, the Children Act 1989 (s. 5 para. 2) allows only for authorities to assist perpetrators of child abuse to leave the home. Social workers in the Uplands team operate on the principle that the only realistic way of removing an abuser in the absence of a criminal charge or conviction is to entreat a woman to issue him with an ultimatum that will force him out. O'Hagan and Dillenburger (1995: 172–3) argue that this is mainstream practice.

They have to choose

Women's responsibility for protection against abusive men is expressed as a clear choice: him or the kids.

> If domestic violence has a high profile within the family I am sure that as a department we would be saying to the woman that you must make a choice about whether you want to stay with this man or leave him. (interview with Margaret)

> Where women are faced with the choice 'it's your children or your partner' quite often they don't make the choice. They choose the partner. (interview with Claire)

> *Margaret:* I mean we have asked Nicola to make the decision about ...
> *Lisa:* Jason or the children.
> *Margaret:* Exactly.
> *Lisa:* And she has chosen Jason.
> *Margaret:* Well she is choosing both isn't she, she won't make that decision. She is choosing the both. (Lisa's supervision with Margaret)

> The child is actually with an adoptive family and to see her now, and how she has developed confidence, stature, that is rewarding. She is not a sad little girl now; she is brave and bubbly. It is sad for her mother, but her mother had choices and chose her partner. That's the kind of process that you go through. It is not always as clear cut as that. (Lynne, Docktown)

Lynne, in the last of these extracts, acknowledges there is not always a clear-cut 'choice'. Claire's view that women often 'don't make the choice' and Margaret's comment that Nicola is 'choosing both' also accept that women do not necessarily make a calm, rational choice to give up their children. Despite these notes of caution, there is a strong culture of laying down ultimatums to women living with abusive men: if it is bad for the children, you have to get him out. Farmer and Owen's research (1995, 1998) has shown that many women living with violent men are afraid to go to social services departments for help, for fear their children will be taken into care. Coming forward for help is viewed positively, but failure then to throw the man out can indeed result in these fears being realised. Ultimatums do not consider the complex reasons why women may want men to stay, or why they are persuaded or coerced into letting them stay. This approach to the presence of violent or abusive men fits with Howe's observations that, in contemporary social work, change in clients is expected in response to the laying down of rules, rather than any therapeutic intervention (see Chapter 4).

Coercion

To enforce responsibility, the authority of the statutory social worker is often invoked:

> We used to have a very good relationship. Then they slipped considerably. We had to start threatening really. You'll have seen some threatening letters, pleading letters. Requests become pleas become threats. (Pete, from fieldnotes, 3 July)

> Brian said . . . it is not their role to work with men who abuse, but rather to make sure children are protected by getting the man out. He repeated the point later and it became clear that he took 'abuse' only to mean child sexual abuse. I asked on the second occasion whether they were often involved in getting men out of the house. The answer implied that this was not often, but that he was referring to a particular recent situation, and in this one case there were not any statutes used. Margaret said, 'let's face it, we usually do it by threatening to case conference'. (team meeting, from fieldnotes, 1 July)

Coercion can be presented as 'concern'. This is a term which signifies risk, which Parton (1998), amongst others, has claimed is the rationale for most of the interventions of local authority child and family social work in the late 1990s. The term 'concern' is inseparable from the possibility of coercion, because investigations into children at risk are conducted with parents fully aware of the context of the child protection register and legal orders.

> I wasn't sure how, if he started pleading with her, 'look I've got nowhere to live, I'm an innocent man', this, that and the other, I wasn't quite sure how well she'd stand up to that sort of theme. So it was as though she ought to know the score if he did come to live with her, which was basically that we'd get very, very concerned. (Mike's supervision with Margaret)

As much of the material presented thus far has implied, child protection work is emotionally highly charged for the staff involved (Morrison, 1990; McMahon, 1998). The chapter will now go on to consider the issue of empathy with women clients, which includes consideration of some aspects of the emotional reactions of social workers.

Empathy

Corby and Millar (1997) cast doubts on the possibility for social workers to combine the demands of implementing child protection procedures with traditional social work roles of empathy, sensitivity and support. There are certainly tensions to be observed in the Uplands team; tensions which could be seen as inherent in the child protection role. It seems appropriate at this point to describe some of the important tensions that can be found in relation to the construction of women clients.

Victims of circumstances

As explained above, there is a strong sense in which women clients are constructed as victims of difficult circumstances. Corby (1987, 1991) found social workers to have a general psychosocial view of clients' problems, making reference to emotional deprivation and stressful environments. As previously outlined, as well as recourse to general environmental factors to explain women clients' circumstances, the influence of feminism can also be seen in the social workers' case talk. This construction of women clients provokes an empathetic response from both men and women social workers, who seem broadly in agreement about the oppressed state of the women they work with and the responsibility of the men around them for much of this oppression. The genuine difficulties they cite as causal, explanatory factors encompass trauma from both past and present. The excerpts below, for example, cite experience of childhood neglect, sexual abuse and coercion from a male partner as relevant to explaining current difficulties:

> She had always found it particularly difficult to cope with all the demands of being a lone parent and having had a care history herself,

she has had a very abusive childhood, at the age of three she was left for three days in a flat on her own with her younger brother who spent the whole three days in a cot, whom she basically kept alive by feeding biscuits and pop. At the age of three, which is how old my son is now. (interview with Pete)

She has had really difficult background, childhood herself, had a step-father who's in prison for sexually abusing her and her three sisters which went on for years. (interview with Mary)

He got his own way. He stayed. There was complete denial on his part. I think the mother acted out of fear. I felt angry at him, but sympathy for her, what must have been going through her mind – 'he'll come back and beat me up'. Often people think 'anything for a quiet life'. But she didn't realise the damage it would do to her daughter. I don't know the outcome. When I left she was accommodated. (interview with Claire)

Working with women

Working with women clients forms part of the occupational identity of childcare social workers, and women workers in particular. When asked in interviews about a memorable, rewarding case, the respondents all either talked of a child with a happy outcome or a mother who had changed for the better. One of the social workers, Lorraine, was very clear that her motivation for doing social work in the first place had been a strong interest in working with women. Despite this, when asked what kept her in the job, she spoke only of child clients. When asked to reflect on this potential paradox, she said:

I think I was probably being optimistic, that you could do some work that had benefits for women, that would have long lasting benefits for women. Sometimes I get depressed about the whole thing and wonder actually how much good the work actually does. (interview with Lorraine)

This echoes White's research (1995), that found women speaking of their difficulty in reconciling private feminism with jobs as state social workers. In the field of education, Stanworth (1983) found a similar mismatch between teachers' beliefs about gender and actual practices in the classroom. Lorraine refers directly to this difficulty, as does Mary:

I have to admit in this job I have felt quite often 'what are we doing to women?' Quite often it does feel like you are sort of persecuting women for the inadequacies of society . . . I went through a phase a couple of months ago where I was really thinking 'what am I doing here?' I just felt that I wasn't being helpful to anybody. And it does feel like quite often you are poking your nose in or you know you are being very judgmental on people. (interview with Mary)

There are inevitable tensions involved for feminists working in child protection (Wise, 1990, 1995). Situations will arise where there are conflicts between the interests of women and children, and situations where the worker will have to oppose the woman client. The personal tensions involved in working with women cannot be avoided by women social workers, since many of them are deliberately assigned to work with women and girls. In particular, it is a belief of social work culture that only women should work with sexually abused girls.

Exasperating women

Women who cannot act when a particular action would make all the difference to their future with their children can exasperate social workers. The reaction seems to be one of 'why couldn't she just do it?' There seems to be a lack of empathy with women whose behaviour is incomprehensible. In particular, it seems that women social workers find it difficult, if not impossible, to empathise with women clients remaining in situations that they themselves would not tolerate. The excerpts below illustrate this. Mary cannot really understand why something as simple as keeping the house clean and safe should be so paralysing. Lisa and Margaret both show their disdain for a woman's inconsistency in failing to keep to her resolve in breaking with her violent boyfriend.

The obstacles to her having the child back are really quite minor and yet somehow or another her attitude is not allowing her to overcome them, so it is really frustrating sometimes. You feel like shaking her, you know, 'if you just clean up this house and keep it that way, that is one major obstacle gone'. (interview with Mary)

Lisa: Jason went out and got drunk the next night and came back and
          she wouldn't let him in, and basically phoned the emergency ser-
          vices at twenty to four in the morning and said 'sort me out with
          somewhere to go'. Nothing came of that. And she then said that
          she was okay, that she could stop Jason from coming into the
          house, which lasted (her body language says 'a very short time').
Margaret: Basically she wasn't offered a refuge because she said she had
          thrown him out and then she would have the house and she was
          advised that if he tried to get in then she must call the police.
Lisa: I mean she had him up the next morning. (Lisa's supervision
          with Margaret)

Whilst there does seem to be a lack of empathy in terms of a failure to
imagine how women could let themselves live in such bad situations,
there is empathy on another level. The background to Mary's frustration with her client is Mary's desire for this woman to keep her child
living with her, and the knowledge that the woman's failings will count
against her when her performance is evaluated through child protection procedures. So the frustration is perhaps inspired by her imagining the trauma of having a child removed.

The lack of empathy with women who fail is linked to the ideology
of mothering as natural, mentioned at the beginning of the chapter.
Women who cannot simply do what the social services department
tells them they have to do in order to keep their children safe from
harm are constructed as unnatural, when the necessary action is seen
to be straightforward. You would simply tidy the house, or make sure
he did not come back, if you were behaving like a natural mother.
Other qualitative research has found similar recourse to the natural
motherhood ideology. For example, Hall et al.'s work (1999) on social
work talk claims there is a parent–mother dichotomy. You can learn
how to parent, whereas motherhood is a natural bond, and a woman
who is seen to reject it is a 'monster'.

Difficult women

As discussed above, in the context of women who 'choose' to transgress, some women clients are experienced as aggressive. These
women are amongst those cited as 'difficult'. The social workers were

specifically asked in the interviews about women and men clients they had found difficult for any reason. Aggression creates barriers to communication, and serves to mark the client out as transgressing both informal rules of social working and gendered expectations of women's behaviour, although aggression does fit a popular expectation of 'rough' working-class women. Women who present in other ways can be constructed as difficult too. The excerpts below are examples of such women. The first concerns a woman who is superficially co-operative ('saying the right things'), but is thought to be deceptive, or concealing important information. The second extract is someone who followed the rules of interaction with a social worker up to a point, but was found wanting by not fully accepting the official line on her failings (not confessing her wrong) and by not showing observable change in her behaviour. Mike says that aggression is easier to handle because it is more straightforward.

> I mean going back to what you were saying originally she is saying the right things. However, we were saying this after the core meeting yesterday about how she was saying the right things but there are lots of hidden agendas there really that we are aware of. (Lisa's supervision with Margaret)

> I think the most difficult thing to deal with really is evasiveness. I can certainly think of one person who at times of crisis will get in touch with me, usually for financial help, to deal with that immediate crisis. But there are a lot of concerns around; a lot of concerns being expressed from school and police about standards of child care. In terms of actually trying to deal with those issues she is very, very evasive, and either simply won't be there with quite alarming regularity, or else will minimise everything. Even if you can actually get her to acknowledge the existence of a problem, she'll then say 'everything is going to be all right now, yes I will sort that out, yes the kid will go to school every day from now on' or whatever. You know full well that nothing is actually going to change, and you can't get past that level of interaction where you are never actually communicating, it is all about 'what can I do to get rid of this busybody from the welfare?' It never gets any further than that really. I think that is perhaps the most difficult reaction to deal with. You get other people who will react with aggression towards you, but at least there is a communication there. At least you can actually have a discussion, even if the discussions in part are being conducted in a very

high volume. You can actually get somewhere with that kind of a response.
Evasiveness is very difficult to deal with. (interview with Mike)

Conclusion

The picture of the construction of women in the social work office is
a complex one with conflicting perspectives influencing practice.
Whereas the next chapter is explicitly structured around 'discourses of
masculinity', I chose not to structure this chapter in a similar fashion.
In some respects the picture of constructions of women is more complex than that of constructions of men. As will be seen, much of the
masculinity discourse is negative (although there are also some
important contrary influences). Constructions of women are, however, more genuinely mixed between positives and negatives. More is
expected of women, but when they fall they fall from a greater height.
Not much is expected of men anyway. Traditional notions of respectable femininity exist alongside more recent ideas derived from feminism. Both the traditional and the newer discourses feed into an
occupational culture that can only really conceive of women as the
adult clients. Men are simply not as much clients as women are.
Despite the complex and conflicting picture of women's clienthood, it
is possible to identify some defining discourses of femininity. These
are women as oppressed, women as responsible for protection, and
women as making choices.

Women are seen as oppressed by the men they live with, the wider
community they live in, and potentially by welfare services. This
belief, however, is overridden by the powerful discourse of women as
responsible for protecting children. It is women who have to be the
protectors, even if very difficult family situations are seen to be
caused by other individuals, by the woman's oppressive history, or by
socio-economic conditions. This protection of children is seen as the
natural course of action in response to the demands of the authorities
for change. This change is regarded as within a woman's grasp
because she can choose to change. Stenson (1993) has commented
that what he calls the 'educative' discourse in social work aims to
produce a client who is a unitary subject, the author of her actions;
a client who can change, and not get stuck in the same old patterns.
Clients are, in the last analysis, regarded as able to change if they
have to.

Many of the *outcomes* of the child protection process are gendered, but obviously not all aspects of the *process itself* are explicitly gendered. The effect of some aspects of organisational procedures and professional practice are only indirectly gendered. Others are not particularly gendered at all, arguably impacting equally on men and women. The key insight to hold onto is that the system is set up to assess and manage risk, and where perceptions of risk differ between parent and professionals, inevitably some coercive practices are used, so those subject to the system, the 'clients', will experience coercion. The adults in the front line are far more often women. Given the continuing gendered division of labour in the care of children, any system set up to scrutinise child-rearing will inevitably bear down on women, since it is women who do the work (Parton and Parton, 1989).

Implications for practice

The constructions of women described above have important implications for social work practice. The general question of the relevance of the material in the book for practitioners is addressed in Chapter 9, including the issue of theory for practice, but here I outline some of the most immediate implications of the particular research findings highlighted in this chapter.

- As previous research has shown, women tend to be the focus of child protection interventions for several different reasons. The most important implication of this research evidence for practice is that social workers should constantly question how they spend their time with client families and, in particular, question the attribution of responsibility to women for protecting children from the abusive behaviour of men.
- There is some tension between the view that women are trapped by their circumstances and the belief that they are able to act decisively when it is crucial for their children's welfare. Practitioners have to struggle with this tension and there is no easy resolution. Chapters 7 and 9 return to this theme. At this point, however, it is worth noting that these two perspectives are, on the face of it, contradictory.
- In the light of the majority of research evidence on domestic violence, social workers should question the construction of cases where violence is seen as women's responsibility.

● Social workers ought to consider how women get themselves into situations where they seem to act against their interests by staying with abusive men. There are many complex possibilities here, including fear of the consequences of leaving and regarding men as in some respects a resource for their children, despite the violence.
● A critical perspective on routine practice with women who mistreat children is needed. Social workers ought to be aware of how they view 'bad mothers' in comparison with how they view 'bad fathers'.

As stated at the outset, the construction of gendered others is inherently relational. Social workers construct others in relation to their self-perception. This can be seen throughout the chapter above where women and, to an extent, men social workers are both implicitly and explicitly comparing women clients' expectations, beliefs and actions with their own. Women clients are also constructed in relation to a notion of client masculinity. The next chapter moves on to discuss this. There is reference back to the themes of this chapter and continued reflection on the implications of constructing gendered others for social workers' sense of self.

5

Working with men

The discussion of working with men clients in this chapter is structured as follows. I introduce the topic by summarising how the 'problem of men' has come to be a matter for social policy development in the UK. I then explain my use of the term 'discourses' of masculinity, and the rest of the chapter is taken up with a description of six different discourses of masculinity in the social work office. Some conclusions will be drawn. I then summarise the implications of the research findings for social work practice.

The 'problem of men'

Collier (1998) and Connell (2000) remind us that in relation to a range of issues, including crime, parenting, working with children, child support, sexuality, marriage and divorce, the behaviour of men has been called into question in media, academic and political discourse. The fact that the topic of masculinity seems to be considered 'good copy' in much of the media, and not just in the intellectual press, is an indication of its currency and accessibility. Whilst the 'problem of men' is not a unitary discourse, and does not arise from a homogeneous set of concerns, but comes from several different directions and focuses on a variety of behaviours, it is possible to outline two fundamentally different approaches that define this social problem. This distinction is rather crude, but may be of some use to people in navigating this increasingly complex terrain of masculinity discourse. The two approaches are men as perpetrators and men as victims. According to the first approach, men are a source of danger and disorder, an antisocial influence. There is, here, an emphasis on the privileges of masculinity (Messner, 1997). According to the second approach, men are facing greater disadvantage in society than women. It is men who are the 'unprotected sex', to cite the title of Patrick Jones's play that was performed in Cardiff during 1999 (P. Jones, 2001). Here the emphasis is on the costs of masculinity (Messner, 1997).

The dominant notion in the mainstream media seems to be that of the 'crisis of masculinity'. Some widely disseminated examples of popular academic writings which rely on this notion are Faludi (1999) and Clare (2000). Typically, this crisis discourse draws on both approaches outlined above, in that men are described as exhibiting antisocial and destructive behaviour, but that this is in response to insecurity about their 'role'. In general, there is a fairly heavy emphasis within this discourse on the costs of masculinity. Ros Coward (1999), a journalist with a feminist heritage, goes as far as to claim that it is men who are now the primary victims of the gender order, rather than women.

Hearn (1998) noted that masculinity was, in 1998, 'just about' on political and policy agendas in the UK. By the time this book is being written (2001), masculinity is very firmly on the agenda of some UK government departments, although not all (Featherstone, 2001). Across the Western world, there is increasing attention being paid to the 'problem of men'. Messner (1997: 1) has observed that 'in the past few years the United States has discovered men'. The intersection of masculinities and social work is an increasingly mainstream topic in the social work literature, if not in social work offices (see Cavanagh and Cree, 1996; Pease, 1997; Pringle, 1998b; Courtenay, 2000; Christie, 2001).

In the light of my stated emphasis in Chapter 2 on contextual constructionism, I should make it clear that I believe many men *are* in fact a problem. It is possible to discuss how men are constructed (or problematised) by social workers, whilst also accepting that not only are some dominant societal notions of maleness barriers to sex equality, but also real men do cause real problems. One current project of the network called Critical Research on Men in Europe (CROME) has the necessarily long title of 'the social problem and societal problematisation of men and masculinities' (Critical Research on Men in Europe, 2001). This phrase is close to describing my dual interest in the social construction of masculinity as a social problem and the actual behaviour of many men that causes problems – for women, children and men themselves.

Two substantial concerns about men and masculinity that have come to the fore in the UK in recent years, and have featured to differing degrees in academic, political, media and popular discourse, are dangerous young men and dangerous fathers. Interesting overviews of these debates are provided by Hearn (1998) and Williams (1998). The issue of fatherhood is particularly pertinent to the ethnographic data described below. Williams's chapter outlines the debates about fatherhood that form the context to social workers' constructions of men as clients.

She divides social policy discourse on fatherhood into concerns about absence and distance. The concern about absence is often accompanied by fears about the 'dangerous' masculinities of socially marginalised men who are leaving women with delinquent children; Charles Murray's 'underclass' (Murray, 1990). The concern about distance is expressed by a wide range of different commentators, but is usually sympathetic with the feminist goal of reducing sex inequality through men spending more time on childcare. Williams divides this group according to whether they seek to achieve their goal by increasing men's rights or by challenging men's lack of active involvement in childcare.

The key legislation that frames childcare social work in the UK is the Children Act 1989. This holds the 'welfare of the child' (inevitably loosely defined) to be paramount. As previously stated, this concept is crucial to the occupational culture of social work, and is often used as professional justification where the interests of parents and children are seen to conflict. There are ambiguous messages about masculinity in the Children Act 1989. Williams (1998) claims it draws on a relatively new discourse of shared parenting. She observes that the term 'parent' is used, providing apparent gender neutrality that obscures the reality of the gendered division of domestic labour in most households. However, until changes being brought in by the Adoption and Children Bill 2001, the central concept of parental responsibility on which the Children Act is based has only been available as an automatic right to married fathers. The unmarried father has had to apply for legal parental responsibility.

The position of men in work with children, and in caring work in general, has been up for debate (see, for example, Pringle, 1992; Carter, 1993). Hearn (1990) has pointed to a major tension, that the call for more men to work with children conflicts with a much higher degree of awareness that some men pose a risk of abuse. As Christie (1998b) observes, the European Union Council of Ministers has committed itself to increasing men's involvement in the care of children, and in some European countries this increase is seen as relatively unproblematic. In the UK, however, scandals of child abuse in residential care have led some to question whether or not men should be employed at all in certain roles with children (Pringle, 1992).

These and other debates on men and parenting are reflected in the occupational culture of social work that I shall now go on to discuss.

Discourses of masculinity in the social work office

> To speak legitimately of a discourse of masculinity it would be necessary to show that a particular set of usages was located structurally within a clearly defined institution with its own methods, objects and practices. (Middleton, 1992: 142)

It can be argued that child protection social workers do have to negotiate discourses of masculinity according to Middleton's definition. Knowledge about men is located in institutional practices such as case conference decisions, use of the law, reference to social scientific concepts and research evidence.

To set the context for a typology of constructions of men, some introductory comments about the profile of the client group are needed. The male clients of childcare social workers either come into the category 'children', or 'parent/carer'. This chapter does not discuss how boys are constructed. My concern is with the construction of men as parents or carers. With a few exceptions, these men have a socially and economically marginal class status. They are usually unemployed or working casually and probably illegally. Most live in stigmatised social housing estates, which are relatively remote from public services and shops. A high proportion seem to have criminal records.

Because I chose to focus on 'child protection' cases (not all clients are thus categorised), inevitably there is a high proportion of men in this system that are suspected of, or found to be responsible for, some form of child abuse or neglect. As might be expected, therefore, a dominant discourse that influences much of the representation of men in office talk, interview and case files is that of dangerous masculinities. It is important to repeat the observation that one would not expect an infinite number of different gender constructions, since social workers are responding to material reality, or men's actual bodily practices. However, notions of masculinity, femininity and childhood are socially constructed. The material realities of poverty and men's bodily practices feed into wider discourse about dangerous underclass men. Collier (1995) tells us that the notion of the 'good father' in family law is set against the idea of the unrespectable men of the dangerous classes. Lupton and Barclay (1997), in their discussion of discourse on fatherhood, have pointed out that the 'dangerous' father, who has become a figure of moral panic, is a poor, working-class, perhaps non-European father. However, they write in an Australian context. The Uplands fathers are white, and in fact much of the popular British underclass imagery is of whiteness (Collier, 1998).

There are exceptions to the class profile of men clients summarised above. It was explained to me early on that within the children and families service the place where middle-class men were most often encountered was in advocating, often in highly articulate fashion, for their disabled offspring. Also, it seems to be accepted wisdom on sex offending that it goes on across class boundaries. Other types of abusive behaviour are understood as being more class-specific in the sense that they can be responses to social stress. I was allocated to this particular social work team (one of a possible three) by the senior managers partly on the basis of there being more men than usual in this particular team. They thought this would help me with my topic. There is a connection made in social work culture between the sex of the worker and the sex of the client, as with the idea of women working with women (see also Christie, 1998b). The discourses of masculinity outlined below are as follows: men as a threat, men as no use, men as irrelevant, men as absent, men as no different from women, and men as better than women.

Men as a threat

There is not one unified discourse on men clients in the social work office. There are some tensions and contradictions. However, the discourse of men as a threat is a particularly powerful one. There is, therefore, considerably more space given in this chapter to discussion of this discourse. Men are seen as a potential threat to children, social workers and women clients. Social workers are frequently faced with reports of men's violence against women, and, less often, with tales of their violence towards children. The possibility of sexual abuse is also an important influence on the discourse of men as a threat. A women social worker explained her general expectation that men clients would be a threat to the well-being of women and children:

> I find that working in the area I am working in, which is usually sexual or physical abuse, emotional abuse, and at the high end of the scale as well, most of my mothers are victims in their own lives and have been targeted by manipulative men with their own agenda that would target vulnerable women. So my experience of working with men is probably tainted by that; the fact that their agenda for being there is not conducive for the best for the children or for the mother. (interview with Lynne from Docktown)

The discourse of 'men as a threat' is discussed in two parts: firstly, discourse on sexually abusing men and, secondly, discourse on violent men. Whilst recognising that sexual abuse can be seen as a form of violence, in the discussion that follows it is necessary to distinguish occupational constructions of physical violence from those of sexual abuse. This is necessary because of the notable differences in how social workers understand these two categories of behaviour.

Sexual abuse

The 'discovery' of sexual abuse in the 1980s and 90s has been a major influence on the culture of social work (Parton et al., 1997). It has been so all-pervasive that the general terms 'abuse', 'abuser' or 'abused' are sometimes used to refer specifically to sexual abuse. Popular discourse on sexual abuse in the UK can be summarised in two main strands: the predatory 'paedophile' and the abusing male relative. Social workers make reference to both. The former has been particularly prominent in the British media in the last couple of years, with many stories of offenders being hounded from communities. The predatory paedophile is seen as coming into families from outside, preying on children in public spaces, or inviting them into his home. The discourse of the male relative as abuser is less rooted in the popular imagination, but its acceptance as mainstream social work knowledge demonstrates the success of feminism in convincing the profession of the ordinariness of child sexual abuse. In social services there is the added dimension of scandals of abuse by staff in residential homes for children, some of which, it is alleged, may have been organised through sophisticated networks. These men are both predatory, in that they seek out positions where they can abuse vulnerable children, and 'familial' in a sense, because they are part of the organisation.

There was experience within the team both of cases of fathers, stepfathers or other male relatives sexually abusing children, and also cases of child victims of abuse by an 'outsider'. The potential for discovering sexual abuse is thought to be ever present. This became clear to me during negotiation of research access, when a gatekeeper expressed his concern that I might be a 'paedophile' wanting to make contact with like-minded people through my research. His concern is based in the predatory paedophile discourse, but also illustrates the extent to which the threat is seen to be close at hand, and potentially within the organisation. It also illustrates the extent to which the 'discovery' of sexual abuse has influenced organisational constructions of masculinity in general. Stainton Rogers and Stainton Rogers (1992) use the term 'whole gender blaming' in connection with the new focus on men as potential sexual abusers. This gatekeeper's concern was triggered by a one-page summary of my research questions that simply stated I was interested in studying work with men. There had been no mention of sex offenders.

Unlike other men responsible for abuse of children, sex offenders are constructed as a homogeneous group in the Uplands team. Featherstone and Lancaster (1997) argue that the range of masculinities amongst men who sexually abuse children in fact makes them indistinguishable from other men, but there has developed an agreed set of assumptions about offenders which has achieved hegemonic status in the culture of social work. This, they argue, has come about because the issue of child sexual abuse is much less open to question than other areas of child protection intervention (see also Stainton Rogers and Stainton Rogers, 1992).

The Faithfull Foundation, formerly the Gracewell Clinic (see Wyre, 1990), has been a particularly influential UK organisation in reaching social workers with these messages. During my fieldwork, a social worker presented to the team a summary of one of their courses that he had attended, and the ideas were clearly very familiar to them. There were several references to the same concepts during the rest of the fieldwork period. The key concepts are as follows: an offence is 'never a one-off', but is deliberate, and planned; the offence is committed as part of a 'cycle' which involves fantasising about the child and self-justifying beliefs; the child is 'groomed', that is, gradually introduced into abusive situations and persuaded to keep quiet; abusers will minimise and deny their abuse, so are generally not to be believed, whereas children are always to be believed if they apparently disclose abuse; abusers are often clever and charming; you would not expect them to change their behaviour, at least not without intensive therapeutic input such as that provided by the Faithfull Foundation.

Social workers do not expect to spend time working with sex offenders. The only acceptable strategy, if it is decided that abuse has taken place, is to get the man out of the home. In practice, the social workers testify, this is done either through imprisonment or by pressure being applied through the threat of legal action if he does not leave. In many cases this involves the woman having to 'choose' him or the children.

> There is only one strategy really to start with and that is him leaving the home … so really you are talking of separation then. It is very difficult to work with a family when there are children in the family and you know about the abusive cycle. (interview with Lynne from Docktown)

As Featherstone and Lancaster (1997) have argued, social workers whose practice is governed by such a template miss out on the opportunity for their response to be informed by theory and research on the social construction of masculinities (for example, Connell, 1995; Kimmel and Messner, 1998). Messerschmidt, for example, in his analysis of life history research with young sex offenders, describes how they use sexual violence as a response to 'masculinity challenge', gaining 'a contextually-based masculine resource where other masculine resources were unavailable' (Messerschmidt, 2000: 293).

Imagining seems particularly important in constructing sexual abuse. There is often a suspicion that secrets lurk in families; possibly secrets about men's dangerous sexuality. Social workers will talk of having strong suspicions that a man is abusing a child, even in the absence of any evidence. The following excerpts are examples of this:

> It's only when there's a smell of sexual abuse, you get a feeling about it. (Brian, from fieldnotes, 7 August)

> I don't know but the kid reckons he was locked in the car boot at one stage. I don't know. I think what was probably going on was that he was a very

possessive man and I think wanted to develop a relationship with the boy especially, and just wasn't prepared to actually put the work in. He really thought that he could have the relationship just like that. So I think that is the most charitable explanation of what he was doing really. I mean there were a lot of other possibilities, but I really don't know, and I don't think we will get to the bottom of what went on. (interview with Mike)

Talk of this kind of suspicion is specific to sexual abuse. There is not the same discussion of lurking secrets in relation to other forms of abuse. This must be due in part to the hidden nature of the abuse. There is also, perhaps, an assumption that sexual abuse is necessarily more traumatic to children than other forms of abuse, a perception that would be supported by research such as that undertaken by Kelly et al. (1991). It also seems that sexuality has cultural power in the organisation (Hearn and Parkin, 1987). Stainton Rogers and Stainton Rogers (1992) have observed that the topic of sexual abuse creates a profound emotional reaction in people, what they call a 'visceral clutch'.

A case that vividly illustrates the role of the imagination and the emotions in relation to sexual abuse was described by Lynne in one of the pilot interviews in Docktown. She described a family where, despite no mention from the daughter of her stepfather having sexually abused her in any way, she became convinced that there were secrets of sexual abuse to be unearthed. She said 'I'm ninety-nine per cent certain that he is abusing this girl.' One of the main reasons for this belief was that the man had sent letters to a former employer that were 'full of religious intimidation in a way, witchcraft, Satan and God'. This case is the only one I heard of during the fieldwork with any mention of satanic links, and I do not intend to digress onto a major discussion of satanic abuse on the basis of one social worker's mention of one case. It is an interesting example, however, of how sexual abuse is associated with fears that are culturally deep-rooted. La Fontaine (1998) has argued that the allegation of satanic abuse needs to be understood as a contemporary manifestation of the traditional societal belief in witchcraft. Her work is highly controversial. The 'discourse of disbelief' she represents has been challenged by Sara Scott (2001), for example. Whatever the material reality of this case, Lynne's firm belief in the reality of sexual abuse without any allegation of such from any party indicates to me the connection in the popular imagination between sexual abuse and 'dark forces'. I now address another aspect of the discourse of men as a threat, namely men's violence against women and children.

Violence

Violence against women is regarded as dangerous to women and children alike. Again, the message of feminism that it is serious and damaging has become accepted in mainstream child protection knowledge. If a case is categorised as a child protection case because of a man's violence towards the children's mother, it is typically labelled as a situation of likely physical or emotional abuse of the children. It is often stressed that the risk of physical abuse is not direct, but that the children might get 'caught up' in the violence towards their mother. Although it is regarded as damaging to women and children, 'domestic' violence is also seen as fairly routine, and is often not the target of intervention if there are thought to be other problems in a family (see also Swift, 1995). Neither is there the consistency in explanations of violence that we find with constructions of sexual abuse. Social workers' explanations reflect the diversity of academic discourse on violence in the home.

Featherstone and Trinder (1997) have claimed that the feminist explanation that men's violence is a tactic for gaining control over women (they label this 'radical feminist') has attained hegemonic status in the culture of social work. This assertion is not supported from the Uplands team data. Violence as men controlling women does form *part* of the repertoire of explanations in the social work office, but alongside this, sometimes as part of the same assessment of a family, run other interpretations. These include the notion of a cycle of violence that the *woman* is trapped in, the idea that alcohol is a causal factor, and the idea that in some families the man and woman are 'both as bad as each other' (see also Chapter 4). Usually, however, the responsibility for the violence is attached to the man. Violent men are variously described as possessive, controlling, heartless, obsessive, resentful of women, and not safe to look after children. Responsibility for the children's safety, however, is firmly with the mother. It is children that are the priority.

Mullender's article (1997) is interesting to note here. She describes the shift from social workers trying to keep families together in the 1970s and 80s (see also Maynard, 1985) to the current orthodoxy, which is to expect the woman to remove him from the home (see also Humphries, 1999). The approach in childcare teams has changed as the man's violence has come to be seen as a threat to the children's safety, rather than a threat to the stability of the relationship. So a successful outcome is the woman 'choosing' the children rather than the man, and leaving home, or insisting that he leaves. If she does not do this, she is 'failing to protect' the children. This aspect is discussed in more detail in Chapter 4.

There is no common construction of domestic violence across the social work profession. For example, Hester and Radford (1996) found that, in the court welfare practice they investigated, a man's history of violence was not seen as jeopardising his contact with his children, regardless of the quality of that contact. I found in researching probation culture (Scourfield, 1998) that although social work trained officers referred in interviews to men using violence to control women, in court reports the dominant constructions were of 'volatile relationships', and the orientation was to mitigation of men's behaviour; the discourse reflected the task and the audience. In the Uplands team we find diverse explanations of violence, but orthodoxy of institutional response.

Men clients who are known to be violent towards women partners are also assumed to be a threat to women social workers. In such situations, male social workers are seen to provide protection. Interestingly, both these assumptions are questioned by certain research findings. O'Hagan and Dillenburger (1995, citing research by Rowett and by Norris) point out that most assaults on social workers are in fact from women clients. Balloch et al.'s research (1998) into assaults on social workers found that men were much more likely to be assaulted than women. Women's greater fear of violence, and the material reality of the threat to women is well documented (for example, Stanko, 1990). In the following excerpt, Lorraine recounts an example of an assault on her car which she saw as a result of challenging a man:

> You can quite understand as well, you know, I think probably half of us have been threatened in fairly serious ways by men. I mean I have had my car scraped from head to tail once – absolutely scraped – and the windscreen smashed. And it was never proved, but I had a good idea who did it. And that was directly as a result of challenging this man. (interview with Lorraine)

Unknown men are thought to pose a potential threat to children if they have some kind of negative connection, or suspicious history of their own. An example is the case of the children accommodated by the local authority because of risk of physical abuse (an infant's leg had been broken, apparently by the stepfather) when the father of the violent stepfather was willing to take them instead. Use of the extended family is standard procedure in these situations, but this man was not trusted because he was unknown and had a violent son.

> Margaret said 'but we don't know Jason's father'. They mention the fact that he has a girlfriend, but they are not sure if she lives with him or not. It seems that social workers will now have to assess his suitability to have the children. (fieldnotes, 30 September)

Another man, who had not been met by social workers because he had been in prison, was assumed to pose a risk to a child because of reports of his violent and controlling behaviour in the recent past, but was well regarded when he was actually met.

The discourse of men as a threat rests on images of embodied masculinity. On one occasion a senior manager used the expression 'hairy beast' to describe a hypothetical violent man. This is a stark image, and does not accurately represent the manager's visual construction of the client. It does, however, indicate the importance of spectral as well as iconic imagery in the construction of clients. Swift (1995) found in her Canadian research that social workers were making overt judgements about client's bodies, with reference to excess weight and lack of care to physical appearance. In the Uplands team, there was little evidence of such overt judgements, but on the basis of comments such as the 'hairy beast' remark cited above, I would speculate that physically and sexually violent men conjure powerful embodied images.

Men as no use

Another powerful discourse of masculinity in the social work office is that of men as no use. These are men who are not seen as usefully employed in any activity, either legitimate paid employment or help with child-rearing and housekeeping. Dicks et al. (1998) found in their research that service providers spoke of an unemployed man's presence in the house all day creating problems for women and children. In the Uplands team, whilst some women clients are described as viewing the men in their lives as no use to them if they are unemployed, this view is not shared by the social workers. There is not such a direct connection between paid employment and worthwhile male activity. Men who spend their time looking after children are highly regarded. Such men are only rarely, however, seen to feature in the caseload. Men clients are more generally described by the social workers as not contributing to childcare, not helping with work around the house, and spending all the money. This contrasts with Swift's (1995) research, where she found fathers' failure to care generally producing no comment from social workers. Men are also often described as always being away from the home. Their time tends not to be taken up with legitimate working, which would be considered an acceptable absence from home, but with either looking for work, working illegally or socialising. The implication is that these activities are probably excuses for avoiding family responsibility. Pete sees the phenomenon of men being out of the house while women do the childcare as a national trend, but one that is particularly strong in the local area:

> In some cases the male is out of the house either working on the alternative economy or legitimately. And that again is quite a cultural thing around here that the male is the person that goes out and earns or is the first name on the claims. Unless it is child benefit in which case it's the mothers' name that appears first. I know that is nationally common, but it is considered very much that the woman is at home looking after the children while the man, even if he is not employed, is out and about with his friends. (interview with Pete)

There is a certain exasperation expressed about men's incompetence as carers and as clients. They are variously described as unable to cope, childlike, deluded, obsessive and stubborn. They are difficult to work with. They refuse to take responsibility for problems that are of their own making, instead blaming their partner or the social worker. They lack commitment to the social work plan, which means they lack commitment to their children. Although they are of little practical use in terms of family life, it is difficult to talk to them about problems with their behaviour, because they only want to talk about practical matters, such as housing. 'Hopeless' men can be the butt of office humour and irreverent comment. The excerpts below illustrate some of the ways in which men clients are described as of little or no use to families.

If you can persuade him to look after the two younger ones while Jade is going to the hospital to be monitored he thinks he is doing you a big favour, you know. The last day that I was arranging this he was saying to me 'well what will you do for me for this?' I said 'nothing, they are your children so you look after them, it is as simple as that.' He obviously thought that she was going to owe him a big favour for doing this. If he is there, then that is fine but she doesn't expect him to be there. (interview with Lorraine).

Women tend to be into service provision and men into care management. If he has the kids for the weekend he's more likely to take them round his new partner's or to the funfair. I've always been interested in these issues, that the man opts out. I'm a man. They want to talk about work or something like that. If you give them specific tasks they can carry them out. They'll take him out for a burger, they'll do what you tell them to do. They have to be tasks that are acceptable to them as men. Women tend to meet other women and there's lots of kids around. It doesn't tend to be like that for men. When they've got their kids they tend to do things with them. (Pete, from fieldnotes, 4 July)

Lorraine describes a man who she regards as reluctant to help with the children, rather than opting out all together; he doesn't really see it as his job. Pete outlines what he sees as differences in style between men as fathers and women as mothers. He does not so much see men as of no use, but sees their involvement with children as limited by 'what is acceptable to them as men'. In general, the discourse of men as no use portrays fatherhood as a fundamentally problematic experience.

Men as irrelevant

There is a sense in which men can be non-clients. The concept in the Children Act 1989 of parental responsibility is a crucial one for the organisation's definition of who is and is not a client. It seems that many of the men that the social workers encounter do not have this status in law, because they are not married to the children's mother. In this situation, they will not necessarily be involved in the child protection process. There seem to be occasions where it does not occur to a social worker to involve a man without parental responsibility, and also occasions where it is a convenient to have recourse to this legal concept to avoid involving a man who is, for whatever reason, undesirable. Social workers also spoke of situations where a man was not relevant to their work because the children's mother did not want him involved.

There were various ways in which it was explained that working with men is not always part of the job. If a man is in prison, it is not part of the job to go and see him. Pragmatic considerations can mean that men are not worked with. For example, in the case of a man who is violent to his woman partner, it is not considered part of the job to work with him to change his behaviour, but rather to pressurise the woman to leave him, thus protecting the children.

> You have got to be working with a woman to say 'do you want to, why are you staying with this man, do you want to stay with this man, do you want help in moving away from this man?' I have yet to meet a social worker who would say 'let's you and me and your husband or partner look at the violence that is going on between you.' I don't think a social worker is actually trained for that, I don't think that they have got the resources to do that, in terms of time and I think that there are too many other demands. (interview with Margaret)

The priority is child safety, and that can mean deciding to concentrate on the children's mother, because it is her that spends time with them and does most, perhaps all, of the work of caring.

> Sometimes we work with the woman to get to the children quicker. If you can't change the actual childcare you work with the women because they're the actual providers of childcare. (Lorraine, from fieldnotes)

Men as absent

As well as men whose legal status or behaviour renders them non-clients, there are men who are potential clients but are thought to avoid engaging with social workers through their absence. They are often seen to absent themselves when social workers come to call. They may well either not live with the family full time or at least not declare themselves as living there because of their assumption that a reduction in welfare benefits would follow. Men are also absent through imprisonment, and moving on to new partners and new families. Some of the ways in which men are constructed as absent are portrayed in the following excerpts:

> In some families, the stable figure is the mother who is there with the children, and over the years there have been several partners. I suppose you can't generalise. Or you just have the mother figure, and he has left, and she is on her own, battling with everybody; battling to get any kind of support and that kind of thing with the benefits agency, battling with us, battling for the kids in school. There are quite a few where the father is actually living at home but where the father will always attempt to go out when he knows that you are coming. (interview with Lorraine)

> If you contact a family, the wife is usually there. You'll ask for the husband and he's tinkering with the car. He comes in and stands sheepishly and wonders why he's there. The more you try and involve him the worse it can be. (interview with Brian)

> The child is our client, and in cases where there is a single parent family, where perhaps there is a boyfriend but he doesn't live there, he may not enter into the dimension at all. (interview with Margaret)

Despite the negative constructions of men as a threat and as useless, their absence is usually considered to be a bad thing (see also Edwards, 1998). Men should be there for the children, and to help the mother with the work of caring. A man's abdication of responsibility can contribute to a neglect categorisation. There is general sympathy with women clients who are left to do the work themselves. Absent men can 'make themselves look good' as prospective parents, without having the daily struggle of caring work. There are echoes here of the concern in social policy discourse about father absence described by Williams (1998).

> At the time of the last conference and for some time afterwards, Mr Wheeler was working fairly regularly. More recently he has been at home more and helping with the children. In recent weeks Mrs Wheeler has seemed happier and plays with the children more. (case conference report, Wheeler family)

> It's not fair on the kids. He's out before they're up and back after they've gone to bed. I'm going to write and lay it on the line to him. (Pete, from fieldnotes, 11 September)

The tone of the discourses of masculinity outlined so far has generally been pejorative. Constructions of men in the Uplands team are not, however, uniformly negative. In particular contexts, men can be constructed as no different from women, or fathers as better parents than mothers. I shall move on to describe these aspects of gender construction next, starting with how men come to be seen as no different from women.

Men as no different from women

This discourse comprises two rather different aspects. One relates to cases where a man and a woman are said to be 'as bad as each other'. The other reflects a notion of equality in social work culture that involves viewing men as no different from women. There is recognition that child protection procedures, involving as they do some confrontation and intrusiveness, can be equally difficult for both parents.

> And obviously you are questioning somebody about how a bruise happened or how this injury occurred and obviously people become very, very defensive, but that is equally the same for women as for males. (interview with Jane from Docktown)

As mentioned above, the social workers' explanations of violence in the home reflect the diversity of academic discourse on this topic. There are certain cases where domestic violence is understood as being to some degree the responsibility of both partners. This construction seems to be particularly strong where the problems are long-standing and the case has been active for many years. Typically the children are described as 'pulled all ways' between warring parents. This construction of a violent household tends to be linked to the presence of a woman who is seen as aggressive (see Chapter 4).

The other aspect of the discourse of men as no different relates to tensions in the interpretation of concepts of equal opportunities and anti-discrimination. These can be seen in the mixed reactions to my stated research topic, social work with men. There was general interest, rather than hostility, but more than one different interpretation of the purpose of the research. Some people immediately made reference to feminist critiques of masculinity. Of these there were some that assumed 'the problem' to be located with the difficult behaviour of men clients themselves. Others assumed it to be an issue of the organisation failing to confront men's difficult behaviour. Finally, there were some social workers that wondered whether men were being disadvantaged in the social work process. In the excerpts below, Mike reflects this discourse of equal treatment when he questions whether he should have treated a man as a victim of domestic violence. When he says 'it's a good example' he is directly referring to my research topic. Jane showed during her interview and after it (see second extract) that she was resistant to the idea of men as difficult.

> Mike was on the phone for 15 minutes when I arrived. He came off the phone exasperated. It was a man who says his wife is mentally ill and attacks him, scratching his face. Mike said 'there's no kids there', to emphasise how inappropriate it is for the man to phone a children and families team. The man refuses to take out an injunction or use the fact that the tenancy is his to get her out. The mental health team has done an assessment and she has not been found to have any mental health problems. Minutes later Mike came back into the room, having popped out briefly, to say 'I suppose I could have put him in touch with the domestic violence unit. It's a good example. If it had been a woman, would we do something different?' (fieldnotes)

> At the end of the interview she asked 'so why are you interested in men anyway?' I am not sure what was behind this, but it implied scepticism. I had explained my rationale at the outset, and the general tone of her interview was that she did not see the problem – she resisted the notion of men as difficult. (from fieldnotes, 10 July, following pilot interview with Jane from Docktown)

There are clearly different versions of gender politics available to the social workers. The issue of gender bias in social work practice can be one of unfairness to men because they are not fully involved in procedures that determine children's futures, or unfairness to women because they are held responsible for the bad behaviour of men. Tensions surrounding concepts of gender equality and justice in social work relate to different emphases in social work knowledge, as well as the range of perspectives on masculinity outlined by Clatterbaugh (1990). I shall return to this issue in an extended discussion in Chapter 7.

Men as better than women

> We do assume as a department that women are the natural carers, and you
> can see it, the occasional time that there is some crisis and a man is looking
> after his children, it gets so much more attention because it is seen as,
> 'gosh, isn't he wonderful? He is looking after the children.' (interview with
> Lorraine)

Lorraine is critical of what she sees as a tendency in the organisation
to praise men for mundane and expected childcare work. Despite
this view of Lorraine's, I did not in fact find that the work of the
Uplands team echoed Swift's (1995) finding from her Canadian
research that virtually any childcare performed by a father produces
a positive view of him. As explained above, the Uplands social workers
often seem to note men's neglect of childcare duties. Where a man is
singled out for positive comment, it tends to be in relation to a woman's
failings. Men are constructed as better, or as surprisingly good,
where the mother is seen to be deficient in some way. This might
mean failing to cope with the tasks of mothering: housework, nurturing
and the servicing of the child's body. The following excerpt is an
example of this:

> She makes an effort in that her clothes are clean and her personal hygiene
> is good. The home is also clean and tidy. Neil undertakes all of the cooking
> and possibly all of the cleaning...Helen has some insight. The parti-
> cipants reiterated that Neil is more in tune with the baby. He is less
> egocentric and immature than Helen. (case conference report, Warren
> family file)

Positive constructions of men are more easily explained in relation
to ideologies of mothering than in relation to any particular discourse
of masculinity. For a father to be constructed as capable and committed he needs to be connected to a 'bad mother'. However, a 'bad
mother' case does not necessarily involve positive constructions of
men, although gendered constructions of parent clients are always
relational in some respect. Women who are failing as mothers are also
seen as victims of oppressive men, weak or unnatural in refusing to
leave such a man 'for the sake of the children', or 'as bad as he is' in
cases of mutual hostility.

Conclusion

Munro (1998: 93) writes that the scrutiny of mothers in child protection work is

> surprising ... since men are considerably more likely than women to be violent and so, one would think, professionals would give them more, not less, attention than women in assessing danger to children.

The ethnographic data described above go some way towards addressing this surprise. The study found that in the occupational culture of child protection social work, men are constructed as a threat, as no use, as irrelevant, as absent, as no different from women, and as better than women. In general, men clients seem to be constructed as a negative influence unless there are bad mothers with whom they can be contrasted. Where they are a negative influence, it tends not to be seen as part of the job to work with them.

Men are often invisible or silent in child protection practice. This phenomenon has been observed in the UK (Stanley, 1997), Australia (Parton et al., 1997) and the USA (Edleson, 1998). Hall et al. (1997b) have analysed the various ways in which voices are silenced in social work narratives. This process of silencing can affect children as well as women and men who are in receipt of social work services. It seems to be very often the case, however, that men are effectively silenced in accounts of social work. The discourses of men as a threat, men as irrelevant and men as absent are particularly relevant in explaining this silencing.

In many ways constructions of men are strongly influenced by some particular feminist accounts of masculinity. There is frequent reference to men's power over women and children, and the inequality of domestic labour. It is interesting to note, however, that this feminist influence does not seem to have reduced the scrutiny of women. Abusive men are seen as a danger to women and children and should be removed, but it is the responsibility of *women* to do this, and not doing so constitutes 'failure to protect', so it is women's actions and attitudes that are scrutinised (see the previous chapter). There is a feeling that women clients would be better off without these particular men (although not necessarily without men at all), and little empathy when they do not wish to be.

It is interesting to compare constructions of violence against women and those of sexual abuse. The most striking aspect of the constructions of men and sexual abuse is the homogeneity; the view that 'they are all like that'. There is a marked difference between the way the social workers respond to sex offenders and the diverse ways they respond to other men clients, including those who are constructed as a threat. Sexual abuse is seen to warrant an extraordinary response (Scott, 1998). It is not considered possible for children to remain in a household where a man has sexually abused unless the mother rejects him absolutely. Men who are abusers are only engaged on the cynical basis of the need to get them talking to find out their 'grooming' tactics. As Featherstone and Lancaster (1997) point out, these men are seen as exempt from entitlement to the 'universal respect' said to be a core traditional social work ethic.

It needs to be remembered that constructions of men as clients of childcare social workers are constructions of socially and economically marginalised men. The dangerousness of rough working-class men is implicitly contrasted with the respectability of other men (Hearn, 1990; Edwards, 1998), and male social workers themselves are among the respectable men. Collier (1995) has observed that in the last century a respectable, middle-class family man was constructed as a 'dad' who was sexless, safe, rid of the natural force of male sexuality, and could be set against the sexually licentious 'dangerous classes' of the Victorian imagination. It is these men of the 'dangerous classes', Collier asserts, who are the other of respectable familial masculinity. It is worth considering the application of Collier's (1995) argument to child protection work. Social workers are operating in a wider discursive context where the 'problem' of masculinity is increasingly becoming a matter of public debate, and a specific occupational context where there is a particular connection between men and sexual abuse. It could be argued that in the light of these discursive contexts, pejorative discourses of masculinity have some value for the staff in making social worker men seem all right, seem safe.

The discourses of men as a threat, men as no use, men as absent and, to an extent, men as irrelevant relate to the increasingly powerful discourse of the 'problem with men', mentioned at the beginning of the chapter. The Uplands social workers' constructions of men as clients should not be seen as simply a straightforward reflection of the material practices of the men they encounter. Nor should they be taken to reveal a tightly bounded occupational culture of social work. Rather, the process of constructing men in child protection work ought to be understood as rooted in a wider discourse of masculinity as problematic. The problematising of masculinity has its roots in feminist activism, academia and women's life experiences (although men have also contributed). It is possible that its influence on social work culture indicates the extent to which front-line practitioner culture is, in origin at least, a women's culture.

Implications for practice

Whilst the general issue of relating my research to practitioners is addressed in Chapter 9, at this point I outline some of the most immediate implications of the discourses of masculinity.

- There is a tendency to underestimate the extent to which domestic violence can be explained by men's coercion of women. For example, cases where a couple are seen to be 'as bad as each other' should be re-examined in the light of feminist research on domestic violence.
- Applying a rigid template to all sex offenders hinders the development of a richer understanding that is rooted in the specific social context of particular men. A formulaic approach will not be sensitive to the perspectives of particular women and particular children either. Each case should be seen as unique, within the context of knowledge of relevant research on sexual abuse.
- Social workers ought not to be too preoccupied with whether or not a man has parental responsibility. Much more important is whether he is a significant part of the life of the family, regardless of his legal status. Neglecting men without parental responsibility runs the risk of underestimating the potential for stepfathers and mothers' boyfriends to cause harm in families and can also deny participation in key decisions to unmarried men who *are* important to children.
- 'Equal treatment' of men and women will not lead to justice for clients, when the lives of most women and most men are so very different. I return to this theme in Chapter 7.
- Social workers should see working with abusive men as part of their job. Not doing so is simply too dangerous to women and children and will lead to more pressure being put on non-abusing women.

Overall the picture of gender construction in this and the previous chapter is a complex one of multiple discourses, albeit one where certain discourses are more powerful than others. There is a different discourse for different audiences, and for different kinds of cases. Not all kinds of cases are given the same attention, however. Amongst the diversity of family situations that social workers face, and the diversity of academic and professional perspectives on child abuse, the organisation inevitably chooses to prioritise certain kinds of cases above others, and this process is also inevitably gendered. It is this issue of the organisational prioritising of child protection issues that the next chapter tackles, providing an extended discussion of one category of child maltreatment as a vivid example of the gendered nature of child protection social work.

6

Child protection priorities

The scope of child protection work is potentially huge. The manifestations of child maltreatment range from inappropriate diet through to
rape. There has to be a paring down of this mass of allegations and cases
competing for attention. The choice of child protection priorities is
what preoccupies this chapter. The discussion centres on the gendered
nature of this choice and its gendered implications. The most mean-
ingful way to discuss the gendered nature of child protection priorities
is with reference to an actual example of prioritising which had major
implications for increased scrutiny of mothering. This is the 'new' interest in child neglect in the local authority where I carried out my research.
This chapter proceeds, then, with a focus on a specific categorisation
of child maltreatment, that of 'neglect', but this focus is designed to
illustrate much broader issues about the implications of child protection policy for gender inequality.

Investigating gender in social work inevitably requires attention to
the process of institutional categorisation. In child protection work
the most important one is the categorisation of the nature of actual or
likely harm to a child, decided by a multidisciplinary case conference.
One of these categories is 'neglect'. I found attention to the categorisation of neglect impossible to avoid in the social work team where
I conducted my research (the Uplands team). It was an issue that was
very much on the minds of social workers. The question of what does
and does not constitute neglect was the subject of almost daily discussion. The social services department of the local authority, River County,
had made a decision to prioritise the identification of child neglect, as
such cases were seen as underrepresented in the past in the department's workload. This chapter uses the issue of child neglect in the
Uplands team as a case study of the construction of gender. Since, as
has been asserted throughout the book, gender is not the only factor

of social organisation that is pertinent to understanding child protection work, some other concepts are brought in to help to explain the current focus on child neglect.

The chapter is structured as follows. I begin by explaining the circumstances in which child neglect has become a priority issue in the authority. I then outline two influential professional discourses of child neglect, the lack of emotional warmth and physical care. The section that follows this then describes how the latter of these professional discourses, the importance of physical care of children, is currently dominant in the Uplands team. I then explain the implications of this for questions of gender, and consider some other social and political factors that may help to explain the concentration on physical care.

The rediscovery of child neglect

The new focus on child neglect in River County constitutes a rediscovery of the issue in more than one sense. In the decades between the world wars and in the immediate post-war period, child welfare concern in the UK was focused on the issue of child neglect (Parker, 1995). The focus then shifted to physical abuse in the 1970s, following the growing influence of the work of the Kempes (for example, Kempe et al., 1962) and, more specifically, the inquiry into the death of Maria Colwell. The 1980s saw an increased interest in child sexual abuse. These last few decades have seen the marginalisation of concern about child neglect. Wolock and Horowitz (1984) have called this 'the neglect of neglect'. River County social services' decision to prioritise neglect does, then, constitute a rediscovery.

The other sense in which this can be seen as a rediscovery is related to social work's capacity for the social control of socially and economically marginalised people. Arguably, an awareness of this capacity has been mainstream among social work practitioners since the 1970s, resulting in an awareness of how class-based assumptions can influence practice. This in turn has led to a reluctance to bring families into the child protection system because they are poor, shabby and dirty. As the discussion below of the ethnographic data shows, this reluctance is being seriously questioned in the Uplands team. The social workers speak of the need to rediscover their own personal values in terms of the physical care of children.

Child neglect was a dominant construction of new cases when I spent time in the Uplands team. Social workers commonly referred to neglect as 'the flavour of the month' or 'the buzz word at the moment'. The interest in neglect arose from the response to several child deaths in the local area, and one recent and notorious death in particular that attracted the full glare of the media. This death was retrospectively constructed as a 'neglect' case, although the direct cause of death was violence from the mother's boyfriend. The reaction in River County social services department to these deaths was to arrange training for staff in the identification of child neglect. This training was provided by the Bridge Child Care Consultancy, and it seems to have had a profound effect on the social workers.

The rediscovery of child neglect is a specifically local example. River County social services have targeted neglect, with the result that the proportions of children thus categorised on the child protection register increased threefold between March and July of 1997, the months preceding my fieldwork. All data from an ethnographic study can be seen as locally specific, and clearly not straightforwardly generalisable. However, the data on constructions of child neglect highlight many of the general themes outlined in the previous chapters and a lot of the problems of gender that I argue are inevitable in this work. The rediscovery of neglect in River County is also an interesting phenomenon in its own right, and one that is not happening in isolation, but represents an attempt to respond to national guidance and, according to Parton (1995), illustrates a national trend to treat neglect as a child protection issue. Government statistics (in Corby, 2000: 89) show that the proportion of children on child protection registers in England and Wales for neglect rose from 5 per cent in 1978 to 42 per cent in 1999. Neglect has become the highest category of child protection registration.

What is neglect?

There is a wealth of literature from medical, psychological and social work disciplines that debates the nature of neglect. Summaries of the field can be found in Stevenson (1998) and Swift (1995: 68ff.). This chapter does not attempt to review this literature, because its concern is how social workers construct child neglect in their everyday work rather than with academic child neglect discourse. There are two important professional discourses on child neglect that the social workers make reference to in their case talk, interviews and written records. There is some tension between these discourses. They are connected with the literature of specific organisations, but this literature does not impact on the practice wisdom of social workers in a straightforward way. The social workers take up the selected and condensed messages from this literature, which are passed on to colleagues through occupational socialisation.

The first is what is taken to be the message of the Bridge Child Care Consultancy. This independent, UK-based profit-making organisation has been prominent in raising the profile of child neglect, with the claim that the neglected child can suffer longer term emotional difficulties than children abused in other ways (Pritchard, 1996). Their emphasis (or at least the social workers' version of it), in defining neglect, is on physical care, or the servicing of the child's body. Their neglected child is dirty and smelly. This seems to ring true for social workers who say they have not previously targeted neglect as a major issue requiring intervention:

> I think research was showing that although in the past some of the worst tragedies have been children where social workers have said 'oh well the house is stinking but the children are happy', research is saying 'are they really happy, are they happy in school?; and 'they are different from other children, their clothes are worse and they can't bring friends home'.
> (interview with Lorraine)

The other important influence on the development of the authority's response to child neglect is the UK Department of Health's *Child Protection: Messages from Research* document. The statement most often quoted by social workers from this summary of twenty commissioned research studies is the finding that individual incidents of abuse are less connected with poor long-term outcomes for children than living in families characterised as 'low on warmth and high on criticism' (Dartington Social Research Unit, 1995: 19). As a social worker put it during an interview:

> Everyone doesn't have to have dirty houses and dirty smelly children to have been neglected, neglect is more looking at 'are the child's needs being met, particularly the emotional needs?' – the holistic picture if you like.
> (interview with Margaret)

To summarise, the emphasis of the Department of Health discourse on neglect, as understood by the social workers, is on the emotional impact of parenting styles. The child neglect discourse of the Bridge Child Care Consultancy, however, is understood by the social workers to be promoting the importance of servicing the child's body. The Uplands team social workers' constructions of families labelled as neglect cases do in fact concentrate on children's bodies, and parental body maintenance work for children, and cleaning and feeding in particular. There is also reference to other factors, which are outlined more fully later in the chapter, but the servicing of the child's body is the dominant concern.

The construction of neglect in the social workers' routine practice suggests that judgements are indeed made about the emotional climate of the home, but that if this is found to be positive, and the standards of body maintenance unacceptable, the family are seen as giving cause for 'concern'. The practical construction of neglect is more influenced by the discourse of the servicing of the child's body. The intention of this chapter is not to claim that the Uplands team social workers are only concerned with physical care and not with emotional well-being, but rather to draw attention to their questioning of the welfare of happy, dirty children, and to discuss the implications of this.

The physical care of children

The dominant concern in the Uplands team has become body maintenance work: 'the permanent and exacting corporal relation between adults and their children' (Foucault, 1986: 279). The next section of the chapter discusses the social workers' responses to failures in body maintenance in relation to dirt, disorder and diet.

Dirt and disorder

For neglect cases to be categorised as child protection cases rather than warranting a preventive response is a new development in this authority, and one that Parton (1995) argues is a general development throughout the UK. A preoccupation with dirt and disorder, however, does not seem to be new. The phrase 'home conditions' has, for many years, been a standard category for comment on the forms for monitoring children on the child protection register in River County, and the phrase appears in many different contexts in files that are more than ten years old. It is seen as a category of professional knowledge, and is often invoked in social workers' discussions of cases. Assessment of 'home conditions' means deciding whether or not this is a tidy house (see Steedman, 1982).

> As far as home conditions are concerned, the front room is perfect. At least it's acceptable by my standards. It's OK, I've seen a lot worse. (Joan, from fieldnotes, 6 August)

> We're investigating neglect. It's mainly to do with the home situation. They're living in squalor. Upstairs there's no carpet, the children are sleeping four to a bed... It's getting the mother to accept that there's a problem. Everyone's to blame bar her. (Debbie, from fieldnotes, 3 September)

> The home conditions are very good aren't they? I don't know if she does any cooking. I never see any food in the kitchen. (Claire, from fieldnotes, 29 August)

> The home conditions had appeared dirty and very untidy as usual. However, Mrs Wheeler had hoovered the living room – again, effort I had not noticed before. (Wheeler family file)

Home conditions are judged against tacit standards. These seem to involve a high level of order and cleanliness, although a small amount of mess or dirt, if caused by children, is considered to be a good thing, giving a house the feel of being homely and 'lived in'.

> I did use the loo... It was acceptable in a way. You know I wouldn't use the loo unless... It'd be worrying if a house was so tidy you wouldn't know they had kids... there's got to be a balance. (Joan, from fieldnotes, 6 August)

Neglect cases invariably involve dirt and mess. Swift's research (1995) into the construction of neglect cases in Canada found that dirt and disorder were constant reference points in case recording, but that they tended not to be the primary factors that precipitated a decision about a family. She found that details of domestic environment were used to justify institutional action. In the Uplands team, however, following their training from the Bridge Child Care

Consultancy, it has become acceptable to use dirt and disorder as primary grounds for child protection procedures. The following excerpts from the data, as well as many of those cited later in the chapter, illustrate the preoccupation with dirt, mess and smell in the identification of neglect:

> It was interesting. It was a bit of a chaotic family but the parents are always extremely well dressed and extremely clean, and present very nicely, whereas the children in the house, at its worst, when there were untrained cats running around the place, there was so much faeces brought in from the cats, trod on by the cats, children crawling in it. At times as well there were visits where the two older children were absolutely dirty with their own faeces, which was smeared on them, on their legs. Obviously, they would always give an excuse and say 'well we are just putting them in the bath, we are just going to give them a bath now', but it was pretty yucky at one stage. (interview with Lorraine)

> We'll do a little scene. Don't eat for a fortnight and don't bath. (Lisa and Debbie discussing the session they intend to run on the topic of neglect for a forthcoming training day, from fieldnotes, 7 August)

> The flat was in a very untidy state. It appeared to be totally disorganised and I had difficulty finding a place to sit down. (from case recording, Wheeler family)

> The kitchen! Well, they said they cooked in it, but I can't imagine how you could. (Debbie, from fieldnotes, 23 July)

As Swift (1995) also found, neglect is seen to be associated with long-term, or chronic problems; families who are in and out of the caseload over many years.

> It's cyclical. They were right back where they were at their worst. Some of the bits like the kitchen were frightening. The environmental health, well, they probably wouldn't even have wanted to go in. (Pete, from fieldnotes, 3 July)

At times social workers have to rely on the accounts of others. Several spoke of other professionals having a 'lower tolerance' of dirty houses. It seems that particular censure is reserved for those parents (mothers) who are thought to be exposing their children to messy or dirty environments. This is illustrated in the extreme case formulation of the referrals of some other professional groups. A police report of their response to a 999 call because of a 'domestic incident' at a client's house had little to say about the alleged violence, but recorded at length their impression that 'the house is uninhabitable to say the least. You cannot see a foot of carpet.'

> Both officers were disgusted with the inhuman conditions in which the children were living in. The living room looked more like a rubbish tip with dozens of flies on the ceiling. The house had a very strong putrid smell. There was a small very scabby dog which appeared to be in the process of being eaten by swarms of fleas. (police report in Brown family file)

There is a sense in which the participants were apologetic about the focus on dirt. There was an awareness that they might be in danger of imposing class-bound values on clients. They were keen to justify their attention to cleanliness as ensuring healthy children, and as related to a concern that smelly children would be isolated from their peer group.

> The poor standard of hygiene in the home and the possible risk this presents to Ian's health. (from core group minutes, Smith child)

> You start to dig, and teachers are saying things like, 'oh Leanne isn't very popular, because she smells.' Teachers don't think a child being isolated because they smell warrants a call to a social worker ... you hear that Leanne has repeated urinary tract infections, and there's no referral because people don't understand neglect. (Pete, from fieldnotes, 3 August)

This focus on isolation seemed to be a recent insight for the team, stemming from the Bridge Child Care Consultancy literature. Whilst seeing neglect as linked with poverty, there was an attempt made to separate out ordinary poor families from neglectful ones:

> Actually being able to distinguish between families who are struggling materially, of which there are a lot around, and families who struggle but despite that they will manage. The kids sometimes go to school with half a slice of toast or something for breakfast because there isn't anything else around but people will always have that half a slice of toast, whereas there are other families who even if they might be well off in terms of income

won't actually be materially as well off because they misspend their money. (interview with Mike)

There is a difference between deliberately not feeding children and the kind of neglect which lets children go to school in clothes that nobody else is wearing or doesn't provide money for them to go on school trips – which is a kind of neglect but it is not wilful neglect. (interview with Lorraine)

The rationale for the comment on disorderly houses is less clear from social workers' talk than the rationale for their interest in dirt. There was one reference (below) to a very young child being at risk of injury. Otherwise it seems to function as a symbol of more generally inadequate parenting.

It was the state of the house. She just felt that it was unsafe for a toddler his age, you know sort of toddling around the living room or whatever and she just felt it was too dangerous, old food lying around, crockery, knives and forks. (interview with Mary)

Diet

Adequate feeding is another abiding concern about the servicing of children's bodies. There is concern about children being given enough food and the right kind of food. As Lupton (1996) observes, domestic cooking is still overwhelmingly women's work, with women providing food for men and children. Silverman (1987: 254) has observed that '"thriving", "well-fed" children testify to the moral worth of their mothers'. The social workers' concerns about diet are illustrated in the passages below:

The other thing that caused her concern was his weight. The health visitor in Coast Town had always said his weight was a bit up and down. That is what she always said to me but on the whole he was okay. And there was always some concern about his diet, was he receiving an adequate diet or not, and she was always giving him crisps and chocolate and stuff like that. There was a question mark basically over whether she was feeding him properly, whether he was getting an adequate diet. The guardian felt that he wasn't and that his pattern of weight gain proved that. (interview with Mary)

Never seen any evidence of food being cooked or prepared, except for empty cartons of 'Indian take away' food. The only time I have seen the children eating has been cereal the day of the hospital appointment. (case recording, Wheeler family, list of 'concerns discussed with team manager')

Issues around Ian's inconsistent weight gain, poor diet and inconsistent feeding routines. (core group minutes, Smith child)

There is an appreciation that judgements about diet are culturally relative, and that the idea that only a 'cooked dinner' is proper food (see Murcott, 1982) should be questioned. Alongside this runs a conviction that some things are measurable:

Joan: If you feed your child pizza, the sort of food they get in school, granny might give them faggots and peas, you know, meat and two veg. She might think you're not feeding them proper food, even though there's not much difference in nutrition.
Mike: What's a lot less subjective is medical things.
Joan: Like development. Absolutely.
Mike: Like the sentile chart. (from fieldnotes, 9 August)

White (1998a) has written of the widespread faith in developmentalism in the child welfare field. It does seem that the field of child development is believed to be an exact science, a belief that is challenged by Burman (1994) and Stainton Rogers and Stainton Rogers (1992), amongst others. As evidence of neglect, social workers make reference to 'developmental delay'.

How are you finding Daniel with regard to his speech? He doesn't to me, he just stares, and he does the same to Julie Morris [health visitor]. You don't find him like that then? (Debbie, on phone, from fieldnotes, 3 September)

Jade's name was added to the child protection register on 30.4.96 following concerns about her failure to thrive. (case recording, Wheeler family)

Other factors

There are other aspects of body maintenance cited as identification of child neglect in the Uplands team that are less dominant than cleaning and feeding. There are also some factors occasionally deployed which move away from the focus on physical care. These will be mentioned below, albeit briefly, because they are notably less central to the construction of neglect than the physical care tasks already discussed.

Two other core tasks of body maintenance referred to less frequently than cleaning and feeding were the clothing of children and seeking appropriate medical attention:

> If we're looking at neglect, we have to look at every aspect of the child.... How are they in school? Are they appropriately dressed and things? In winter they don't come in a t-shirt or things like that. (Debbie, from fieldnotes, 3 September)

> I suppose also, around issues of safety. A hazardous house, failure to take children for medical appointments, to call a doctor when they are ill, that I suppose is around neglect. (interview with Margaret)

Failure to supervise children can constitute neglect. One example was a child alleged to have picked up and swallowed a small amount of cannabis resin. The social worker (Lisa) said there was 'definitely an element of neglect' in this case. Leaving children alone in the house or flat also comes into this category. As Swift (1995) also found, whilst neglect is usually chronic, there can be a 'neglect incident' such as abandonment:

> She wasn't sort of supervising him enough. She admitted that she had left him in the flat while she nipped out to the chippie or something like that but she always asked one of the girls down the road to keep an eye on him. (interview with Mary)

An exception to the emphasis on physical care is the noting of the presence or absence of toys in some cases to back up formulations of neglectful or non-neglectful families:

> There are no toys, no books, there's no evidence of any children there. There's a computer, but nothing else. They've had toys, social services have bought them. (Debbie, from fieldnotes, 3 September)

Domestic violence is occasionally cited as contributing to an overall picture of neglect, although cases of family violence are also often categorised very differently (see Chapters 4 and 5):

It fits the neglect profile so perfectly. Isolation of children in peer groups, developmental delay, domestic violence. It fits this family like a glove. (Pete, from fieldnotes, 3 July)

In almost all the neglect cases I encountered in the Uplands team there were incidents of violence from the father to the mother recorded on the files. However, in these cases, it was not a major issue for monitoring. The key to this is the process of institutional categorisation. The physical care of children comes to be seen as a greater threat to their well-being than other problem factors when a case is categorised as a neglect case.

A general rule about neglect is understood to be parents putting their needs before those of their children:

I think in my experience those families where I have felt that sort of thing was going on, quite often it is about adults with emotional needs which tend to take precedence over the children. I mean adults who will go out and buy a bottle of vodka in preference to paying the electricity bill or buying some food for the kids or whatever. I think that is probably what it is about. Not being able to actually put your needs second to the needs of the children when it is required. (interview with Mike)

As noted earlier, the emotional climate for children is certainly considered relevant, but a positive emotional bond can be outweighed by lack of physical care:

Conditions have again deteriorated and despite intensive efforts by social worker and team manager to raise standards, the house has now become unacceptable for the children to live in. It is fly-ridden, filthy, cluttered and totally unhygienic. The children themselves are not neglected emotionally, not physically in terms of clothing/food/schooling...However, the situation is now reaching the point where their health must be at risk, living in such dirty surroundings. (child protection referral form for Brown family)

There has always appeared to be a strong emotional bond between Carol and Ian, and until recent months Carol has on the whole put Ian's needs first...However, this strong emotional bond has always been somewhat overshadowed by Carol's difficulties coping with practicalities e.g., budgeting, cooking, domestic tasks, as well as coping with her own emotional needs. (case recording, Smith child)

I have described in this and previous sections how a particular version of neglect comes to dominate the construction of this category of maltreatment. In the rest of the chapter I discuss the implications of this and attempt to find an explanatory framework which should shed light on broader questions about the construction of gender in child protection work. First I discuss the implications of targeting the physical care of children for men and women clients.

Body maintenance work and the scrutiny of mothering

The result of this preoccupation with body maintenance work is that mothering comes under scrutiny. A connection between neglect and mothering is a familiar one. Swift (1995) argues that it is mainstream in the professional literature. The influential work of Polansky et al. (1981), for example, is notable for targeting mothers in its concern about child neglect. Turney (2000) argues that this connection stems from the construction of neglect as an absence of care. When care is so strongly associated with femininity, she observes, it is inevitable that women will be held responsible. Swift captures the gender bias of neglect categorisation:

> while the category neglect appears on the surface to be gender free, impli-cating 'parents' as responsible for the care of children, virtually all people actually accused of neglecting their children, both historically and at present, are mothers. (Swift, 1995: 107)

The attention to mothering in the Uplands team is not, however, in any straightforward way, a conscious decision on the part of social workers to avoid men and pressurise women. As the extracts above show, there is a tendency in case talk to slip into only mentioning mothers as culpable. This slippage also needs to be understood, how-ever, in the context of an occupational culture where a feminist critique of men's power over women in families is mainstream social work knowledge. The focus of mothering needs to be understood on many different layers; as the outcome of pragmatic decisions, as the inevit-able result of a system based on risk management, and as connected with the social workers' gender and class identities.

Social workers' explanations of neglectful families tend to refer heavily to the negative influences of fathers, or mothers' partners, often in terms of their lack of engagement with the routine tasks of parenting. As observed in the previous chapter, this contrasts with Swift's research (1995). A manager, in reference to his recent survey of fifteen cases retrospectively identified as neglect cases, said:

> The men in their lives were at best an impediment, and almost always a negative influence. Either there was domestic violence or they ruined the household, through spending the money on drugs or by being in prison. There was not one of the fifteen [cases] where a man was a positive role model. (senior manager, from fieldnotes, 8 July)

In practice, intervention is usually focused on women, however. As outlined in Chapters 4 and 5, social workers declare that there is little choice within the current routines of home visiting, because men absent themselves from the family for much of the time, and perhaps especially when the social worker is due to call. Social workers make pragmatic decisions about who they can realistically work with, deciding that they will not get very far with changing men's entrenched patterns of behaviour.

Parker's (1995) overview of the history of child protection in the UK suggests that periods of attention to neglect have historically meant more attention to bad mothering than periods when abuse has been targeted. Gordon's historical work on child protection in the USA also shows that:

> when child *abuse* had been emphasized, and individual vice blamed, men were the spotlighted culprits. When neglect was emphasized, and social conditions blamed, women were responsible, because they were in charge of children's care. (Gordon, 1988: 73)

Unlike the earlier decades of the century that Parker refers to, the current cultural and legislative climate in the UK is generally more supportive of fathers' involvement in child-rearing. This is reflected in the social workers' view that they should ideally be working with both parents. Formal documents, such as minutes of meetings and social workers' reports, typically use gender-neutral language, referring to *the parents'* responsibilities. In fact these formal documents have the effect of masking the gendered reality of the work. Discussion of the construction of clienthood by professionals and procedures cannot escape the material reality of the gendered division of labour in client families and elsewhere. Housework, and the physical and emotional care of children are, in practice, women's work. So a concentration on dirt, mess and food is a concentration on mothering.

It can be argued that, given the gendered division of parental labour in client families, scrutiny of mothering is inevitable in the current child protection system, whatever the case categorisation. The system is based on the management of risk; the future possibility of harm to children (Parton et al., 1997). Any attempt to assess and manage a case defined as 'high risk' will be intrusive and interventionist, and it is women who are bodily present in households, taking responsibility for childcare, so they bear the brunt of this intrusion (Parton and Parton, 1989). Some social workers are uneasy about the intrusive and coercive nature of their work, and its focus on women. As cited in Chapter 4, one said 'quite often it does feel like you are sort of persecuting women for the inadequacies of society'.

It is clear that the local authority's choice to target the neglect of body maintenance when there is a host of potential new child protection targets, men's violence, or men's abdication of responsibility, for example, is a choice with implications for the gender and class composition of the client group. It means in practice that more poor women will have their housekeeping and child-rearing skills scrutinised. The interesting question to ask is why this particular target? Why physical care, and why dirt, disorder and diet? The next section will discuss these questions.

The gendered implications of a decision to target physical neglect are fairly clear. It is possible that a failure on the part of senior managers (almost all men) to seriously acknowledge men's abuse of women and children contributed to that decision. However, the data suggest that some aspects of feminist discourse on the family are also mainstream at management level. The words of the senior manager cited above that the men in cases of neglect were 'almost always a negative influence' are an illustration of this. Whilst the practice of child protection work which prioritises physical neglect has gender and class implications, gender as an explanatory framework does not tell us everything we need to know about the preoccupation with dirt, disorder and diet. We need to go beyond the issue of gender to understand more thoroughly the choice of this particular target.

Why dirty, hungry children and untidy houses?

I now offer some other possible reasons for the dominance of one particular professional discourse on neglect. The discussion makes reference to anthropological work on the social meaning of dirt and cleanliness, the influence of physical and emotional responses, traditional notions of respectability, the usefulness of the observable body as evidence, and the rediscovery of child neglect as a response to conflicting but unavoidable pressures in contemporary child protection work.

Dirt is culturally very powerful. When a social worker records that 'the smell of cat faeces was overwhelming', we share the horror of that smell. Mary Douglas's work on the social meaning of dirt and cleanliness (1966) might point to some clues as to the preoccupation with dirt. Rather than describing dirt within the medical framework of hygiene, she sees it as 'matter out of place'. An interest in dirt and pollution arises in response to the ambiguity caused by the challenging of social boundaries. Child abuse is certainly an example of the challenging of internal societal boundaries. There are multiple ambiguities and insecurities inherent in the child protection role. Risk to children is not provable, but social workers are under a great deal of pressure to get it right. The shift in emphasis towards neglect arose from a child death where the social worker was found to be at fault; every social worker's worst nightmare. Perhaps the interest in dirt is explained by this context. Certainly in the face of this kind of uncertainty and insecurity, dirty, hungry, ill-clad children are bodies of evidence. They are concrete proof of parental failure to clean, feed and clothe.

To understand the interest in dirt, we need to consider its capacity to provoke physical and emotional responses as well as cognitive ones. The importance of embodied cultural responses has been convincingly asserted by Bourdieu (1986). Peile (1998) has argued a case for applying bodily and emotive knowledge to social work practice. 'Carnal knowledge' is the term used (albeit in a very different context) by Mellor and Shilling (1997) to describe the link between the physical body and the mind. The reaction of social workers to some households is certainly an emotional and physical one:

> There were times when I felt that if somebody had gone in there who didn't have a strong stomach as maybe I had, they would have probably removed

those children just because of the stink, the smell in the house. (interview with Lorraine)

If you saw the state of this property. The state of the toilets downstairs. I took a housing official with me. He almost threw up. It's the only house I visit I just can't wait to get out of. (Debbie, from fieldnotes, 3 September)

This is, of course, a culturally specific physical reaction to particular smells. A paper by De Montigny (1995) discusses at some length the one line in a social work case file 'the apartment smelled of urine'. He first describes his own embodied response to the apartment (he was the social worker), as well as the complex power relations behind this reaction and its translation into a mundane 'fact' in a social work file.

The construction of neglect should perhaps be understood in the context of traditional preoccupations in working-class communities, namely the importance of the tidy house, well-dressed children and proper food as markers of respectability (Steedman, 1982). The backgrounds and regional origins of the social workers vary, but the Uplands community values are seen strongly in the recorded reactions of other professional groups more homogeneous in their local origins, such as police officers and health visitors. In some sense 'home conditions' are familiar territory in a climate of uncertainty. Skeggs's work (1997) captures the crucial significance of respectability in the construction of gender and class identities. She states her case neatly in the following passage:

Respectability is one of the most ubiquitous signifiers of class. It informs how we speak, who we speak to, how we classify others, what we study and how we know who we are (or are not). Respectability is usually the concern of those who are not seen to have it. Respectability would not be of concern here, if the working classes (Black and White) had not consistently been classified as dangerous, polluting, threatening, revolutionary, pathological and without respect. (Skeggs, 1997: 1)

The Bridge Child Care Consultancy message on neglect that the social workers remember most vividly is the danger of believing that families are dirty, but happy. Several of the research participants spoke of the need to question their existing professional values on parenting, described as 'minimum standards' and reclaim their own higher personal standards of what would be acceptable for children of their own. I return to discuss this issue at greater length in the next chapter.

It seems that the social workers are both interested in the issue of child neglect, experiencing a sense of novelty, and also feel uneasy about it. One said that it raised 'huge dilemmas'. Perhaps because of the newness of neglect as a priority issue, and because of the particularly overt links to poverty, there is more of a sense that social workers are struggling to get it right than with other types of cases:

I am never convinced that if I lived in one of the dump houses in say Hilltown or Valleytown that I would be any better than anybody else. I am sure that if I was left on my own with a couple of small children, a very limited income, no car, no expectations, I don't think I would do a very good job. (interview with Lorraine)

Neglect is a difficult one anyway. With neglect it's over a period of time. With physical or sexual abuse you've got it there. We've all got different views on what neglect is. I find it the most difficult of the categories. What might be acceptable to me in the home, a health visitor might think 'oh my God'. Where I might think 'well, I've seen worse'. We've not got a clear definition of neglect. (interview with Claire)

As already stated, the version of neglect being taken up in River County is what staff perceive to be the message of the Bridge Child Care Consultancy. The effectiveness of this discourse warrants some preliminary discussion. Bridge are successful in getting across their message through the use of powerful emotive rhetoric. For example, one of their publications (Pritchard, 1996) compares a passage from *Oliver Twist* with one from the 'Paul' report (Bridge Child Care Consultancy, 1995) and asks the reader to consider how far society has progressed. The training delivery is very effective in striking a chord with social workers' experiences, and making the message stick through fear: the fear that the same could happen here:

We've had this training day. It was excellent. You could just picture cases in your mind. (from fieldnotes, Debbie, 3 September)

Pete said that the description of the Paul case made him 'go cold' because of the Brown family. (author, from fieldnotes, 5 August)

Despite the emotional content of the child protection role, much of the daily work is fairly routine. A new professional mission, packaged in an exciting way and combined with the crucial element of fear, can be highly effective:

> He's the best speaker I've ever heard. When you compare it with some of the boring training I've been on. (from fieldnotes, Lorraine, 21 August)

Bridge are not alone in this kind of approach. Child protection is a highly contested field, and the competing philosophies have to battle to persuade social workers. There are financial vested interests where profit-making organisations increase custom through the success of charismatic presentations. This is not to suggest that Bridge are different from other organisations in respect of the above comments. It is to argue that the rhetorical construction of child abuse discourse needs to be questioned by social workers and social services managers. The Bridge version of child abuse and neglect is controversial, after all. An NSPCC spokesperson commented that the new dangerous families checklist written by Bridge was 'a throwback to practice before the current trend, supported by the Government, of a less confrontational approach to families in need' (Brindle, 1998: 11). It is worth restating that the dominant version of neglect in River County is only what they *perceive to be* the Bridge message on neglect. A good example of where errors are made was one of the Uplands social workers mentioning the death of Sukina Hammond as an example of a neglect case. He rightly associated this case with Bridge – they wrote the report (Bridge Child Care Consultancy, 1991) – but there is no suggestion in the Sukina Hammond inquiry report that this is a neglect case. It is clearly identified as having been a problem of a violent man.

So why the attention to the physical care of a child at a time when the official message (from the Department of Health) is that a rounded view of a child's welfare is needed; one that includes consideration of emotional attachments? It is of course easier to monitor the observable body. You can see and smell dirt, check a child's weight. It is certainly easier to monitor than other parental deficiencies; men's violence, for example, and easier to measure than emotional well-being. As Howe (1992), amongst others, has asserted, monitoring and the gathering of evidence have become the chief tasks of child protection social workers. Howe (1996) has also characterised contemporary social work as concerned with surface, rather than depth. In the Uplands team it seems that social workers want to get beyond the surface of observable family situations to find unpleasant secrets rather than locate causes of problems that can lead to helping strategies. There are frequent references to 'digging', or even 'ferreting' for what is hidden. In gathering evidence, bodily signs are crucial. Evidence of 'development' is written on the child's body (White, 1997a). It is perhaps difficult for social workers to shift to the holistic view of child welfare recommended by the Department of Health when there are compelling practical and cultural reasons for scrutiny of the child's body.

The switch to a protectionist approach with neglect could be seen as a surprising development, when the thrust of UK government guidance is towards reducing the time spent on investigations and increasing support to families (Dartington Social Research Unit, 1995). Obviously the implication of the rediscovery of neglect as a child protection issue is that more children will be brought into the child protection net rather than more kept out. The rediscovery of neglect in River County is a response to two very different pressures. It represents increased scrutiny of families, or at least scrutiny of different problems, in response to local furore at child deaths. It is also an attempt to follow the government guidance that it is unwise to focus on specific incidents of abuse rather than children's overall welfare. Although a preoccupation with physical neglect does represent a move away from specific incidents of abuse, the result is a very partial view of children's welfare, albeit one that is easier to establish than the more holistic picture. The authority's predicament illustrates very neatly the difficulty of responding to the Department of Health's *Messages from Research* in a climate of preoccupation with risk. Parton (1997) has pointed out the tension between attempts to move away from child protection and the continuing influence of inquiries into child deaths. He cites the Bridge report on the death of 'Paul' (Bridge Child Care Consultancy, 1995) as an example of forces pulling back towards protectionism. The local inquiries in River County, albeit not public ones, have had the effect of putting pressure on the authority to step up investigation rather than reduce it.

Observing the Uplands team at work suggests, in keeping with the findings of Parton et al. (1997) and Kähkönen (1999), that the attention of the child protection system is on standards of parenting, which usually means mothering. But the bodies of children can be the focus for judgements on parenting. They are easy evidence in a system which is based on the gathering of evidence and the management of risk. They are tangible and concrete in a climate of risk, insecurity and uncertainty. And they are visible signs of the quality of mothering.

Conclusion

This chapter presented an analysis of ethnographic data on the construction of child neglect in the Uplands team, as a particularly vivid and topical example of the gendering of child protection work. The dominant construction of child neglect was seen to be the failure to provide adequate physical care for children and their environment; in particular an emphasis on dirty, hungry children and untidy houses.

The chapter went on to discuss the implications of this dominant construction for the gender and class profile of the primary clients. The rediscovery of neglect was seen to increase the scrutiny of women living in poverty. Various perspectives were then brought to bear to explain the emphasis on body maintenance work. These were as follows: anthropological work on the social meaning of dirt and cleanliness; the importance of physical and emotional responses; traditional notions of respectability; the rhetorical power of vested interest groups; and the usefulness of the observable body as evidence. Also, the rediscovery of child neglect in this authority is a response to the dual pressures of public reaction to a child death and government guidance on reducing investigations of alleged abuse incidents, both inescapable pressures in contemporary child protection work. The gendered effect of a concentration on body maintenance is particularly stark, but this concentration has to be explained in the context of the political and social context of child protection in the late 1990s; a context which makes the scrutiny of mothering an inevitability.

Implications for practice

As with the previous two, this chapter concludes with some summary points about the implications of the above discussion for practitioners.

- Managers and practitioners need to be aware that the target of organisational prioritising in child welfare services will have profound implications for the question of whether interventions target men or women or both.

- There are gendered implications of choosing to weight interventions towards either child abuse or child neglect, since the responsibility for child neglect has in child welfare services traditionally been ascribed to women and child abuse more often to men.
- There are strongly gendered implications of focusing on domestic labour – feeding, cleaning and clothing.
- Managers and practitioners should be aware of the potential injustice of reconstructing men's abusive behaviour as something that women are responsible for stopping.
- 'Parents' are never gender neutral but always actual men or women. Social workers should be specific about which parent they are really referring to wherever possible.

In this chapter I aimed to provide a sustained example of gender construction. The initial reason for the inclusion of this particular example was the impossibility of avoiding the issue of child neglect in River County, such was its topicality and novelty. Over and above this local dimension, however, as an example of gender construction, child neglect cases are illuminating for several reasons. They illustrate how choices about child protection priorities at a management level are gendered. They illustrate how the outcomes of some ostensibly non-gendered practice can in fact be highly gendered. They also emphasise that gender relations can never be considered in isolation from other explanatory factors. In particular, the more general social, political and historical location of child protection policy and practice has to be brought into the analysis. The next chapter moves away from the specific frame of this one, and back to a more general level of analysis. It focuses on social work knowledge and values in practice, and their gendered implications.

7

Knowledge and values in practice

The aim of this book has been to unpack and examine the occupational culture of child protection work. Chapter 3 set out the context of the construction of clienthood. Chapters 4 and 5 gave overviews of the discourses of masculinity and femininity in the social workers' case talk, recording and report writing. Chapter 6 focused on the gendered construction of child protection priorities. This chapter goes on to address how social workers draw on professional knowledge, ethics and values, and the implications of how they do this for work with men and women. Reference has already been made to social work knowledge, ethics and values in each of the previous chapters. This chapter tackles the topic in a more sustained fashion, having as its central question: On the basis of what knowledge, ethics and values do social workers construct gender?

The Central Council for Education and Training in Social Work (CCETSW) sees the 'competences' necessary for good social work practice as comprising the separate elements of skills, knowledge and values (CCETSW, 1991). In this chapter I do not make much of the distinction between 'ethics' and 'values'. Dictionary definitions link both professional 'ethics' and 'values' to 'moral standards' that are considered correct in a social group (although what social workers refer to as 'values' should in fact be understood as much, if not more, within a political framework as a moral one [Butler and Drakeford, 2000]). It could be argued that ethics come into play in relation to specific practice dilemmas, whereas values are overarching working principles. I tend, however, to collapse the terms together, using either the phrase 'ethics and values' or just 'values'. My interest at this point is not so much in social work theorising in the academy, although I do make reference to relevant debates in academic literature. Rather, I aim to explore how social workers draw on knowledge and values in their *practice*.

Relating knowledge and values to practice is unavoidable, since knowledge in the social work office is not disembodied. Individual social workers have to process the dilemmas and discussions in child protection work, and these ultimately relate to individual children, and adult carers – women and men.

My concern is with the social workers' 'knowledge-in-action' (Schön, 1991). This involves not only 'official' professional knowledge, but also lay knowledge. As Swift expresses it:

> the practices of child welfare workers . . . reflect the knowledge, values, and beliefs of the larger society. In other words, child welfare workers import and apply their experiences as members of society to their everyday reasoning and decision processes. (Swift, 1995: 13)

There is of course much more that could be said about the relationship between lay and professional knowledge. For a discussion of some broader debates on the nature of knowledge and the application of lay and professional knowledge in the Uplands team, see Scourfield (1999). So far most of the book has been concerned with the discursive interaction of lay and professional knowledge. This chapter focuses rather more on professional social work knowledge, and especially tensions that can be observed in the case talk and case recording of the Uplands team. These are tensions that could be seen as inherent in social work knowledge and values – tensions between a focus on individuals and a focus on their social context. The topic here is not so much knowledge about gender as knowledge about social work and knowledge about personal and social problems, with the implications for the question of gender drawn out. To begin the chapter I start with an introduction to the inherent tensions in social work knowledge and values.

Inherent tensions in social work knowledge and values

Sibeon (1990) argues that the theoretical ideas behind social work can be organised into three sub-sections: theories of what social work is, theories of how to do social work, and theories of the client world. The discussion below will refer to two of these areas, theories of how to do social work and theories of the client world. I will argue that tensions exist in both levels of theory over the relationship between the individual and the social; tensions which are central to under-standing the gendering of child protection work. I refer to 'the social' not as the domain of professional intervention between the public and the private that Donzelot (1980) describes (see Chapter 2), but rather to mean a focus on society and collectivity; a sociological perspective.

The tensions between the individual and the social take several forms. There is the tension between the disciplines of psychology and sociology, both of which inform social work theory and practice. Then within sociology there is the tension between structure and agency, and the discipline of psychology encompasses a range of perspectives from an emphasis on individual neurology through to a focus on socially produced cognition. These tensions are in some ways related to that which Sibeon (1990) calls the distinction between generalising (nomo-thetic) knowledge and particularising (idiographic) knowledge and between what Berger and Luckmann (1967) term the intersubjective and the intrasubjective meaning of events. There is also tension between the dual promises of impartiality and an individualised service, which Murray et al. (1983) see as the Janus character of professions:

> On the one hand, it is publicly asserted that they offer an impartial, objective and freely available way of resolving problems of social or natural order. On the other, a private promise is given of a service that is personal, individualised and oriented to the resolution of private problems to the satisfaction of particular rather than general interests. (Murray et al., 1983: 219, cited in Atkinson and Delamont, 1990: 97)

There is also the tension between working with the individual or working on a collective level: casework versus community work. This tension is seen in the debates between those who believe that social work has to focus on individual and family difficulties and those who believe that community action and radical political change should be the priority (Rojek et al., 1988, summarise these debates). Philp (1979) attempts to circumvent this debate by arguing that the underlying discourse of social work requires the production of knowledge of people as subjects:

> Social work has an ambivalent relation to any form of determinism, for deter-minism suggests forces beyond individual control. At the same time it utilises determinist theory to explain why an individual has become, for example, anti-social. It solves the problem by ultimately denying an absolute nature to determinism and by showing that, with compassion and an understanding of

the individual's essential humanity, these forces can be transcended, thus realising the individual's inherently social self. (Philp, 1979: 92–3)

Many commentators have argued that social work has to have a dual focus on the individual and the social (Howe, 1996, is just one example); that social work necessarily involves engaging with individuals, but that what distinguishes the profession from others is its location of individuals in their social context. One version of this is the ecological model (see, for example, Barber, 1991), which assumes intervention on several levels, from the microsystem (the client's immediate, phenomenological environment) up to the macrosystem (the norms and rituals of a culture or sub-culture). Despite the fact that there have been some interesting attempts to integrate the individual and the social in social work theory, this chapter aims to explore the tensions at the level of practice reasoning. And tensions there undoubtedly are. Jordan (1991) argues that there are unavoidable tensions between an appreciation of structural inequalities and an emphasis on the individual's right to dignity, privacy, confidentiality, choice and protection.

All of which is relevant to gender because gender is a social category. However far deconstruction of the terms 'sex' and 'gender' takes us, and whichever we decide comes first (see Delphy, 1993), we are dealing with social identities and social inequality. If you accept that there is inequality and imbalance in child protection work with men and women, and aim to change that situation, you cannot do so unless you have a social analysis. Neither, if that is your aim, can you offer a service that is 'gender sensitive', that is, geared towards the 'different needs' of men and women.

In terms of gender issues, manifestations of the individual–social distinction include equal treatment versus anti-oppression, and structural theories of male power versus an emphasis on individual gendered identities. In the culture of social work the two oppositional pairs are linked, as will be explained below. The discussion that follows is structured around theories of how to do social work and theories of the client world.

Theories of how to do social work

One of the most interesting tensions around gender is caused by the enduring legacy of what can be termed 'traditional social work ethics'.

Concepts such as respect for clients, valuing individuals, partnership, confidentiality and equal treatment are important elements of the ethical basis that social workers draw on, and they cause some confusion and conflict in child protection, with important implications for work with men and women clients.

Biestek's (1961) classic formulation of social work values includes the concepts of unconditional acceptance of the client as a person, a non-judgemental approach, and clients' self-determination. As Hugman and Smith (1995) point out, by the time the basis of the UK Diploma in Social Work was set out thirty years later (CCETSW, 1991) the emphasis had changed. The CCETSW document reflects the influence of radical critiques, including feminism. It also reflects an increasing recognition both of the need for an authority role in certain contexts and also of the limits of what social workers can achieve. So unconditional acceptance becomes respect for clients' dignity and strengths, self-determination becomes the promotion of choice. Non-judgementalism becomes non-discrimination and anti-oppression. The theme of commitment to the value of individuals is a consistent theme in Biestek and CCETSW's Paper 30, and the Code of Ethics of the British Association of Social Workers states:

> The social worker's basic values must relate to individuals, whether working with individuals, groups or communities, since it is the welfare of the individuals in a group or community which is the social worker's basic concern even if indirectly. (BASW, 1996)

Studying the work of the Uplands team shows that all these different emphases are present in the social workers' knowledge-in-action. The acceptance of clients as they are is reflected in the optimistic refusal of some to talk about clients as 'difficult'.

> I do not have difficult clients really. I have clients who may be in crisis when I go to see them, and therefore they may be quite angry and looking for help, but I don't generally see clients as being difficult clients. I see them more as clients with difficulties, which then means that I become a sort of an enabler, a facilitator and that sort of thing. So it is not very often that I do have, although I remember, you know they spring to mind as being difficult clients, it is almost as if that has become part of the job and you expect people to be difficult at different times. (interview with Pete)

Although an optimistic acceptance of clients is an important stream of professional rhetoric, there are notable exceptions. As Featherstone and Lancaster (1997) have claimed, sex offenders are in many respects exempt from the traditional social work ethic (with roots in Kantian ideas) of 'respect for persons'. This exemption seems to be made on the basis that it is the child that is the client. This ethical stance, expressed in the phraseology of the Children Act 1989 that 'the welfare of the child is paramount' has become something of a mantra in child protection work. The child is the client, so deserves respect, whereas disregard of parents' wishes is justified on the grounds that they are not the key client. Sex offenders do not receive individualised service, because their behaviour is understood according to a fairly rigid template (see Chapter 5). Social workers do not expect to spend time working with sex offenders. The only acceptable strategy, if it is decided that abuse has taken place, is to get the man out of the home. In practice, the social workers testify, this is done either through imprisonment or by pressure being applied through the threat of legal action if he does not leave. In many cases this involves the woman having to 'choose' him or the children.

Philp's work (1979) is relevant here. He argues that social work cannot speak for those whose objective status overwhelms their subjectivity. Social work cannot operate when an individual's act has removed him from the right to be perceived as human. The examples he gives are the psychotic or the mass murderer. In the current climate of particular horror being reserved for those who sexually abuse children (Stainton Rogers and Stainton Rogers, 1992), this category of people (mostly men) can be added to Philp's examples.

This brings us to the key dilemma about gender in the knowledge and value base of social work. How can social workers incorporate an understanding of social inequality alongside an individualised service that treats each client as unique? Most interpretations of inequality point to the profound effects of this inequality on social identities. If social workers accept that there are social trends in men's and women's behaviour resulting from the different opportunities given to each sex, and that informs their practice, how do they also then treat each client as an individual? Margaret, in the following excerpt, resists the idea that you can talk about men and women in collective terms:

Jonathan: Are there any common differences between the men clients that you work with and the women clients you work with?

> You know, could you describe, for example, what the women
> clients are kind of typically like?
> *Margaret*: Oh gosh, I don't think I can generalise to that extent. No, I don't
> think I could describe what women are typically like. I think we
> endeavour not to discriminate between men and women. (inter-
> view with Margaret)

She equates generalising about clients on the basis of their sex with
discrimination, although at other times she is happy to talk about the
effects of social structural inequality on clients' lives. The dilemma of
negotiating both individualisation and a focus on collectivity and
social forces in social work has led to much debate. On one side is the
argument that social work too often explains situations that are at root
social problems (for example, violence against women) with individualised therapeutic discourse (Dobash and Dobash, 1992). In opposition
to this argument, some authors have claimed that a rigid interpretation
of social structural oppression can dehumanise social work and result
in formulaic interventions (Featherstone and Trinder, 1997).

Inevitably, the complexity of the picture of social work practice in
the Uplands team means it does not neatly justify either critique. As
stated above, constructions of sexual abuse are formulaic, whereas
knowledge about other kinds of abusive behaviour by men is more diffuse. The discourse of men as a threat is a powerful one, but some
men are constructed as caring and capable in contrast to their women
partners.

The tension between knowledge of social forces and knowledge of
the individual echoes, in some respects, the debate about the gender
order between those who emphasise structural power and post-struc-
turalists and others who emphasise fluidity and diversity. These are
the different emphases of, for example, Walby (1989) and Butler
(1990) or, in the social work literature, Mullender (1996) and Fawcett
et al. (2000). All these authors write from within the broad school of
feminism. Practice wisdom about gender in social work teams
includes notions that are pro-feminist, pre-feminist, non-feminist and
anti-feminist. The analogy with academic debates is a fair one,
however. It is not always possible to maintain firm boundaries
between conceptions of what constitutes theory and what practice.
Also it is arguable that anti-discriminatory discourse within social
work practice is now so mainstream that we can talk about feminism
as a major influence.

Mention of anti-discrimination brings the discussion round to another key gender tension about how to do social work; the tension between equal treatment and anti-oppression. There is a general acknowledgement in the Uplands team, informed by feminism, that the lives of the women they work with are very often made much more difficult by the oppressive behaviour of the men they live with. There is also, though, a strong assumption that practising in a gender-aware and anti-sexist fashion requires an 'equal treatment' approach. This is an essentially liberal strategy of non-discrimination; men and women should not be treated differently. The following extract from an interview with Pete illustrates the tensions between equal treatment and an approach tailored according to the gender differences that clients present. This social worker has been asked if he sees any differences in the way he works with women and with men:

I'd like to think not. And I think it would only be by being directly observed that we would know if there was, but I would like to think not. I don't believe that I have a different approach in that I try and approach every one as – God this sounds crass! – but as an individual. I try, whether they are a child or adult male or female, I try and approach them as an individual and relate to them in the best way that I can. I am aware of anti-discriminatory practice, obviously because of my practice teaching, but I try and be conscious that the way I relate to people is not in a discriminatory way. I know inevitably that I do and sometimes I am conscious of that and can address it and sometimes I am not conscious of it. But I don't think I could say that I was totally non-discriminatory because I just think, well the sheer fact that I am fallible, that is inevitably going to creep in. But I try and make sure, as best I can in my dealings with people, that I am dealing on an individual level rather than dealing with things on a gender basis. But, sometimes you have to, in that dealing with or engaging some clients you are not going to engage the father by talking at great length about the child care, about the nitty-gritty of babies. If they have just had a baby into that family, I am saying in some cases because that is not what that father considers his role or that family considers that father's role to be. And he will want to talk about and discuss other things and that is the 'I want to provide' bit. So he might want to discuss with me bits about help with providing certain bits of equipment or problems with the money, whereas the mother might want to talk about difficulties in coping with the physical demands of caring for a baby. But what I try and do where possible is address people where they are coming from. But if they were a couple I would address my answers to both regardless of who fired a question. But if they are on an individual level then I will address the sort of problems that they are raising. (interview with Pete)

His response reveals several distinct professional discourses. He refers to the need to deal with people as individuals, drawing on a traditional social work ethic. It is interesting to note that he is embarrassed to voice this. It is possible he sees this tradition as associated with the pejorative, sandal-wearing, 'woolly liberal', popular image of social workers. There is perhaps, in the culture of child protection, a fear of being seen to be 'soft on parents' (see White, 1997a, on scepticism about parental accounts). He may even be apologising to another man for an approach that might be seen as feminised. His acknowledgement of fallibility feeds into a discourse of reflexivity that is increasingly influential, particularly where it overlaps with anti-discriminatory discourse, in terms of the need to be aware of your own inevitable discriminatory views. He talks of the importance of equal treatment 'rather than dealing with things on a gender basis', but then goes on to argue that it can be necessary in some situations to tailor your approach according to client's gendered behaviour. This approach, to 'address people where they are coming from' or work at the client's own pace, is also a familiar element in social work discourse.

A distinction has been made in the social work literature between anti-discriminatory and anti-oppressive practice, the former being a strategy to avoid treating any group unfairly, and the latter a more proactive approach which acknowledges structural power differentials and oppressive forces (Phillipson, 1992). Pete, in the extract above, refers to anti-discrimination in his stated desire to deal with people as individuals with equal rights to a service, and he refers to anti-oppressive practice in recognising the reality that men often want a limited role in child-rearing. He does not advocate challenging men, as do some commentators on social work (for example, Stanley, 1997), but rather believes you should begin by responding to the man as he is.

So much of the anti-oppression discourse in social work has taken for granted that it is the clients of social workers that will be the oppressed people in the power relationship; oppressed by the state, including the social services, and oppressed by a racist, sexist, homophobic society. One of the reasons that child protection social workers spend little time actually working with abusive men may be that this anti-oppression discourse, that has become mainstream in social work culture, cannot understand these clients. It cannot understand clients as the oppressors, the abusers of power. In fact, such men are often excluded from social work services. Women are expected to remove them from the house (Mullender, 1997; Humphries, 1999), and there is thereafter no notion that they should be engaged in any way. The idea, advanced by some, of challenging abusive men is perhaps alien to mainstream social work knowledge. It does not fit with the traditional notion, as found in Biestek (1961), of unconditional acceptance of the client. Neither does it fit with newer ideas about anti-oppressive practice.

The excerpt below from Debbie expresses the limits of mainstream social work discourse in responding to gender inequality, and more broadly the inherent difficulty in child protection practice of attempting to work co-operatively with people whose behaviour you find problematic:

> There's a clash of values when you're supposed to work in partnership but he may have no idea that it's his role to give her any support. (interview with Debbie)

Theories of the client world

There are of course many different theories used by social workers in practice to explain the child abuse and neglect they work with. Many have been mentioned already in previous chapters. The brief discussion below will again highlight the tensions between the individual and the social, and draw out the implications for the construction of gender.

The trend towards a liberal non-discriminatory ethic resists knowledge about social characteristics. There is a view that to incorporate into practice a version of the gender order which acknowledges oppression of women by men would be to stereotype, label, and therefore discriminate. The excerpts below illustrate this reluctance to talk about social trends, or to talk about one sex in negative terms:

> No I don't think I could describe what women are typically like. I think we endeavour not to discriminate between men and women. I say we endeavour to, that is not to say that we probably don't end up doing so. (interview with Margaret)

> I don't think I have specifically difficult male clients. I have been into difficult situations where it could have been dodgy with either mum or dad

but they turned out okay in the end. And obviously you are questioning somebody about how a bruise happened or how this injury occurred and obviously people become very, very defensive, but that is equally the same for women as for males. (interview with Sarah, Docktown)

There is, however, a great deal of social categorisation in routine child protection work. Some of this is tacit categorisation of clients (Howitt, 1992), some is categorisation for bureaucratic purposes, and some is a more consciously theoretical explanation of client problems that draws on sociological ideas. More individually based psychological explanations are also frequently employed. Psychodynamic ideas continue to be referenced in mainstream social work practice, and developmental psychology is unquestioned as a foundation for decisions about children (White, 1998a). Psychological and sociological explanations are also often combined. The excerpt below from one of my pilot interviews in 'Docktown' is an example of this:

I must say that I am sure that there are different reasons why there is physical abuse in families. A lot of it can be behaviour, it was what was the norm in the childhood that they had. And there are lots of views about, you know, you hit a child and you tell a child that it is all right to hit. There are lots of kinds of theories that we could look at about why. There is also I believe a lot of pressures on people today, coping alone. You haven't got the social networks of family networks that you had before. Where you had a gran around the corner or auntie you haven't got that. People are a lot more isolated. I think there is demand to have a television, it has to be a colour television, so there is the demand on the financial implications. I think that they all put pressures on how families cope with everyday living, and with fractious children that could be around at the wrong time when things are going wrong for you and you lash out, so there are those kinds of reasons. (interview with Lynne, Docktown)

She makes mention of social learning theory from the psychological realm ('it was what was the norm in the childhood') and also the more sociological comment on the state of social networks and the pressures of poverty. Another social worker, in the excerpt below, references both ideas about the origins of domestic violence in men's social power and also, switching the focus to the woman as cause, more psychological ideas about learning to have a low self-esteem:

> In my previous job, not so much here, alcohol and domestic violence were rife. If we look at the mother, look at the parents, what I see is the man having control, power, being in charge, perhaps drinking quite a lot of the income. The mother has low self-esteem, a poor self-image. She's grown up with a father who's violent. (interview with Claire)

Despite this combining of individual and social theories, the data tend to support Philp's argument (1979) that social work requires the production of knowledge of people as subjects (also see Stenson, 1993). Philp writes:

> Essentially, any theory which suggests forces permanently beyond the individual's control is either ignored by, or subverted to, social work's regime of truth. (Philp, 1979: 93)

There is a sense in which, in the final analysis, social workers cannot see a situation as socially determined. The extract below quite clearly illustrates this belief in relation to alleged child neglect in a situation of poor housing:

> Debbie tells Margaret 'It's about protecting the children, a safer environment. There aren't any locked doors, they aren't deprived of affection.' It turns out there is a man after all. Until today I assumed it was a single mother. Margaret notes that 'the woman says she has housing problems' and Debbie replies 'that's no excuse'. (from fieldnotes, 23 September)

This insistence on clients' agency has implications for work with men and women. It perhaps explains the expectation that women should be able to release themselves from oppressive situations, by leaving or by removing the source of the oppression. It also suggests a belief that abusive men should be able to change, unless (again echoing Philp, 1979) their objective status overwhelms their subjectivity. Into this category of those beyond redemption fall 'proven' abusers, such as perpetrators of sexual abuse and people whose physical or psychological abuse of women or children is seen as 'serious'. It is important to combine Philp's argument with the assertion in Chapter 3 that redeemable clients are expected to change solely in response to the threat of losing the care of their children. Although social workers make frequent reference to social and psychological causes of client problems, there is a belief that if they are told what needs to change in order to keep their children, they will be able to do this.

Discussion

The tension between individualisation and social context warrants further discussion at this point, particularly in as much as it reflects on the construction of gender in the childcare social work office. The discussion above has related throughout to the material in the previous four chapters. One obvious point of connection between the tensions in social work knowledge and values described above and the multiple discourses of masculinity and femininity described in Chapters 4 and 5 is fluidity. The fluidity of gender construction and the presence of multiple discourses are both central to my theoretical base in this book, and I would reject Philp's (1979) structuralist assumption that it should be possible to identify a unitary discourse for the social work profession. I do agree with Philp, however, that the production of knowledge about subjects – subjects who can act and not get stuck (Stenson, 1993) – does have a great deal of discursive power in the culture of social work. Gordon's (1988) study of gender and violence in historical case records also found that:

> despite the environmental analysis, child protectors continued to feature moralistic appeals to will power, as if individual determination could hold off the centrifugal forces of modern urban life. (Gordon, 1988: 74)

In fact the application of Philp's theories to the Uplands team shows that women are expected to have willpower and men, when seen as abusers, are beyond subjectivity and therefore beyond clienthood. The emphasis on the subject who can act, despite a lifetime of identity formation and overwhelming circumstantial pressure, is problematic for feminist social work. Inevitably, it means a downgrading of social information that might explain a 'case' and makes interventions on a governmental or a community level seem irrelevant. As Swift observes:

> the contextual information that might help to explain problems in child care is stripped away from the mother, and she is looked at as an 'individual'

a process that warrants the efforts of the state to focus its change efforts on her – in fact, which makes any other effort appear off the point. Poverty, class and race relations, gender issues, and fathers all vanish. Mothers are produced and reproduced as the 'causal variable'. (Swift, 1995: 125)

Arguably, the emphasis on the 'willpower' of the subject does not take account of how gender works. It does not consider the effects of long-term oppression on the formation of social identities, the difficulty of thinking you ought to do one thing, but finding yourself doing another – the very thing you believe you should not be doing. It does not take account of limitations on opportunities for action, for example, the immense difficulty for a woman in acting to force a man to leave her house when he has threatened her life and she fears homelessness and the stigma of single parenthood. This form of subjectification of clients does not allow for a social understanding of gender relations, but brings everything back to individual responsibility. Croghan and Miell express it thus:

Social work, with its foundation in humanist principles of self-actualization and personal autonomy, has tended to treat individual experience as both ahistorical and asocial, and has thus emphasized individual (and particularly female) responsibility for child welfare. (Croghan and Miell, 1998: 446)

The tensions between the individual and the social experienced by social workers in trying to explain their clients' circumstances mirror my own struggles to conceptualise the social workers' constructions of gender. The question they have to face as to whether clients are trapped in an oppressive social context neatly matches one of the most important theoretical dilemmas of my research, namely: Are the social workers trapped in occupational discourse or can there be alternative, oppositional constructions of men and women clients? Not surprisingly, there is a symmetry here, since this is the oldest problem of social inquiry, the activity the social workers and I are engaged in. This is the dualism of sociology–psychology, structure–agency, work with individuals or work with collectivities. Because this is the oldest problem, it will not go away just yet. The next two chapters will continue to grapple with it.

Before concluding, I should return to the issue of 'gendered knowledge'. Knowledge about gender preoccupies me in this book, and this chapter is no exception. I do not see much relevance, however, in the idea of knowledge as connected to biological sex – the way in which the term 'gendered knowledge' is sometimes used – the idea that men and women think differently. In the case of this research, the question as to whether men or women social workers construct their clients as gendered in different ways is an important one to address. It has already been asserted that this is not my position. I did not find in the Uplands team that there were substantial differences between men's and women's constructions of clients. I also find the idea that there could be a knowledge–body link to be a flawed one which implies biological determinism.

I do not accept wholesale the rejection of the categories 'woman' and 'man' in postmodernist feminism and queer theory. I agree with Oakley (1998) that such theorising tends to be distanced from

> the situation of women out there in a world that definitely does exist, and that remains obdurately structured by a dualistic, power-driven gender system. (Oakley, 1998: 143)

I do find, however, that postmodernist feminism, such as Butler's (1990, 1993), has successfully exploded the connection between knowledge and the body. I believe that such theorists have ensured the notion that certain types of thinking are associated with possession of female or male body parts is no longer tenable. Because of this, I do not consider such a version of 'gendered knowledge' to be a helpful framework for this book. I have tried to explain in which ways I do see knowledge about clients and social work values to be gendered. I explained in Chapter 2 that I use the term 'gendered' in relation to child protection practice and office culture to refer to the different implications of that practice and that culture for men and women clients.

Conclusion

This chapter explored some aspects of the 'knowledge-in-action' of practitioners in a child protection team. The premise of the research has been that whilst social work is circumscribed by discourse, there is not one fundamental discourse but rather multiple discourses, some of which oppose others. Multiple discourses can pull in very different directions. For example, discourse on the family that is conservative about gender relations, and discourse that is challenging and radical, can simultaneously influence the culture of the social work office. An important discursive tension discussed in this chapter is that between individualisation and a focus on social context. The discussion focused on the social workers' ways of dealing with the dilemma of how to provide an individualised service whilst considering the impact of social inequality. Overlapping discourses of the individual and the social can be found throughout practitioners' case talk. Whilst not all the discussion above has been about gender, the particular implications of these tensions in social work knowledge, ethics and values for working with men and woman were highlighted.

Particular aspects of the use of social work knowledge and values were highlighted. Social workers find a tension between the discourses of anti-discrimination and anti-oppression, and they are torn between a reluctance to categorise their clients as a 'type of person' and a need to understand them in terms of what is known about social trends. This tension goes to the heart of the problem of understanding gender relations, since gender is an inherently social concept. There is a tendency to use rigid social categorisation for some problem behaviour (sex offending) in contrast to the perception that other types of behaviour, whilst constructed as abusive, are nonetheless thought to be heterogeneous. Challenging abusers (more often men, in terms of the daily work of child protection teams) is not seen as part of the job of childcare social workers. The roots of this limitation of the social work role in the occupational knowledge and value base were discussed. The intention has not been to preach any particular line about social work knowledge or values, or to criticise practitioners, but rather to point to some of the difficulties of attempting to apply social work knowledge, ethics and values to the practical task of child protection work.

8

Understanding gendered practice

This chapter aims to discuss why child protection practice is gendered in the way it is. Parton and O'Byrne (2000) make the useful distinction between theory *of* practice and theory *for* practice. The concern of this chapter is theory *of* practice. The next chapter will consider theory *for* practice as well as summarising the lessons of the book.

There are four sub-sections to this discussion. It starts by reconsidering how useful the concepts of social structure and discourse might be for understanding the occupational culture in child protection. Following this, there is consideration of the influence of social workers' gender identities and the gendered organisation of social services. The discussion then moves on to the preoccupation with the body in late modernity, and the intersection of current discourse on gender, class and crime. The first two sections deal with the two ends of the continuum of feminist work on gender relations. Firstly, I tackle the structuralist idea of patriarchy and, secondly, the notion of gendered identities favoured by post-structuralist and postmodernist writers.

Structure and discourse

One of the most interesting theoretical questions on this topic is how we explain the persistence of gendered practices in child protection work, when anti-oppressive rhetoric has become increasingly dominant in the formal knowledge base of social work. I tackle this question by exploring the nature of occupational discourse, through a consideration of notions of social structure. I start by discussing the usefulness of the concept of patriarchy for understanding child protection, and then go on to examine the extent to which occupational discourse prescribes social work practice.

Patriarchy has been consistently used in feminist conceptualisations of structures of masculine domination in and beyond the state (Walby, 1990; Charles, 2000). As Pollert (1996) observes, it is interesting that, whilst in sociological writings, structures and causes seem to have been taken over by fragments and contingencies, the grand narrative of patriarchy has survived. That is not to say that the concept is without its critics, including Pollert (1996) herself, who has argued that the poverty of patriarchy is an analytical concept (see Gottfried, 1998, for a response to Pollert). There are etymological, definitional and theoretical problems with the concept of 'patriarchy' (Waters, 1989) and poststructuralist and post-modernist challenges are now well established in feminist theory (Weedon, 1997; Flax, 1990; Waugh, 1998). However, the concept continues to be widely used, even within sophisticated accounts of the gender order such as those of Connell (1987, 1995), so it deserves some attention at this point. Potentially, an emphasis on the continuing social structural oppression of women could be useful in explaining the persistence of gendered practices in child protection work despite the increasing influence of feminism in the social work profession.

If someone employs the idea of patriarchy, they are claiming relevance for the generalisation of men's dominance of women. Whilst many who employ the concept of patriarchy (for example, see Walby, 1990) acknowledge the historical specificity of forms of male domination, and the effect of other power relations such as class and race, it is more of a challenge to apply this generalisation to situations where women exert power over other women. Undeniably, women social workers exert power over women clients. As well as individual women social workers having authority over individual women clients, it can also be argued that child protection involves, to some extent, a group of professional women with power over a group of poor working-class women. As Abbott and Wallace observe:

> Whilst sociologists have commonly drawn attention to the power exercised by social workers... and criticized them for being agents of social control, they have ignored two key interrelated factors: first, that clients of social workers tend to be predominantly female, and, second, that they are mainly working-class... most social workers... are female and they exercise control over women – much of the time working within patriarchal ideologies. (Abbott and Wallace, 1990: 6–7)

Although the higher management of social work is male (see next section), the front-line culture can be seen as a women's culture. However, this does not necessarily make the concept of patriarchy redundant. Whilst individual social workers may well be women, there are those who would continue to conceptualise the organisations in which they work (particularly the state) as patriarchal – representing patriarchal interests and furthering these through action (Walby, 1990). Moreover, a feminisation in terms of numbers does not automatically lead to a feminisation of theory or practice (Coffey and Delamont, 2000). However, it could be argued that it is front-line social work culture, rather than policies from central or local government, that is most crucial to the everyday construction of clients. As Lipsky's work (1980; see also Hill, 1982) has shown, the decisions of street-level bureaucrats, and the routines they develop to cope with the uncertainties and pressures of their job, effectively *become* the policies which they carry out. Tacit knowledge about client families in the social work office has developed from a front-line staff base that is still largely dominated by women. This causes problems for a simple version of patriarchy as 'men controlling women'. It is possible to incorporate the dimension of women working with women into a more nuanced version of patriarchy if we take account of the gendered division of labour in social services departments (see next section). There is also a possible argument that women social workers are controlling women clients *in the service of* patriarchy; inducting other women into the role of second-class citizens (Eichenbaum and Orbach, 1983, cited in Lawrence, 1992; see also Charles, 2000).

Some commentators have used the term 'mother blaming' to describe the gendered nature of child protection intervention (Hooper, 1987; Davies and Krane, 1996). In the research project on which this book draws, this phenomenon was observed in the everyday narratives and actions of social workers. However, there was also a fair amount of father blaming. Men clients tended to be viewed negatively, and much of the scrutiny of women came about because of the initial suspicion of men. This again does not lend itself to an explanation based on a simple and rigidly structuralist version of patriarchy. What I saw in the child protection team was the combined forces of gendered discourses, only some of which were patriarchal. Clients (and gender) were constituted through discursive practices. The interplay of discourse and subjectivity operates in such a hybrid, temporal and situated manner in the social work office as to make a rigid notion of systemic male-dominated power structures indefensible. Events, actions and the (re)construction of the client can be understood in terms of this interplay and its relationships to gender and power. In this sense I would argue that the concept of patriarchy is not a particularly helpful one in explaining either the power of women social workers over women clients or the negative construction of men clients. It does, however, convey the privilege of most men and the oppression of most women, social facts that remain central to this topic. I also acknowledge that the actual bodily practices and representation of clients will in part determine the gendered constructions of professionals. That social workers consistently describe men as having power over women in the families they encounter must bear some relation to material reality. Patriarchy does, therefore, form *part* of the framework for understanding the domain of child protection, as long as the provisos above are taken into consideration.

It is useful at this point to return to the question of whether the interests of patriarchy are being served by child protection practice. One of the contradictions (or inevitabilities) of social welfare is the proliferation of women clients and workers constructed and operating within the (patriarchal) state. It is certainly true that women are scrutinised in and through child protection work and men often slip away. Even feminist discourse in the social work office, where it justifies failure to engage men, feeds into this process. But, as Ferguson (1997) emphasises, some children are protected from violent men and patriarchal families. After all, it is children who will usually be the most vulnerable family members (Wise, 1990). It might be argued that in a world of gender transformations (Walby, 1997), where women are stronger and more protected in many ways, increasing the emphasis on child protection at the expense of child welfare is one of a dwindling number of state functions that allow for increased scrutiny of (poor) women. As Swift (1995: 11) observes, child protection can be seen to serve purposes other than securing children's safety:

> The rescue and saving of children is the apparent reason for allowing scrutiny of family life, but other social purposes are more effectively met through this process – controlling social costs and reorienting the behaviour of particular people in ways that benefit groups other than themselves.

Most feminists will not seriously challenge child protection practice if children are being saved from bad men. However, as Howe et al.

(1992) have observed, birth mothers in the adoption process have not yet become a cause célèbre for feminism, and this could equally be said about mothers with questionable parenting skills who come under the scrutiny of the child protection system. These women (and men) are the poorest of the poor and have no political voice. Their place in the residuum of the underclass renders them subject to both old and new gendered discourses. While social policies and social welfare practices can change family structures and challenge male power, the state (and in this case child protection work) may continue to perpetuate patriarchy and capitalism. I return to the intersection of class and gender discourses toward the end of the chapter.

We have observed that the construction of gendered *others* in the social work office is in part an outcome of patriarchal and feminist discourses. The question remains as to what extent these discourses, played out through discursive practices, constrain the social work 'gaze'. Are social workers free to choose how to construct clients? I would reject simplistic conceptualisations of structuralism, and in turn patriarchy, but embrace instead the insights offered by patriarchal theorists offering a more nuanced version of the complexities of gender and power. Moreover, I wish to situate this embrace within an understanding of discursive practice, noting the constraining, as well as empowering, nature of discourse.

Ferguson (1997) has presented an optimistic application of theories of reflexive modernisation to child protection bureaucracies. Whilst he concentrates on the relation of clients to social regulation, the ideas of reflexive modernisation can also be applied to social workers' use of discourse and knowledge (in that these theories imply social workers themselves ought to be able to challenge and question the expert systems they draw on). My position is somewhat contrary to this, locating social workers' constructions of clients within the limitations of occupational discourses. The feminist post-structuralism offered by Weedon (1997) explains that the power of discourse constrains what can be known and what can be said in specific social and historical contexts. However, Weedon's theoretical framework also allows for fluidity and tensions between discourses. So, for example, it can explain how conservative discourses on the family operate, and it can also allow for feminist challenges. Post-structuralism challenges the liberal humanist notion of the knowing, unified, rational subject (Weiner, 1994; Benhahib, 1995). Rather, subjectivity is seen as socially produced in language and as a site of struggle and potential change. Hence, individuals can be powerful and powerless in different discursive spaces (Blackmore, 1999). So social workers are not free to construct their clients in any way they choose, but do so in contested (and differentially powerful/less) discursive spaces. As Weedon explains:

> Discourses represent political interests and in consequence are constantly vying for status and power. The site of this battle for power is the subjectivity of the individual and it is a battle in which the individual is an active but not a sovereign protagonist. (Weedon, 1997: 41)

There are multiple gendered discourses in the culture of the social work office that constitute the knowledge available to social workers, but I would not wish to argue that there is no scope for resistance to this culture. The application of a Foucauldian understanding of power can encompass the 'shifting and unstable political relations between actors, institution and discourses' (O'Brien and Penna, 1998: 118), and thus relates power to knowledge and discourse (Watson, 2000). It may be helpful here to elucidate an example. The prioritising of physical neglect of children in the social work team can lead to an intensified scrutiny of mothering (see Chapter 6). The prioritising of this particular aspect of child maltreatment can be explained in terms of ease of evidence, but also by dominant professional and lay discourses on child maltreatment. Maybe the choice of men's violence or men's neglect of children as an alternative target for intervention was not genuinely open to the managers of the social services department, because of the power of certain forms of discourse (knowledge). If child neglect is constructed as an absence of care, and care is associated with femininity, then responsibility for neglect will obviously be ascribed to women (Turney, 2000). There is, however, also the feminist discourse which challenges this ascription of responsibility (see, for example, Swift, 1995) and also an alternative mainstream professional discourse which understands neglect in terms of emotional care. Potentially it is open to the social workers to resist the dominant occupational discourse, although it may be difficult (or impossible) to do so within the discursive spaces in which they operate. In research interviews, some social workers showed signs of doubt, if not active resistance, to the dominant discourses (see Chapter 4). Foucault (1984) sees this process as involving the (re)appropriation of elements of the dominant discourse.

In this section I have revisited the usefulness of theoretical perspectives of social structure and discourse. In particular I have focused on the social structural concept of patriarchy, and the discursive regimes and practices of social workers. In the next section I focus on social workers' own gendered identities, setting this discussion in the context of the gendered institutions of social services departments.

Gendered identities in a gendered organisation

The previous chapter dealt with the issue of gendered knowledge and knowledge about gender in the social work office. In the context of constructions of masculinity, Chapter 5 referred to the issue of men working in childcare social work, since this has been raised as a problematic issue in social policy discourse. Chapter 4 also touched on the issue of women social workers' empathy with women clients. I return at this point to the issue of gendered identities as a potential explanatory framework, together with the issue of social services departments as gendered organisations.

It was explained early in the book that there would be little discussion of data on how social workers understood themselves as gendered individuals, because there was found to be far more common ground between women and men social workers' constructions of clients as gendered than there were differences. Nonetheless, at this point it is pertinent to ask whether the social workers' gender identities explain why women are worked with more than men. Do they shed any light on why social workers are positive about the idea of men's involvement in families (and about actual men when they strike up a good relationship with them) but generally negative about actual men clients? Do social workers' gender identities explain how they so often conclude that even where a man is thought to be abusive, it is women who are ultimately culpable if children are not safe? It is not the intention to discuss data on the particular individuals in the Uplands team, but rather to present some theoretical insights about the position of men and women in child protection work, reflecting on both gendered subjectivity and the experience of working in a gendered organisation.

Atkinson and Delamont (1990: 91) contend that any theory of professional work that fails to explain gender divisions within the occupation cannot be an adequate account of the topic. There are certainly marked gender divisions in River County social services, although I would argue that these do not particularly help us to understand the gendered construction of clients. The relative power of men and women within social service organisations has fluctuated over time (Carter Hood et al., 1998) and remains debatable. The Uplands team has three men and seven women. One of the men is a senior social work practitioner and one of the women is the team manager, but the three layers of management above her in the organisation are all represented by men. Women are generally underrepresented in the higher management of UK social services and men overrepresented (Christie, 1998a), and River County is no exception.

Hearn (1982) defines professionalisation as a patriarchal process, with 'semi-professions' such as social work being domains of work where men have achieved only partial domination and full professionalisation indicating complete male control. He sees the process of professionalisation as an attempt by men to take over control of spheres of emotion that have hitherto been private. It is also worth noting that bureaucratic structures themselves are 'sites for the shaping of gender identities and relations' (Morgan, 1996b: 58). As Morgan also notes, feminist critiques of organisations tend to see them as dominated by masculinist notions of rationality. Otway, writing about social services departments, claims there has been a 'masculinisation of the managerial role and hierarchy' and that in work with children and families 'women's experience and values are being replaced by those of men and business' (Otway, 1996: 153). I do not agree with Otway's second point. Women could be seen to be disadvantaged in career terms in the River County department, and it can be argued that the bureaucracy is increasingly masculinist but, as I stated in the previous section, I believe front-line social work should be understood as predominantly a women's culture. Whilst it can be seen as a women's culture, the ways in which men and women social workers in the Uplands team construct their clients as gendered are markedly similar. I would maintain that it is the discursively constructed tacit knowledge of the social workers that is the key to understanding the way they understand and work with men and women clients.

If social work practice is scrutinising women even when anti-discrimination has a high profile within their profession, social workers are in some ways doing what they know they should not do. Some suggested in interviews that they are in fact doing what they believe is *wrong* by not challenging the men who are the root cause of a lot of problems. It may be that the explanation for this can be found in the complex histories of the social workers own subjectivities. Some of the data do touch on interesting aspects of the social workers' selves, and I am sure they would have had some fascinating insights into their own motivations in relation to their personal histories if I had targeted this in my fieldwork. However, an emphasis on individual identities would distract from the commonality of the constructions of clients across the team and across the sexes. I have to conclude that organisational discourse is strong enough to override gendered identities. It is not possible to set up binary divisions between male and female social workers' identities since, as previously asserted, some feminist writings have successfully argued contingency and fluidity in the construction of personal identities. However, a focus on complex subjectivities misses the point that there are some common constructions of clients in particular contexts, which are based, as explained in the previous chapter, on the discursive interaction of lay and professional knowledge. It seems that whether we see gender identities as fixed, or as diverse, complex and not tied to 'sex', we cannot escape the conclusion from the data that the social workers' identities are overridden by a powerful occupational culture of the construction of 'others' (see also Pithouse, 1984 – the chapter on 'Women and the area office').

The removal of the subject that is necessitated by a post-structuralist perspective is appropriate for understanding occupational culture. To refer back to the discussion on social constructionism in Chapter 2, it may seem odd to be asserting the power of the discourse of an occupation, whilst claiming distance myself, with a background in social work practice. My practice experience was not, however, of paid employment in a childcare team, which is a significant factor in the light of the variation in discourses of masculinity and femininity across different settings (see below). Also, I repeat my view that it is indeed difficult if not impossible to truly distance yourself unless you are reflecting from a position of total (me) or partial (White, 1997a) detachment from that occupational culture, achieved, perhaps, through academic affiliation. Those who expressed unease in the Uplands team, such as Mary, still practise within the accepted discourses while employed. Perhaps these people are most likely to take their chance to leave the job, as indeed Mary did within a year of my fieldwork.

So far the discussion has led to a position whereby concepts such as patriarchy, organisational inequalities and gender identities, whilst all offering some useful insights, cannot stand alone in explaining how the

Uplands team works. To summarise, a crude version of patriarchy was found to be too structural a concept to allow for the existence of multiple and contradictory gendered discourses, and was not found particularly relevant to other power dimensions such as women controlling women. Moreover, an emphasis on inequalities between men and women across the social services department masks the central importance of front-line practice culture in the construction of clients, a culture that is strongly influenced by women, who substantially outnumber men. In addition, the idea of gendered identities is not structural enough to account for the greater power of occupational discourses.

The concept that has endured is that of occupational culture as discourse. The term 'occupational culture' suggests social work as a whole. Bearing in mind the diversity in gender construction across the social work profession (see Chapter 5), it is in fact more accurate to talk of organisational culture; the culture of social services childcare teams. Harlow and Hearn (1995) identify 'culture as discourse' as one of several distinct theoretical orientations towards understanding organisational culture, one which focuses on the inclusion and exclusion of knowledge and the regulation of subjects (workers, managers, clients) by the real or imagined gaze of the other. So according to this approach, organisational culture can 'consist of the discourses that are in circulation and their effect' (Harlow and Hearn, 1995: 187). I find this approach helpful in understanding the gendering of child protection work.

The concept of organisational culture as discourse is not in itself solely to do with gender construction of course. Hence the chapter now broadens to consider other analytical perspectives which further illuminate the specific gendered discourses of child protection work.

Regulation of the body

The word 'body' has appeared in several places so far in the book. Social, theoretical and empirical work on the body has burgeoned in recent years. There has, as Davis (1997) has put it, been a 'body craze' in academia at the end of the twentieth century and the start of the twenty-first. Setting aside the fashionable status of the body in sociological writings, I believe that there is real significance in some of the data on the body in preceding chapters. I would further claim that an analytic focus on the body in child protection work is one that has potential for explaining gendered discourses, and is certainly a perspective that warrants further attention. It is argued that we now live in a 'somatic society', within which 'major political and personal problems are both problematized in the body and expressed through it' (Turner, 1996: 1). Twigg (2000) has argued more specifically that attention to the body in social policy is needed for several reasons. These include the need to examine 'disordered, controlled and concrete' aspects of social life (p. 128), the fact that so much care and welfare work is actually body work, and the importance of interpreting our own or others' physical presence. Twigg also argues the relevance to social policy of Foucault's (1977) work on the defining, ordering and controlling of bodies through 'bio-power'. Foucault's articulation of the body as created and reproduced through discourse can be utilised to understand the operation and disciplinary potential of welfare institutions and practices.

The sociology of the body emphasises the effect of social processes on individuals, in contrast with the abstractions of class and structure favoured by traditional sociology (Turner, 1996). Such an emphasis is important if the working of child protection is to be understood both as socially constructed within an occupational culture and as affecting individual clients and social workers. The argument here is that a fruitful approach to understanding the current state of child protection is to focus on the representation and regulation of the body. This perspective perhaps allows more attention to the inevitably gendered nature of the child protection system than other theoretical frameworks allow. It allows attention to the imagined bodies that the social workers construct, the actual bodies that the system regulates and the effects of the system on these bodies – *who* experiences child protection and *how*. The process of constructing and regulating the bodies of clients needs to be considered if we are to better understand the concentration on investigation and risk in child protection work.

Whilst I tend to agree with the postmodernist view that gender identities need to be seen as inherently fluid, social regulation is not so fluid. What is needed is a conception of social structure that can explain social regulation and also allows for the regulation of men as well as women and allows for the presence of multiple discourses. The particular perspective on the body that seems to work in relation to child protection is that of disciplinary power over bodies (Foucault, 1977). Foucault's work demonstrates that discourse is not abstract, impacting on minds only, but has a material relation to the bodies that are the objects of discourse. As Connell (1998: 6) expresses it, 'domination is not a matter of disembodied discourses'. Dyer (1988: 14) has written that 'to represent people is to represent bodies'. It can be seen from Chapters 3 to 6 that embodied images are central to the occupational construction of clients as gendered. As Collier (1998) and Daly (1997) have argued, the criminal body is constructed as sexed through popular and academic discourse. Shilling (1993) has claimed that there is a preoccupation with the body in late modernity. This pre-occupation cannot be gender-neutral. Bodies are inevitably imagined as sexed and gendered, and bodily practices such as violence, sexuality and intimate care for the bodies of others are all strongly linked to societal constructions of gender (Davis, 1997).

The requirement of the child protection system for parental change includes the regulation of women's bodies. Intake of alcohol and drugs is scrutinised. Women are often coerced over choice of sexual partner, when he is considered a threat to children's safety. And above all women are expected to be constantly available for children. Women's responsibility for servicing the body hangs over all cases, but is particularly acute in 'neglect' cases, which are fundamentally about failure to reach acceptable standards of body maintenance. Social workers seem to find maternal abuse particularly horrifying. The replacement of the mother as protective body with mother as abusive body in the social work imagination can lead to a powerful reaction and some of the most intrusive intervention in the child protection repertoire. Women's responsibility for protecting children against the abusing bodies of men is a recurring theme in the ethnographic data. This construction of families with abusive men present is not seriously questioned by the social workers. Women are held responsible for protecting their children from men's bodily excesses.

There are several different discourses of masculinity in the social work office. Dominant amongst these is the imagining of men as threatening bodies. Their violence is seen as a direct threat to the bodies of social workers (especially women) and there are several instances in the data where nasty secrets of men's sexual violence are thought to lurk in families. Discourses of client masculinities are inevitably those of socially and economically marginalised men, influenced by visual images of the underclass. We can only speculate on these visual images: perhaps idle and drunken (or drugged) men, or dirty, hairy and scruffy men (although another underclass image is of cheap and 'tasteless' glamour). There are images of underclass bodies (both men's and women's) and also the social workers' embodied cultural responses (or 'tastes') which are often class-bound (Bourdieu, 1986). As Chapter 5 showed, there are several child protection discourses of masculinity, which conflict and complement. They reflect images of embodiment and both 'known' and imagined bodily practices.

Constructions of children are not sexed/gendered in the same way, but rely on a discourse of the child as a vulnerable body. I shall not rehearse again here points that have already been made in Chapter 3. Most stark in relation to children is the 'new' interest in the dirty, ill-fed child's body described in Chapter 6. This could be seen as tentative support for the idea that there is a preoccupation with the body in late modernity. The culture of investigation in contemporary child protection work could be seen as a preoccupation with the child's vulnerable body and the abusive bodies of adults; men in particular, but also women in 'failing to protect'. Whilst the child's body is not sexed/gendered in the way that adult caregivers are, that body is ultimately constructed as in need of protection from women. It is women who can keep the vulnerable child's body sustained and safe from harm. When they fail in the tasks of body maintenance and body protection they become unnatural – non-mothers.

It is not only clients whose bodies are regulated. The stress created by an investigative culture that is premised on rooting out failing parents takes its toll on the bodies of the social workers. McMahon's study (1998) describes negative physical reactions that include nausea, sickness, depression, nightmares and ulcers. One man in the social work team he observed periodically vomited into a rubbish bin in his office. McMahon (1998: 89) writes that 'their bodies were wearing out because of the way they had to do their work'. The social workers interviewed by Chris Jones (2001) described themselves as completely 'wrung out' by a Friday evening and spoke of how the pressures of work took its toll on their personal and social lives.

The preoccupation with the body in child protection work is an area that needs much more work in terms of specific research and theorising. I only hope to raise it as an issue rather than examining it in detail. To further consider current trends in child protection, the next section will consider the intersection of popular discourse on gender, class and crime.

Gender, class and crime

The focus of this last section is on what occupational discourses tell us about the wider picture of gender and class discourse and the intersection with discourse on crime. The occupational discourses of masculinity and femininity described in Chapters 4 and 5 resonate with wider discourses, which are either implicitly or explicitly class-laden. I label these 'the problem with men' and 'mothers as the root of family problems'. As I argued in Chapter 5, the Uplands social workers' constructions of clients should not be seen as simply a straightforward reflection of the material practices of the men and women they encounter. Nor should they be taken to reveal a tightly bounded occupational culture of social work. Rather, the process of constructing clients in child protection work ought to be understood as rooted in wider discourses of masculinity and femininity.

Feminism's challenge to the behaviour of men has become rooted in the popular imagination in the UK. It can no longer be claimed, as the early new men's studies were keen to stress, that no one is making masculinity explicit. In the UK broadsheet newspapers, men, and the 'crisis' of masculinity in particular, are thought to be good copy and get considerable coverage. Chapter 5 showed that the 'problem with men' is now being considered in New Labour social policy. The discourses of men as a threat, men as no use, men as absent and, to an extent, men as irrelevant relate to this increasingly powerful discourse of the 'problem with men'. Collier (1998) and Hearn (1998) have observed that it is not all men whose behaviour has come under scrutiny. In particular, the masculinity–crime connection has been made in relation to poor working-class men. Journalist Nick Cohen describes a conference on men and crime he attended in 1993:

> Middle-class feminists who thought of themselves as paragons of left-wing rectitude displayed a hatred of working-class men that seemed indistinguishable from coffee-morning Conservatives' loathing of single mothers. (Cohen, 1999: 2)

Whilst this statement relies on journalistic hyperbole, he conveys accurately enough the class dimension of the 'problem with men' discourse. The poor working-class men who are clients of the Uplands team are constructed through several different discourses, some of which can be seen to contradict others. These multiple discourses cannot be summed, or reduced to one unifying theme. However, I would maintain that constructions of men as a threat, as absent, as irrelevant and as no use all need to be understood with reference to this wider discourse of problematic working-class masculinity. As mentioned in Chapter 5, the discourses of men as no different and as better than women have different origins. The former is rooted in both the individualising ethos of traditional social work and a general pessimism that believes 'they (adult clients) are all as bad as each other'. The discourse of men as better than women is explained by the powerful connection between femininity and child-rearing.

The 'problem of men' discourse comes from the political Left and feminism, but could be seen to overlap with aspects of the New Right discourse on the underclass family, referred to in earlier chapters. For example, both Charles Murray (1990) and Bea Campbell (1993) are critical of fathers on poor estates, although as Williams (1998) has observed, the origins of the critique and the aims these commentators pursue are very different. The Uplands social workers would strenuously resist the idea that their approach to either men or women echoes that of the political Right. Whilst I agree it does not in any straightforward sense, there are connections to be made. The 'single mother' panic on the Right, initiated by John Redwood's speech in Cardiff in 1993 (Bates, 1993), places responsibility for family problems, and the social problems that 'inevitably' result, firmly with women. For example, a strong connection has been made with the crisis surrounding the 'explosion' in youth crime. As Young (1996: 17) expresses it, this has been a discourse of 'the maternal relation as potentially criminogenetic'. What we see in the Uplands team is not so much a reflection of this discourse of the Right as of a wider discourse of women as ultimately responsible for things that go wrong in families, including the bad behaviour of men.

The New Right, 'single mother' discourse is saturated with assumptions about class. The problem women being addressed are, again, from the poor working class. It is perhaps inevitable that, given the high profile of this discourse and its partial incorporation into New Labour policy, a disquiet about the mothering of 'underclass' women will surface in the culture of a social work team. After all, this is not a new discourse. It draws on concerns about the morals of the unrespectable poor that go back to the origins of the social work profession.

To maintain the theme of class and gender discourse and its connection with discourse on crime, Alison Young's work (1996) on the 'crisis in the crimino-legal complex' can potentially be applied to contemporary child protection. Whilst she is writing in relation to criminal law, and most of the child protection process comes under family law, there are many overlaps between popular discourse on child abuse and more general crime discourse. Young sees the name 'victim' as signifying 'our' community and simultaneously expelling the criminal as outlaw: 'the symbolically sacrificed outlaw is thus the victim of our desire for community (through shared victimisation)' (p. 9). The idea of shared victimisation mimics the recognition of the yearned-for, pre-modern community, and 'recognition is not based upon shared friendship, but upon the awareness of risk and danger' (p. 10).

There is potential for exploring these ideas in relation to child pro-tection. There has been an explosion in referrals of alleged abuse, and considerable resources are spent on investigating these allegations and monitoring children 'at risk'. This investigation is more often of alleged abuse by men, but in fact it is women who bear the brunt of it. The child victim and the adult perpetrator, according to Young's theories, help us to maintain a sense of community in times when this is seen to be under threat. We could all be seen as either real or potential victims of child abuse, on the basis that everyone has a childhood, so the idea of shared victimisation can apply to these private and domestic crimes as well as to public crimes by strangers. Perhaps in times of increased awareness of men's abusive behaviour, we are all also potential victims of violent men.

Young writes of the importance of boundaries, the making and breaching of borders. This connects with Mary Douglas's ideas (1966) about pollution concern arising when there is fear that boundaries will be breached (see Chapter 6). To Young, 'crime is elsewhere and criminality is Other' (p. 58). Child abuse is also other and elsewhere (usually in unrespectable and very poor homes, and usually on certain estates – see Chapter 3) but is also potentially in social services departments in the form of sexually abusive male care staff.

Young suggests that woman might be 'constituted as a surrogate for the originary outlaw of the community' (p. 9). It is men who are very clearly the 'outlaws' of child abuse. Stainton Rogers and Stainton Rogers (1992) have termed the association of masculinity and child sexual abuse 'whole gender blaming'. But men are very often not held to account. Both when they are and when they are not, it is quite possible that women will be thought to have failed in comparison with an idealised model of motherhood. So in a sense perhaps women will always be the 'originary outlaw' of child abuse whilst child-rearing is so associated with societal constructions of femininity.

Young's work is one example of how gendered social control can be theorised in such a way as to account for social structure without the restrictive limitations associated with simplistic versions of patriarchy. Her ideas lead to the question as to whether the child protection system is really as much about protecting children as it is about regulating masculinity and femininity; maintaining the respectable father and the protective mother. To ask that question is not to claim that the control of masculinity and femininity is some kind of hidden *aim* of the child protection system. This would look rather like a conspiracy theory. But the result of its practice, governed as it is by organisational cultures (themselves products of wider popular, academic and legal discourse) is that mothering is scrutinised while men disappear from view.

Conclusion

In this chapter I attempted to draw out some theoretical perspectives that might help to explain what I found in the social work office. I examined theoretical perspectives of patriarchy, inequality in the workplace, and gender identities. Each of these captures something of the nature of gendered social control in the Uplands team, but also has shortcomings in explaining the research findings. Structuralism cannot account for some of the dimensions of power, such as the negative constructions of men. Simplistic versions of patriarchy cannot explain the central relationship of women social workers controlling women clients. An emphasis on gender identities misses the commonality of the construction of others. Crucially, any explanation needs to appreciate the strength of organisational discourse in overcoming complex identities. I offered some more fruitful theoretical perspectives, which maintain a focus on power and social constraints whilst avoiding the rigidity of crude structuralism. These were the preoccupation with the body in late modernity and the intersection of wider discourses of gender, class and crime. It has been asserted throughout the book that the construction of clients will be constrained by the material reality that social workers encounter. The final chapter, which follows this, returns to materiality, by focusing on implications of the research for practitioners.

9
Conclusion

This final chapter has two main themes: the current state of child protection work and an overview of implications for social work practice. The first section of the chapter deals with questions such as 'what is child protection practice like these days?' and 'how do staff and clients experience the child protection process?' The second section considers the implications of the book's material in two respects: theory for practice and practical implications. I preface these discussions by summarising the previous research-based chapters.

Summary of research findings

The discussion of the research project began in Chapter 3 by looking at divisions of the potential clientele other than on a gender basis. The vast majority of all active child protection cases are poor working-class clients. They are often stigmatised even within very poor communities, and their socio-economic status is understood by the social workers within a variety of discourses, including those of the underclass and the unrespectable working class. There was seen to be rhetorical power in the assertion of the primacy of the child's welfare and the child's needs, although it was professionals who ultimately decided what these needs were. A key parenting philosophy emphasises parents putting their children's needs before their own. Social workers will proudly say that it is the child that is their client, rather than the parent or parents, although a great deal of the routine talk about clients actually refers to adults, since it is adults the social workers spend most of their time with. Children are constructed as essentially vulnerable, with the child's body in particular being a current target of concern. The child's body reflects judgements about parents.

There are aspects of the work that could be seen as gendered in effect rather than intent. An example would be where a woman becomes the principal point of contact in a family not because the social worker has targeted her in particular, but because she bears the brunt of day-to-day responsibility for the childcare. There are also aspects of child protection work that show deliberate choices being made that, whilst again not consciously targeting women, have the effect of screening out men and increasing the scrutiny of women. The extended example given in Chapter 6 is that of the construction of child protection priorities. Where a wide range of types of child abuse could be targeted, including those which may be more likely to involve men as perpetrators, the local authority I studied chose to target the physical neglect of children. The concern with dirty children and houses that resulted led inevitably to attention falling on women as the primary carers. There are, also, explicitly gendered constructions of adult clients. Two of the chapters were given over to discussing these constructions of women and men.

There is more than one gendered discourse on women clients. The picture is complex. Most are thought to be oppressed in the extreme, often by men partners who are lazy, domineering and possibly violent. This experience of oppression is thought to affect their parenting, although where women transgress by not putting their children's needs before their own they are seen to have made a deliberate choice to do so, regardless of the influence of their social context. On the one hand the social workers come to expect little change in cases, but where a woman is given an ultimatum about her children's future, it is expected that this will galvanise change, that she will act immediately to keep her children. It is seen to be women's fundamental responsibility to protect children, so that 'allowing' a violent man to stay in a household constitutes 'failure to protect'. There is empathy with women clients, but only up to a point. When a woman fails to act in response to an ultimatum, the empathy ends. The defining discourses identified in Chapter 4 were women as oppressed, women as responsible for protection, and women as making choices.

There is, also, a variety of discourses of masculinity in the social work office. There are constructions that are broadly negative and those that are broadly positive, although negativity predominates. These can all be seen as responses to the 'problem of men' that has emerged in academic, popular and now political discourse, and also as responses to discourses of anti-discrimination and anti-oppression in social work. The negative constructions identified were men as a threat, men as no use, men as irrelevant and men as absent. The first of these is particularly powerful in relation to child protection cases, and draws on popular and professional ideas about violence and sexual abuse. There was also the discourse of men as no different from women, coming both from an ethic of non-discrimination and also from the perspective that both parents are 'as bad as each other'. Finally, in a small number of cases, men are constructed as better than women, where the woman had been identified as failing in her expected role.

Chapter 7 focused on gender tensions in the knowledge and values employed in routine social work practice. Overlapping discourses of the individual and the social were identified in case talk, with implications for working with men and women. There is tension between anti-discrimination and anti-oppression, that is, between an ethic of equal treatment and an attempt to incorporate into practice an understanding of social inequalities and social trends. So, for example, there is a tendency to a rigid social categorisation of sex offenders, who are seen to fit a clear template of behaviour, whilst other people alleged to have abused children in some way are seen as heterogeneous. There exists simultaneously a reluctance to categorise clients, on the basis that all should be seen as individuals, and a perceived need to understand people in their social context. The issues of knowledge and values that were left unresolved at the end of Chapter 7 will be addressed later in this chapter.

The aim of the next section is to make some general evaluative comment about the current state of child protection work in the UK. Whilst it was made clear in the book's introduction that the primary aim of the research was understanding rather than evaluation, I do not believe it is possible to discuss the theoretical implications of the research findings without straying into the territory of evaluative comment. The premise of the research was, after all, that the gender bias of child protection practice is unjust. I will attempt to locate child protection work within a continuum of gendered social control.

The current state of child protection work

Child protection procedures and interventions must not only be seen as constraining, but viewed also in a positive light as enabling, creating new opportunities for protection from violences that were traditionally repressed and for reflexively organised life-planning. (Ferguson, 1997: 230)

My warning to people now is that if you need help the last people you should go to is to social services. We warn anybody we can. They are not there to help. (one of the women labelled 'bad mothers' who were interviewed by Croghan and Miell, 1998: 454)

The judgements expressed in these two extracts illustrate the range of possible conclusions in the evaluation of child protection. The former extract comes from an academic commentator and the latter from a former client. It is not intended to set the opinions of clients against those of researchers, but only to show the scope for opposing views from all parties on the child protection system. In fact, a similar range of opinion can probably be found between academics and between clients. The conclusion a researcher reaches about the extent of coercion in family welfare services is principally determined by his or her position in relation to the respective rights of parents, children and the state (Fox Harding, 1997). Dingwall et al. (1995) conclude that the organisational orientation remains one of optimism about parenting whereas White (1997a) found the accomplishment of the social work role to require a display of scepticism about parental accounts. These almost opposite findings can perhaps be explained less by differences in research methodology or regional and temporal variations in workplace culture than by the different stances of the researchers on what constitutes optimism or scepticism in relation to standards of parenting (Corby, 1987). These stances will depend on the researchers' baseline for good enough parenting, and also on whether they incline to a parents' rights, children's rights or other perspective.

Since any attempt at reflexivity required me to declare my perspective at the outset, I noted in the introduction that, according to the family welfare paradigms outlined by Fox Harding (1997), I would have to acknowledge mine as a parents' rights perspective. This is not, of course, to say that I have no regard to the welfare of children. However, the book set out to shed light on the problem of gender bias in relation to child protection practice with parents. In making that statement, I am asserting that there is bias and that this is a problem. I have, to an extent, taken as read (based on existing research and commentary) that child protection social workers spend more time working with women. The concern about gender bias assumes that women, who are the object of services, are having a rough deal, rather than men, who are not the object of social work intervention. This in turn is based on the assumption that being in contact with child protection services is a negative experience, at least for adults. This next section aims to further explore this assumption in the light of the ethnographic data. It also aims to reach some conclusions about the influence of feminism on childcare social work, since the persistence of gender bias is all the more interesting in the light of the dominance of the anti-discriminatory discourse in social work training.

Clearly there are methodological limits to what can be claimed about the current state of child protection work. I did not research the views of either parent of child clients on their involvement with social services, and theirs are surely the most important opinions on whether that involvement has been a good or bad experience. I have also only studied one team of social workers, but I can comment on what the culture of the Uplands team reveals about the current preoccupations of child protection practice. Waddington (1999), writing on police canteen culture, criticises researchers' claims that what the police say about their work amongst peers reveals how they perform their duties in public. I believe my research in the Uplands team avoids this pitfall. Firstly, as Pithouse and Atkinson (1988) assert, social workers' accounts of practice *are* work, since good work is only known through good accounts. Secondly, the analysis of documents shows something of front-line practice. Whilst case records are, of course, particular retrospective versions of worker–client interaction, documents such as case conference reports constitute actual social work intervention. Reports are a written summary of a social worker's judgement of a case that strongly influences the conference decision. So whilst there are limitations to what can be claimed from my data, I maintain there is a basis for some initial comment on what can be learned about the current state of the child protection system.

All state welfare work can be understood as social control in some way or another. As Abbott and Sapsford (1990: 120) boldly state, 'it is now widely accepted that social workers are "soft policemen"'. Marxists would emphasise the pacifying of the working class to diffuse opposition to capitalism (Leonard, 1978). The work of Foucault (1977) and Donzelot (1980) has shown that helping professions have a crucial role in disciplining populations. The theoretical concerns of the book could be summed up in the phrase 'gendered social control'. It is the premise of the book that gender relations, whilst not the only social relations relevant to the topic (class, in particular, is crucial), do inevitably impact on every aspect of the job of child protection. So of course child protection is about social control and of course it is gendered. The question remains, where should contemporary child protection practice be placed on a continuum of gendered social control?

My concluding evaluation of the child protection system is that social control of parents and children is fairly overt and that some gendered practices will result in negative experiences for both men and women clients. Whilst I tend to side with the child protection pessimists, I should of course like to avoid the unrelenting negativity described by Pithouse and Williamson:

> the unrelieved gloom that sometimes characterises academic accounts of practice, particularly social work, whereby oppression, neglect, and incompetence are unerringly found by those whose intellectual fascination with welfare is to ensure they find little that is positive or liberating about it. (Pithouse and Williamson, 1997: xiii)

The picture of social control of clients in the Uplands team is, of course, a complex one and a one-dimensional summary would be unfair and inaccurate. For example, some clients' fear of social workers revealed vividly in extracts in Chapter 3 needs to be balanced against some indications of warm relations and the fact that many parents (especially mothers) come to social services to ask for help. But when this complex picture is weighed up, there are features that stand out to create an impression of overt social control that is heavily gendered.

As was explained in Chapter 2, there is something of a consensus in the research on child and family social work that the emphasis shifted from child welfare to child protection in the late twentieth century, with a great deal of time being absorbed by investigation of alleged abuse. At the turn of the twenty-first century some new policy initiatives have attempted to refocus services towards family support, but there is no sign yet of these having a major impact on the culture of front-line child welfare work. An initiative in Western Australia has resulted in fewer substantiated allegations of maltreatment, but many families where there are concerns about children are still missing out on services altogether (Parton and Mathews, 2001). The overwhelming impression from anecdotal evidence in the UK is of front-line practice being as investigative and protection-oriented as ever at the start of the new century. It has been observed several times during the course of the book that in such a climate women will feel the heat of the investigation because they are far more likely to be the primary carers of children.

A narrow interpretation of the welfare of the child only serves to intensify this process. Social workers tend to be very clear that their responsibilities are to children *rather than* adults. It is a clear and open organisational ethic that helping parents for its own sake is not part of the job, and in child protection cases children's interests are quite often thought to clash with those of parents. Certainly there is a belief that parents should be supported for the sake of improving children's quality of life, but we know from existing research that support services are often lacking (Dartington Social Research Unit, 1995). Women do most of the caring, so are more likely to be the parents needing and asking for some kind of support service. They are also more likely to be victims of abuse from violent male partners and, arguably, less likely to cause serious harm to children (see the summary of this debate in Chapter 2). But if support services are few, and primarily for children, or at least for the sake of children, then women will inevitably experience investigation more than help, and experience this more than men.

Whilst my research has not had representations of children as its focus, Chapter 3 took an initial look at this issue, as essential context for the examination of the construction of adult clients. This showed that the rhetorical power of 'the child's needs' and 'the welfare of the child' does not necessarily lead to child-centred practice. There was a stark example given of how it is held to be relatively unproblematic that children's welfare should be determined by professionals. I did not encounter any instances of children going home to parents against their will, but there were examples of children being taken away from home against their stated wishes. Where a family home is considered by social workers to be unsafe, children's opposing views will not affect the action taken.

As Chapters 4 and 5 showed, some aspects of feminism have influenced the culture of the social work office, but not always in ways that have improved women's experiences of social work. The social workers believe domestic violence to be a harrowing experience for women and children, and *part* of the repertoire of explanations within the team is the argument that this violence is rooted in men's determination to control women. However, the stock response to violent situations is to hold women responsible for getting men out of the house. This is one example of a general trend of giving clients ultimatums about making changes that are arguably not within their control. It is generally the case that whilst poor environments and oppressive personal circumstances are thought to explain problems with parenting, they are ultimately thought to be 'no excuse' for continued parental failure, especially when professionals have been very explicit in pointing out where exactly changes need to be made. To an extent, telling adult clients clearly where they are going wrong has become the dominant social work intervention. In response, it is thought that anyone with the potential to look after their children (and any natural mother) will simply act, and do what they are told, regardless of any factors working against change. Social control is, therefore, quite overt. There are relatively few helping interventions to soften the control. Pointing out responsibility or, less euphemistically, allocating blame, is thought to be enough of a help in itself. Swift (1995: 87) expresses this starkly: 'the only helping tool society has provided itself is to find parents guilty'.

Rose (1987) sees society as regulating parental conduct not through obedience to the threat of sanction, but through the activation of guilt and anxiety. Rather than power operating on the family, it suffuses the family. This is Donzelot's (1980) notion of government *through* the family, rather than government *of* the family. Whilst this is no doubt a fair judgement on the regulation of parenting across social classes, and I am generally happy to accept this Foucauldian understanding of power, I would argue that the practice of child protection needs to be viewed rather differently. Power is not simply uni-directional in the child protection process, but clients do not tend to have much of it in relation to crucial decisions about children (rightly, some would argue). The control of parents in this arena is overt and relies on the existence of threats, which are often quite explicit. Since the child protection system affects poor working-class families more than any others, the nature of the regulation of parenting can be seen to be class-specific. Certainly parenting is regulated through anxiety about children (see Scott et al., 1998), but the parenting of those under scrutiny of the child protection system is regulated by threat of sanction.

The choice of child protection priorities is amongst the most obviously gendered dimensions of the preceding data analysis. In response to the panic at a child's death, the decision was taken to prioritise a particular form of child maltreatment that would inevitably result in women being further scrutinised. In theory, an alternative decision was open to the department, particularly since the most talked about child death was caused by a man's violence, a decision that would have shifted social control towards men.

For much of the book, discussion of the data has concentrated on the effects of gendered constructions on women, since they are more often primary carers and therefore more obviously affected by what social workers do. But where men have some kind of stake in the upbringing of children, they too are obviously affected by social workers' gendered practice. As Edwards (1998) has pointed out, professionals' failure to involve men in childcare interventions has the effect of both absolving them from responsibility and excluding them from discussion about the welfare of their children. It is impossible not to stray into realism when discussing constructions of clients. Just as we cannot ignore the overwhelming research evidence on women's responsibility for the work of caring, we cannot ignore the likelihood of behaviour by men that will cause harm to others. So it is not appropriate to start discussing constructions of men in terms of some concept of justice unless the material reality of men clients' behaviour is brought into the equation. It is possible, though, to draw out the implications of the Uplands team data for the social control of poor working-class men. The discourses of masculinity outlined in Chapter 6 spanned a range of positive and negative constructions of men, but the dominant discourse in a child protection context was men as a threat. There were three other pejorative discourses identified, and the two that were more positive about men featured relatively rarely in case talk and case recording. Certainly men are socially controlled. It may be women that are more often expected to act, and women that spend more time under direct pressure from professionals in face-to-face encounters. It is men, however, who are more often denied contact with the rest of the family, and it is men who are less likely to be trusted with the care of children if they are not known to the social services department.

Although I did not myself research the views of clients, my reading of other researchers' work on child and adult clients' experience of the child protection system is that they broadly support my relatively pessimistic conclusions that much practice is coercive and gendered (see Hooper, 1992a; Butler and Williamson, 1994; Cleaver and

Freeman, 1995; Thoburn et al., 1995; Scott, 1996; Croghan and Miell, 1998).

Messages for practice

Whilst discourses of masculinity and femininity in the social work office should not be crudely understood as reflecting directly what men clients are 'really like', neither are they creative inventions formed in a social vacuum. They reflect wider societal discourses and are also limited by the actual bodily practices of clients. No study of the culture of child protection can forget that there is a material world beyond the social work rhetoric; there are actual embodied children out there and real men and real women (White, 1998b). There are of course some highly relevant social facts about gender relations: for example, that more men *do* pose a physical threat to partners and children than women, and women *do* look after children more than men.

A recognition of materiality makes it imperative that I should address the potential implications of the research findings for practitioners who have to make important decisions about families on a daily basis. I do not believe that there should be any overly prescriptive conclusion to a study of this kind. The intention was not to crudely pass judgement on whether constructions of gender are right or wrong. But that is not to claim that there is nothing to conclude that can speak to practitioners.

The job of a childcare social worker, increasingly dominated as it is by child protection, is one where the continual task of balancing the rights of different parties takes a heavy toll in terms of stress (Balloch et al., 1998). McMahon (1998), whose research vividly describes the experience of this stress in a specific setting, conveys the double bind of child protection work with his book title *Damned If You Do, Damned If You Don't*. Social workers are criticised if they intervene in families to protect children, and criticised if they leave a situation alone. It would not be defensible for me to add to this pressure with a heavily prescriptive list of yet more changes that they should make in their daily practice. Neither would it be defensible to deconstruct their workplace culture and leave it at that, without addressing the question of what this might mean for their practice.

In speaking to practitioners, I must consider what they might find useful. It may be that many practitioners would appreciate 'practice tips' of the kind that are difficult for me to provide since I did not set out to study 'good practice' with men and women clients. I also believe that caution is needed about prescriptive recommendations for practice. Sue White argues that such judgements are not necessarily helpful:

> I have no intention of exercising normative judgement on the activity of social workers, nor of providing a set of prescriptions for 'better practice'. Social work is shot through with the traces of previous such attempts ... In my opinion, piecemeal change can take place in this way, but there is scant evidence that it leads to wholesale and cost-free positive change – a newer and purer order. Rather, policy shifts often bring in their wake another set of theory-driven prescriptions which practitioners either embrace or spend their time fighting off. (White, 1997b: 17)

I do not think that prescriptive recommendations are never appropriate, but do not believe it is the role of a study of this kind to make such recommendations. Rather, its most useful role might be in preparing the ground for others to put together a 'practice guide' or in prompting practitioners to reach their own conclusions. It is arguably necessary for any changes in practice to be based on the kind of detailed observation of social *work* that this book has entailed. Sibeon makes this point:

> it can be argued that ... prescriptive statements are better grounded if based upon empirical awareness of which forms of knowledge are 'actually' employed by social workers in their everyday practice. (Sibeon, 1990: 32–3)

White (1998b) recommends dialogue between research and practice based on attention to *how work gets done*, rather than to how it *should* be done. Gendered tacit knowledge is unavoidable in any organisation. What perhaps can be avoided is an unquestioning acceptance of workplace culture. If injustice in social work provision is to be addressed, gendered constructions of clients have to be made explicit and their implications understood. Social workers need to be reflective about their own practice and the gendered discourse of their office culture:

> epistemic reflexivity may only be achieved by social workers becoming aware of the dominant professional constructions influencing their

practice. For example, within contemporary child care services these pivot around notions of parental dangerousness and fragile childhoods. (White, 1997c: 748)

Bloor's understanding (1997) of the relevance of qualitative research to social problems is that it can speak more to practitioners than to policy makers. He argues that practitioners will recognise themselves in the detailed description of a research setting. In considering the nature of policy, he notes the argument that 'policy is a situated discourse, a set of tacit assumptions and implicit meanings found within particular offices and occupational groupings' (Bloor, 1997: 234).

However, despite having taken some time to express these reservations about prescribing good practice and explained how I see this book's role rather differently, I am in fact going to make some tentative suggestions for practitioners: both practical measures and ideas about theory for practice, with more emphasis on the latter. I do not claim these to be definitive, of course, but I believe that to avoid struggling with the implications for practice would be to retreat to academic irresponsibility.

Practical measures

I hope that the term 'practical measures' is not misleading. My points below are not detailed prescriptions for practice, but are concerned with the practice orientation of social workers. It is distinct from the section that follows because that is about a rather more abstract theoretical framework which might help social workers to grapple with the complexity of gender relations. My suggestions in both sections below relate to occupational culture and the gendered construction of clients, and are therefore of a general nature to do with the orientation of social workers towards understanding and responding to clients. For more specific suggestions about justice to women across the child protection system, see O'Hagan and Dillenburger (1995) and Farmer and Owen (1998). For more detailed suggestions for gender justice in relation to domestic violence in particular, see Hester et al. (2000). I do not in any of what follows mean to suggest that changes in mainstream practice would be easy. Featherstone (2001: 185) has noted that the culture shift required in services is 'deep and potentially painful'.

The most important practical measure has to be the involvement of men at all stages of the child protection process, to take the pressure off women. Obviously, part of the rationale for involving men is that they can potentially be a resource for children. This is a controversial issue that gives rise to many claims and counterclaims in debates about the family. Just as some feminist rhetoric on fathering is entirely negative, some other approaches are overoptimistic. For example, Fathers Direct and the NSPCC jointly ran a conference in London during 2001 on fathers and child protection, the publicity for which only mentioned the potential for fathers to protect children, not the potential for them to cause harm (Fathers Direct/NSPCC, 2001). I believe Oakley and Rigby (1998) reach the most helpful conclusion here, which is that men can be of use to women and children, but not regardless of what they do. These authors reach the conclusion from their research that it is patriarchy that is bad for women and children. The discourses of masculinity discussed in Chapter 5 tended towards a negative picture of men. This is understandable, given the issues that these social workers are dealing with on a routine basis. However, these discourses may result in workers not considering men as a resource for families when indeed they do have the potential to be of help. As Featherstone (forthcoming) has argued, social workers should reject 'either or' thinking about fathers. Fathers are not simply either a threat or a resource for children. Most fathers encountered in child protection cases are probably both at once.

So often, though, it is the behaviour of a man that is the cause for concern in a family. As Hearn (1999) observes, men's violence against known women in particular is the cause of a great deal of referrals to social services. Social workers have to deal with the consequences of this violence on a daily basis. Social work teams need to consider a shift in approach to the violence and abuse of men. There is a powerful historical legacy of women being the primary clients, and even where it is men that pose a risk to children, it continues to be women that social workers spend most of their time working with. If social workers and their managers were to actively seek to engage relevant men, even where they do not have parental responsibility or do not live with the family full time, some of the heat might be taken off mothers. Engaging abusive men is not condoning their behaviour. It is possible, although admittedly difficult, to work with them in such a way as to skilfully challenge them whilst maintaining a working relationship.

A useful model for working with abusive men in general is the pro-feminist cognitive-behavioural work used in the Duluth approach to men who are violent towards women (Pence and Paymar, 1993). This approach has been developed specifically to challenge the physical abuse of women and, although developed in the USA, has become increasingly popular in the UK (Scourfield and Dobash, 1999) and there are cautious grounds for optimism about its effectiveness in changing men (Dobash et al., 2000). Despite its specific origins, there is potential for applying both the general principles of this work and the specific tools developed in these groupwork programmes (if adapted for cultural context) to work with abusive men more generally. Various feminist analyses are useful to help us to understand the behaviour of men who intimidate women and children, or who spend the family's limited resources on themselves, or who avoid all domestic responsibility. Therefore pro-feminist cognitive-behavioural work, which aims to change the patriarchal assumptions and rigid thinking that underpin abusive and coercive behaviour, can potentially be useful in addressing a range of problems associated with the privileges of masculinity.

Where women are living with abusive men, I found social workers to be empathetic up to a point. There was, however, little appreciation of the extent to which living in an abusive environment can have an impact on the woman's ability to respond to social workers' demands. It is possible that, for instance, the threat of violence from the man might cause a woman to stay out of fear. It is also possible that a woman can be so defeated by the abuse as to find it extremely difficult to act to change the status quo. For some women the stigma they perceive from making public their experience of abuse by leaving a man is a powerful reason to preserve the status quo. Others will hide violence from social workers not because they do not take seriously its impact on their children, but because they fear that they may lose their children if they tell anyone (a justifiable fear). Social workers should perhaps question their judgements about women's decisions when those women are living in a profoundly oppressive home.

I found the approach to child sexual abuse to have become rather formulaic. The abuse is understood according to a fixed template. This does not help us to understand the complexity of abusive situations and, more importantly, it can lead to formulaic decisions about children's welfare. For example, the fixed template for understanding abusers could lead to an assumption that children can never be safe if the alleged abuser is still around them in any way. This could in turn lead to the removal of children from their mothers if their mothers do not unequivocally agree with the social services line and completely reject or remove the alleged abuser. What I would suggest here is not so much a specific practical measure, but a general practice orientation that assesses each case of alleged child sexual abuse separately, and appreciates the variation in individual children and their relationships with their carers.

Child neglect was raised in Chapter 6. In relation to physical neglect, social workers could consider the wider causes of a physically neglectful environment. They could consider whether physical neglect should in fact be seen as the most important issue, or whether the problem could be reframed as, for example, one of an unequal distribution of domestic labour. I cannot say whether the tendency I found for social workers to concentrate on *physical* neglect, in response to training from the Bridge Child Care Consultancy, is a nationwide phenomenon or not. However, any other authorities that are prioritising the investigation and monitoring of physical neglect could consider how well this fits with the holistic picture of children's welfare that is required if services are to be refocused to family support. This holistic picture can be seen in, for example, the UK Department of Health's Assessment Framework (DH, 2000).

Furthermore, some slipping of responsibility from men to women could be avoided if the term 'parents' were not used inappropriately. Where responsibility for abusive behaviour lies firmly with one parent, this should be stated. So where a woman and children are suffering from a man's violence, this violence is not the responsibility of 'the parents' but of the man. Equally, responsibility for making changes in families could be named as that of all individual adult caregivers rather than the apparently gender-neutral 'parents', meaning in practice, mothers.

Justice for men and women in the child protection process: practical measures for social workers

- Consider parents to be clients as well as children.
- Consider involving men at every stage of the child protection process if they are involved with children's lives, whether or not they have parental responsibility.

(Cont'd)

- Consider abusive men to be appropriate targets for intervention.
- If the cause for concern is a man's behaviour, he could be the main focus of intervention rather than the woman (although she will need support).
- Men can of course be engaged by social workers for challenge as well as for support.
- Innovative pro-feminist cognitive-behavioural work with violent men can be used as a model for work with men who abuse or coerce women and children in other ways.
- Women who live with abusive men cannot necessarily act to remove them because social workers tell them to, for all kinds of reasons. In responding to such women, social workers perhaps need to try and understand the world from the women's own perspectives, whilst of course having regard to the well-being of the children.
- Every family is different and every child will experience their situation differently. Formulaic responses to any kind of child maltreatment should be avoided.
- Managers should be aware of how choices about targeting particular forms of child maltreatment can impact differentially on men and women.
- Inappropriate use of the term 'parents' should be avoided.

Theory for practice

The book has raised some important theoretical issues that I believe are relevant for those engaged in social work practice. Many practitioners would no doubt resist the offer of more theory. The earlier quotation from Sue White reminds us that social workers are, if anything, over-loaded with theory. But Chapter 7's discussion of the use of knowledge in practice indicated that some attention to theory for practice might be helpful because of the difficulties in applying knowledge about gender relations to social work practice.

The analytic practice of social constructionism itself has parallels with social work practice and has much to offer to practitioners, as Payne (1999), Witkin (1999) and Parton and O'Byrne (2000) have argued, but I will not dwell on that connection here. I will, however, make some links between some of the theoretical frameworks reviewed in the book and opportunities for social work practice. The theoretical debates mentioned in the previous chapter reflect the difficulty of understanding the gender order. How might social workers attempt this in practice? How are they to respect individual persons whilst taking social power into account? It needs to be acknowledged that juggling the individual and the social in professional practice is a very complex matter, and most definitely not reducible to a list of anti-discriminatory practice tips, as most practitioners are well aware. My theoretical perspective allows for the existence of multiple discourses, so social workers are not stuck within any given gender discourse. Foucault's conception of discursive power allows for resistance. To repeat a citation from Chapter 2:

> Discourse transmits and produces power; it reinforces it, but also undermines and exposes it, renders it fragile and makes it possible to thwart it. (Foucault, 1984: 100)

Training can initiate support for alternative discourses, and can encourage the reflection on professional constructions referred to above. There has been a great deal of attention to training social workers in anti-discriminatory and anti-oppressive practice and their influence can be seen in the culture of the Uplands team. It is possible that the approach to these perspectives has been rather too punitive, and has not encouraged social workers to be genuinely open about their constructions of clients. It is also possible that it has left certain occupational assumptions unquestioned, such as what exactly is meant in practice by the mantra of the primacy of the child's welfare. Perhaps anti-discriminatory and anti-oppressive approaches need to be more sophisticated in recognising that there are multiple interpretations of just about everything, including what is best for children, and what it means to be a man or a woman. And, crucially, any approach to gender, whether it is termed anti-discriminatory, anti-oppressive or whatever, needs to encompass both individual and structural dimensions.

Rojek et al. (1988) sought to recommend a discourse approach to social workers in *Social Work and Received Ideas* as a way of social workers dealing with the complex relationship between the individual and the social. The fact that a prominent professor of social work admitted in a review of the book that she found it difficult to read (Cheetham, 1989) suggests that they may not have been entirely successful in reaching academics with this message, let alone practitioners. This reminds us of how unrealistic it is to recommend yet more complex theory to practitioners with heavy workloads and many competing demands on them. Yet Rojek et al.'s idea about the relevance of post-structuralism to social work was a good one. Post-structuralism accepts the existence of power relations, but insists that these are fluid, complex and multi-directional. It allows for social structures to influence profoundly people's behaviour and identities, but also insists that this process operates through the interplay of multiple (and sometimes contra-dictory) discourses. So each individual has to be understood as *socially* constructed, but that social construction is contingent on *individual* social situations.

Post-structuralism has been criticised from two very different directions. On the one hand, the case has been made by several authors that the emphasis on fragmentation goes too far and fails to account for continuing inequalities between social groups (for example, Walby, 1992). And from a very different direction, there has been the criticism that post-structuralism fails to account for subjectivity (for example, Lupton and Barclay, 1997). Connell's (1987, 1995) is a sophisticated account of gender relations that takes account of these criticisms. Whilst he is best known for his work on masculinities, his ideas are in fact more generally applicable. For the sake of an example, however, I shall explain some of his ideas with reference to men.

Connell does not shy away from using the concept of patriarchy. For example, he is clear that even men who oppose patriarchal beliefs and practices can gain certain social privileges simply by virtue of being men. This is the 'patriarchal dividend'. His is not a crude, mono-lithic version of patriarchy, however. He insists on the post-structuralist plurality of the term 'masculinities'. So there are multiple, possible ways of being a man, and men's practices vary according to culture, class, ethnicity and sexuality and other mediating factors. Becoming a man is not a passive process of socialisation, but an active construc-tion of an identity. Identities and practices are not freely acquired, however, but there are social structural constraints, and power rela-tions are crucial. Gendered discursive practices configure into a hier-archy. So, for example, compulsory heterosexuality is an important aspect of 'hegemonic masculinity' and gay men therefore represent 'subordinated masculinity'. There are multiple discourses, but some are more powerful than others. What distinguishes Connell's from other sophisticated sociologies of gender is that he also appreciates the importance of a psychic dimension. He incorporates an understanding of subjectivity by including existential psychoanalysis in his framework for understanding gender relations. It was explained at the outset that this book has been oriented towards a sociological explanation of gendered practice in child protection, and I have to acknowledge that the psychic dimension that Connell includes in his theoretical framework is not one which has loomed large in the preceding chapters. I do nonetheless believe it is a crucial dimension for a rounded understanding of gender relations.

Whilst I am not suggesting that all social workers should rush out and buy Connell's *Gender and Power* (1987), his is an example of the kind of sophisticated account of gender relations that social workers need in dealing with the complexities of individual clients in a social context. The job of making relatively complex theory accessible to busy practitioners is a difficult one, warranting a whole book in its own right, but I believe it is a job worth doing. Social workers need a framework for understanding gender that can encompass tensions between the individual and the social, and help to resolve them into a realistic and coherent theory for practice.

Justice for men and women in the child protection process: theory for social work practice

- Individual men and women need to be understood in terms of the social context of gender relations.
- Men and women are also all individuals with unique histories, so understanding them requires an individual psychic dimension.
- In general, men still exercise disproportionate power in society, so the concept of patriarchy is still relevant, as long as it is used carefully.
- There are many different ways of being a man or a woman, but not all of these are given equal status in society.
- Any consideration of power relations needs to be based on an understanding of other factors, such as class, age, ethnicity, disability and sexuality.

The discourses of masculinity and femininity in the Uplands team represent a range of ways of conceptualising gender, from the rigid one-dimensional model of understanding sexually abusive men through to the diversity of psychological and sociological explanations for domestic violence. An attempt to think through the implications of these various different models for other areas of the work may prove fruitful. So, for example, social workers' theories of sex offending emphasise the need for constant awareness of the possibility that men will minimise the severity of behaviour and the intent behind it. This may be a useful insight into other types of behaviour, such as physical violence or avoidance of domestic work. Equally, the belief in the importance of an individualised approach (see 'Men as no different', Chapter 5) may be challenging to the blanket assumptions made about men who sexually abuse. What is perhaps needed is gender theorising that can encompass both the material reality of the relative power of most men over most women and also the nuances of gender relations and gender identities, and the complications of multiple and sometimes contradictory discursive practices. Social workers could apply the ethos and analysis of individualisation to structural assumptions and apply a structural understanding to individualised conceptions of problems.

O'Hagan (1997) stresses the need for widening social workers' theoretical base to more fully incorporate feminist perspectives. Equally, there have been calls for the broadening out of the theoretical base of feminist social work (Graham, 1992; Featherstone and Lancaster, 1997; Featherstone and Trinder, 1997). These authors stress the need for acceptance of diversity, fluidity and the multidimensional nature of power relations. Neither a liberal theory of anti-discrimination as equal treatment, nor anti-oppressive theory based on a monolithic notion of men's oppression of women, can capture the subtleties of gender identities and power at the micro-level. Equally, a postmodernist deconstruction of the intersection of gender and power can leave us totally cut off from any notion that most men are, if not actively involved, at least complicit (Connell, 1995) in the oppression of women. The complexity of the social work role and the complexity of gender relations suggest the need for a sophisticated conceptual framework for understanding men and women as clients in child protection work.

References

Abbott, P. and Sapsford, R. (1990) 'Health visiting: policing the family?' in Abbott, P. and Wallace, C. (eds) *The Sociology of the Caring Professions*, Basingstoke, Falmer.

Abbott, P. and Wallace, C. (1990) 'The sociology of the caring professions: an introduction' in Abbott, P. and Wallace, C. (eds) *The Sociology of the Caring Professions*, Basingstoke, Falmer.

Acker, J. (1989) 'The problem with patriarchy', *Sociology*, **23**(2): 235–40.

Alanen, L. (1994) 'Gender and generation: feminism and the "child question"' in Qvortrup, J., Bardy, M., Sgritta, G. and Wintersberger, H. (eds) *Childhood Matters*, Aldershot, Avebury.

Askeland, G.A. and Payne, M. (1999) 'Authors and audiences: towards a sociology of case recording', *European Journal of Social Work*, **2**(1): 55–65.

Atkinson, P. and Delamont, S. (1990) 'Professions and powerlessness: female marginality in the learned occupations', *Sociological Review*, **38**(1): 90–110.

Bagguley, P. and Mann, K. (1992) '"Idle thieving bastards?" Scholarly representations of the underclass', *Work, Employment and Society*, **6**(1): 113–26.

Bailey, R. and Brake, M. (eds) (1974) *Radical Social Work*, London, Edward Arnold.

Balloch, S., Pahl, J. and McLean, J. (1998) 'Working in the social services: job satisfaction, stress and violence', *British Journal of Social Work*, **28**: 329–50.

Barber, J. (1991) *Beyond Casework*, Basingstoke, Macmillan – now Palgrave Macmillan.

BASW (British Association of Social Workers) (1996) *The Code of Ethics for Social Work*, Birmingham, BASW.

Bates, S. (1993) 'Tory attacks fathers who reject family life', *Guardian*, 3 July, p. 6.

Beasley, C. (1999) *What is Feminism? An Introduction to Feminist Theory*, St Leonards, NSW, Allen & Unwin.

Beck, U. (1992) *Risk Society: Towards a New Modernity*, London, Sage.

Beck, U. and Beck-Gernsheim, E. (1995) *The Normal Chaos of Love*, Cambridge, Polity.

Becker, S. and Macpherson, S. (1986) 'Poor clients: research note', *British Journal of Social Work*, **16**: 689–91.

Bella, L. (1995) 'Gender and occupational closure in social work' in Taylor, P. (ed.) *Gender Dilemmas in Social Work. Issues Affecting Women in the Profession*, Toronto, Canadian Scholars Press.

Benhabib, S. (1995) 'Feminism and post-modernism: an uneasy alliance' in Benhabib, S., Butler, J., Cornell, D. and Fraser, N. (eds) *Feminist Contentions: A Philosophical Exchange*, New York, Routledge.

183

Berger, P. and Luckmann, T. (1967) *The Social Construction of Reality*, London, Allen Lane.

Best, J. (1989) 'Debates about constructionism' in Rubington, E. and Weinberg, M.S. (eds) *The Study of Social Problems: Seven Perspectives*, New York, Oxford University Press.

Biestek, F. (1961) *The Casework Relationship*, London, George Allen & Unwin.

Blackmore, J. (1999) *Troubling Women*, Buckingham, Open University Press.

Bloor, M. (1997) 'Addressing social problems through qualitative research' in Silverman, D. (ed.) *Qualitative Research: Theory, Method and Practice*, London, Sage.

Bourdieu, P. (1986) *Distinction*, London, Routledge.

Bowlby, J. (1953) *Child Care and the Growth of Love*, Harmondsworth, Penguin.

Brent, London Borough of (1985) *A Child in Trust: the Report of the Panel of Inquiry into the Circumstances Surrounding the Death of Jasmine Beckford*, London, London Borough of Brent.

Bridge Child Care Consultancy (1991) *Sukina: An Evaluation Report of the Circumstances Leading to her Death*, London, Bridge Child Care Consultancy.

Bridge Child Care Consultancy (1995) *Paul: Death Through Neglect*, London, Islington Area Child Protection Committee.

Brindle, D. (1998) 'Child abuse checklist divines risk in rubbish', *Guardian*, 18 September, p. 11.

Bristow, J. (1997) *Sexuality*, London, Routledge.

Brittan, A. and Maynard, M. (1984) *Sexism, Racism and Oppression*, Oxford, Blackwell.

Brown, H.C. (1998) *Social Work and Sexuality. Working with Lesbians and Gay Men*, Basingstoke, Macmillan – now Palgrave Macmillan.

Burman, E. (1994) *Deconstructing Developmental Psychology*, London, Routledge.

Burr, V. (1995) *An Introduction to Social Constructionism*, London, Routledge.

Butler, I. and Drakeford, M. (2000) 'Editorial', *British Journal of Social Work*, 30(1): 1–2.

Butler, I. and Drakeford, M. (2001) 'Which Blair project? Communitarianism, social authoritarianism and social work', *Journal of Social Work*, 1(1): 7–19.

Butler I. and Williamson, H. (1994) *Children Speak: Children, Trauma and Social Work*, Harlow, Longman.

Butler, J. (1990) *Gender Trouble: Feminism and the Subversion of Identity*, New York, Routledge.

Butler, J. (1993) *Bodies that Matter: On the Discursive Limits of 'Sex'*, New York, Routledge.

Callaghan, G. (1998) The interaction of gender, class and place in women's experience: a discussion based in focus group research. *Sociological Research Online*, 3, 3, http://www.socresonline.org.uk/socresonline/ 3/3/8.html

Campbell, B. (1993) *Goliath*, London, Methuen.

Carabine, J. (1992) '"Constructing women": women's sexuality and social policy', *Critical Social Policy*, 12(1): 23–37.

Carter, P. (1993) 'The problem of men: a reply to Keith Pringle', *Critical Social Policy*, 37: 100–6.

Carter Hood, P., Everitt, A. and Runnicles, D. (1998) 'Femininity, sexuality and professionalism in the Children's Departments', *British Journal of Social Work*, 28: 471–90.

Cavanagh, K. and Cree, V. (eds) (1996) *Working with Men: Feminism and Social Work*, London, Routledge.

CCETSW (Central Council for Education and Training in Social Work) (1991) *Rules and Requirements for the Diploma in Social Work (Paper 30)* (2nd edn) London, CCETSW.

Charles, N. (2000) *Feminism, The State and Social Policy*, Basingstoke, Macmillan – now Palgrave Macmillan.

Cheetham, J. (1989) Review of two books by Rojek, Peacock and Collins, *Social Policy and Administration*, 23(3): 277–80.

Cheetham, J. and Deakin, N. (1997) 'Research note: assessing the assessment: some reflections on the 1996 RAE', *British Journal of Social Work*, 27: 435–42.

Christensen, P.H. (2000) 'Childhood and the cultural constitution of vulnerable bodies' in Prout, A. (ed.) *The Body, Childhood and Society*, Basingstoke, Macmillan – now Palgrave Macmillan.

Christie, A. (1998a) 'Is social work a "non-traditional" occupation for men?', *British Journal of Social Work*, 28: 491–510.

Christie, A. (1998b) 'A comparison of arguments for employing men as child care workers and social workers in Denmark and the UK', *Social Work in Europe*, 5(1): 2–17.

Christie, A. (ed.) (2001) *Men and Social Work*, Basingstoke, Palgrave – now Palgrave Macmillan.

Clare, A. (2000) *On Men: Masculinity in Crisis*, London, Chatto & Windus.

Clatterbaugh, K. (1990) *Contemporary Perspectives on Masculinity*, Colorado, Westview.

Cleaver, H. and Freeman, P. (1995) *Parental Perspectives in Cases of Suspected Child Abuse*, London, HMSO.

Coffey, A. and Delamont, S. (2000) *Feminism and the Classroom Teacher*, London, Falmer.

Cohen, N. (1999) 'Mr Blair has a problem with Mr Cohen', *The Observer*, Review Section, 16 May, pp. 1–2.

Collier, R. (1995) *Masculinity, Law and the Family*, London, Routledge.

Collier, R. (1998) *Masculinities, Crime and Criminology. Men, Heterosexuality and the Criminal(ised) Other*, London, Sage.

Collins, H. (2000) 'What is tacit knowledge?' in Schatzki, T.R., Knorr-Cetina, K. and von Savigny, E. (eds) *The Practice Turn in Contemporary Theory*, London, Routledge.

Connell, R.W. (1987) *Gender and Power*, Cambridge, Polity.

Connell, R.W. (1995) *Masculinities*, Cambridge, Polity.

Connell, R.W. (1998) 'Bodies, intellectuals and world society'. Plenary address to the British Sociological Association Annual Conference, 'Making Sense of the Body: Theory, Research and Practice, University of Edinburgh.

Connell, R.W. (2000) *The Men and the Boys*, Cambridge, Polity.

Corby, B. (1987) *Working with Child Abuse*, Milton Keynes, Open University Press.

Corby, B. (1991) 'Sociology, social work and child protection' in Davies, M. (ed.) *The Sociology of Social Work*, London, Routledge.

Corby, B. (2000) *Child Abuse: Towards a Knowledge Base*, Buckingham, Open University Press.

Corby, B. and Millar, M. (1997) 'A parents' view of partnership' in Bates, J., Pugh, R. and Thompson, N. (eds) *Protecting Children: Challenges and Changes*, Aldershot, Arena.

Courtenay, W.H. (2000) 'Social work, counseling, and psychotherapeutic interventions with men and boys. A bibliography: 1980 to present', *Men and Masculinities*, **2**(3): 330–52.

Coward, R. (1997) 'The heaven and hell of mothering. Mothering and ambivalence in the mass media', in Hollway, W. and Featherstone, B. (eds) *Mothering and Ambivalence*, London, Routledge.

Coward, R. (1999) *Sacred Cows*, London, HarperCollins.

Craib, I. (1992) *Modern Social Theory: From Parsons to Habermas*, Hemel Hempstead, Harvester Wheatsheaf.

Craib, I. (1997) 'Social constructionism as a social psychosis' *Sociology*, **31**(1): 1–15.

Creighton, S. (1987) 'Child abuse in 1986', *Social Services Research*, **3**: 1–10.

Critial Research on Men in Europe (2001) CROME website, http://www.cromenet.org/ (accessed March 2001).

Croghan, R. and Miell, D. (1998) 'Strategies of resistance: "bad mothers" dispute the evidence', *Feminism and Psychology*, **8**(4): 445–65.

Dale, P., Davies, M., Morrison, T. and Waters, J. (1986) *Dangerous Families: Assessment and Treatment of Child Abuse*, London, Routledge.

Dalley, G. (1996) *Ideologies of Caring* (2nd edn) Basingstoke, Macmillan – now Palgrave Macmillan.

Daly, K. (1997) 'Different ways of conceptualizing sex/gender in feminist theory and their implications for criminology', *Theoretical Criminology*, **1**(1): 25–51.

Daniel, B. and Taylor, J. (1999) 'The rhetoric versus the reality: a critical perspective on practice with fathers in child care and protection work', *Child and Family Social Work*, **4**: 209–20.

Dartington Social Research Unit (1995) *Child Protection: Messages from Research*, London, HMSO.

Davies, L. and Krane, J. (1996) 'Shaking the legacy of mother blaming: no easy task for child welfare', *Journal of Progressive Human Services*, **7**: 3–22.

Davis, K. (1997) 'Embodying theory. Beyond modernist and post-modernist readings of the body' in Davis, K. (ed.) *Embodied Practices: Feminist Perspectives on the Body*, London, Sage.

Day, R. (1997) 'Process, protection and practice: an ethnographic study of child protection social workers'. Unpublished paper presented at 'Constructing Social Work Practices' symposium at the University of Tampere, Finland.

Delphy, C. (1993) 'Rethinking sex and gender', *Women's Studies International Forum*, **16**(1): 1–9.

De Montigny, G.A.J. (1995) 'The power of being professional' in Campbell, M. and Manicom, A. (eds) *Knowledge, Experience and Ruling Relations: Studies in the Social Organization of Knowledge*, Toronto, University of Toronto Press.

DH (Department of Health) (1988) *Protecting Children: A Guide for Social Workers Undertaking a Comprehensive Assessment*, London, HMSO.

DH (Department of Health) (1991) *Patterns and Outcomes in Child Placement*, London, HMSO.

DH (Department of Health) (2000) *Framework for the Assessment of Children in Need and Their Families*, London, Stationary Office.

DHSS (Department of Health and Social Security) (1974) *Report of the Committee of Inquiry into the Care and Supervision Provided in Relation to Maria Colwell*, London, HMSO.

DHSS (Department of Health and Social Security) (1985) *Social Work Decisions in Child Care: Recent Research Findings and Their Implications*, London, HMSO.

Dicks, B. (1999) 'The view of our town from the hill: communities on display as local heritage', *International Journal of Cultural Studies*, 2(3): 349–68.

Dicks, B., Waddington, D. and Critcher, C. (1998) 'Redundant men and over-burdened women: local service providers and the construction of gender in ex-mining communities' in Popay, J., Hearn, J. and Edwards, J. (eds) *Men, Gender Divisions and Welfare*, London, Routledge.

Dingwall, R., Eekelaar, J. and Murray, T. (1983) *The Protection of Children. State Intervention and Family Life*, Oxford, Basil Blackwell.

Dingwall, R., Eekelaar, J. and Murray, T. (1995) *The Protection of Children. State Intervention and Family Life* (2nd edn) Aldershot, Avebury.

Dobash, R.E. and Dobash, R.P. (1979) *Violence Against Wives*, New York, Free Press.

Dobash, R.E. and Dobash, R.P. (1992) *Women, Violence and Social Change*, London, Routledge.

Dobash, R.P., Dobash, R.E., Wilson, M. and Daly, M. (1992) 'The myth of sexual symmetry in marital violence', *Social Problems*, 39: 402–32.

Dobash, R.E., Dobash, R.P., Cavanagh, K. and Lewis, R. (2000) *Changing Violent Men*, London, Sage.

Dominelli, L. (1997) *Anti-racist Social Work* (2nd edn) Basingstoke, Macmillan – now Palgrave Macmillan.

Dominelli, L. and MacLeod, E. (1989) *Feminist Social Work*, Basingstoke, Macmillan – now Palgrave Macmillan.

Donzelot, J. (1980) *The Policing of Families*, London: Hutchinson.

Douglas, M. (1966) *Purity and Danger: An Analysis of Concepts of Pollution and Taboo*, London, Routledge & Kegan Paul.

Douglas, M. (1986) *Risk Acceptability According to the Social Sciences*, London, Routledge & Kegan Paul.

Douglas, M. (1992) *Risk and Blame. Essays in Cultural Theory*, London, Routledge.

Dyer, R. (1998) *White*, London, Routledge.

Edleson, J.L. (1998) 'Responsible mothers and invisible men: child protection in the case of adult domestic violence', *Journal of Interpersonal Violence*, 13(2): 294–8.

Edwards, J. (1998) 'Screening out men, or "has mum changed her washing powder recently?"' in Popay, J., Hearn, J. and Edwards, J. (eds) *Men, Gender Divisions and Welfare*, London, Routledge.

Eichenbaum, L. and Orbach, S. (1983) *Understanding Women*, Harmondsworth, Penguin.

Elliott, M. (ed.) (1993) *Female Sexual Abuse of Children: The Ultimate Taboo*, Harlow, Longman.

Ettorre, E. (1992) *Women and Substance Use*, Basingstoke, Macmillan – now Palgrave Macmillan.

Faludi, S. (1999) *Stiffed: The Betrayal of the American Man*, London, Chatto & Windus.

Farmer, E. and Owen, M. (1995) *Child Protection Practice: Private Risks and Public Remedies*, London, HMSO.

Farmer, E. and Owen, M. (1998) 'Gender and the child protection process', *British Journal of Social Work*, 28: 545–64.

Fathers Direct/NSPCC (2001) Press release: 'Vulnerable children failed by exclusion of fathers', 10 September, London, Fathers Direct/NSPCC.

Fawcett, B., Featherstone, B., Fook, J. and Rossiter, A. (eds) (2000) *Practice and Research in Social Work: Postmodern Feminist Perspectives*, London, Routledge.

Featherstone, B. (1997a) '"I wouldn't do your job!" Women, social work and child abuse' in Hollway, W. and Featherstone, B. (eds) *Mothering and Ambivalence*, London, Routledge.

Featherstone, B. (1997b) '"What has gender got to do with it?": Exploring physically abusive behaviour towards children', *British Journal of Social Work*, **27**: 419–33.

Featherstone, B. (1999) 'Taking mothering seriously: the implications for child protection', *Child and Family Social Work*, **4**: 43–53.

Featherstone, B. (2001) 'Research review: putting fathers on the child welfare agenda', *Child and Family Social Work*, **6**: 179–86.

Featherstone, B. (forthcoming) 'Taking fathers seriously', *British Journal of Social Work*.

Featherstone, B. and Lancaster, E. (1997) 'Contemplating the unthinkable: men who sexually abuse children', *Critical Social Policy*, **53**: 51–71.

Featherstone, B. and Trinder, L. (1997) 'Familiar subjects? Domestic violence and child welfare', *Child and Family Social Work*, **2**: 147–59.

Ferguson, H. (1997) 'Protecting children in new times: child protection and the risk society', *Child and Family Social Work*, **2**: 221–34.

Ferguson, H. (2001) 'Social work, individualization and life politics', *British Journal of Social Work*, **31**: 41–55.

Fernandez, E. (1996) *Significant Harm: Unravelling Child Protection Decisions and Substitute Care Careers of Children*, Aldershot, Avebury.

Finkelhor, D. (ed.) (1984) *Child Sexual Abuse: New Theory and Research*, Los Angeles, Sage.

Flax, J. (1990) 'Postmodernism and gender relations in feminist theory' in Nicholson, L.J. (ed.) *Feminism/Postmodernism*, London, Routledge.

Foucault, M. (1977) *Discipline and Punish*, Harmondsworth, Penguin.

Foucault, M. (1984) *The History of Sexuality*, Vol. One: *An Introduction*, Harmondsworth, Penguin.

Foucault, M. (1986) 'The politics of health in the eighteenth century' in Rabinow, P. (ed.) *The Foucault Reader*, London, Penguin.

Fox Harding, L. (1997) *Perspectives in Child Care Policy* (2nd edn) Harlow, Longman.

Freud, S. (1924) 'The dissolution of the Oedipus complex' in Strachey, J. (ed.) *Standard Edition of the Complete Psychological Works of Sigmund Freud*, London, Hogarth Press, 1953–74, **19**: 173–9.

Gallie, D. (1994) '"Are the unemployed an underclass?" Some evidence from the social change and economic life initiative', *Sociology*, **28**(3): 737–57.

Gamble, A. (1988) *The Free Economy and the Strong State: The Politics of Thatcherism*, Basingstoke, Macmillan – now Palgrave Macmillan.

Gatens, M. (1995) *Imaginary Bodies: Ethics, Power and Corporeality*, New York, Routledge.

Gelles, R.J. and Loseke, D.L. (eds) (1993) *Current Controversies on Family Violence*, Newbury Park, CA, Sage.

Gibbons, J., Conroy, S. and Bell, C. (1995) *Operating the Child Protection System: A Study of Child Protection Practices in English Local Authorities*, London, HMSO.

Giddens, A. (1990) *The Consequences of Modernity*, Cambridge, Polity.

Giddens, A. (1991) *Modernity and Self-identity*, Cambridge, Polity.

Giddens, A. (1992) *The Transformation of Intimacy: Sexuality, Love and Eroticism in Modern Societies*, Cambridge, Polity/Basil Blackwell.

Glenn, E.N. (1994) 'Social constructions of mothering: a thematic overview' in Glenn, E.N., Chang, G. and Forcey, L.R. (eds) *Mothering. Ideology, Experience and Agency*, New York, Routledge.

Gordon, D. and Gibbons, J. (1998) 'Placing children on child protection registers: risk indicators and local authority differences', *British Journal of Social Work*, **28**: 423–36.

Gordon, L. (1986) 'Feminism and social control: the case of child abuse and neglect' in Mitchell, J. and Oakley, A. (eds) *What is Feminism?*, Oxford, Blackwell.

Gordon, L. (1988) *Heroes of Their Own Lives. The Politics and History of Family Violence, Boston 1880–1960*, New York, Viking.

Gottfried, H. (1998) 'Beyond patriarchy? Theorising gender and class', *Sociology*, **32**(3): 451–68.

Graham, H. (1992) 'Feminism and social work education', *Issues in Social Work Education*, **11**(2): 48–64.

Greenwich, London Borough of (1987) *Protection of Children in a Responsible Society: The Report of the Commission of Inquiry into the Circumstances Surrounding the Death of Kimberly Carlile*, London, London Borough of Greenwich/Greenwich Health Authority.

Hall, C. (1997) *Social Work as Narrative*, Aldershot, Ashgate.

Hall, C., Sarangi, S. and Slembrouck, S. (1997a) 'Moral construction in social work discourse', in Gunnarsson, B-L., Linell, P. and Nordberg, B. (eds) *The Construction of Professional Discourse*, London, Longman.

Hall, C., Sarangi, S. and Slembrouck, S. (1997b) 'Silent and silenced voices: interactional construction of audience in social work talk' in Jaworski, A. (ed.) *Silence. Interdisciplinary Perspectives*, Berlin, Mouton de Gruyter.

Hall, C., Sarangi, S. and Slembrouck, S. (1999) 'The legitimation of the client and the profession in social work discourse' in Sarangi, S. and Roberts, C. (eds) *Talk, Work and Institutional Order: Discourse in Medical, Mediation and Management Settings*, Berlin, Mouton de Gruyter.

Hallett, C. (1989) 'The gendered world of the social services department' in Hallett, C. (ed.) *Women and Social Services Departments*, Hemel Hempstead, Harvester Wheatsheaf.

Handelman, D. (1983) 'Shaping phenomenal reality: dialectic and disjunction in the bureaucratic synbook of child abuse in urban Newfoundland', *Social Analysis*, **13**: 3–36.

Hanmer, J. and Statham, D. (1988) *Women and Social Work: Towards a Woman-centred Practice*, Basingstoke, Macmillan – now Palgrave Macmillan.

Haraway, D. (1992) *Primate Visions*, London, Verso.

Hardman, K.L.J. (1997) 'Social workers' attitudes to lesbian clients', *British Journal of Social Work*, **27**: 545–63.

Harlow, E. (1996) 'Gender, violence and social work organisations' in Fawcett, B., Featherstone, B., Hearn, J. and Toft, C. (eds) *Violence and Gender Relations. Theories and Interventions*, London, Sage.

Harlow, E. and Hearn, J. (1995) 'Cultural constructions: contrasting theories of organizational culture and gender construction', *Gender, Work and Organisation*, **2**(4): 180–91.

Hearn, J. (1982) 'Notes on patriarchy, professionalization and the semi-professions', *Sociology*, **16**(4): 184–202.

Hearn, J. (1990) '"Child abuse" and men's violence', in The Violence Against Children Study Group (eds) *Taking Child Abuse Seriously*, London, Unwin Hyman.

Hearn, J. (1998) 'Troubled masculinities in social policy discourses: young men' in Popay, J., Hearn, J. and Edwards, J. (eds) *Men, Gender Divisions and Welfare*, London, Routledge.

Hearn, J. (1999) *The Violences of Men*, London, Sage.

Hearn, J., and W. Parkin. (1987) *'Sex' at 'Work'. The Power and Paradox of Organisation Sexuality*, Brighton, Wheatsheaf.

Hester, M. and Radford, L. (1996) *Domestic Violence and Child Contact Arrangements in England and Denmark*, Bristol, Policy.

Hester, M., Pearson, C. and Harwin, N. (2000) *Making an Impact: Children and Domestic Violence*, London, Jessica Kingsley.

Hicks, S. (2000) '"Good lesbian, bad lesbian . . .": regulating heterosexuality in fostering and adoption assessments', *Child and Family Social Work*, **5**: 157–68.

Hill, M. (1982) 'Street level bureaucracy in social work and social services departments' in Lishman, J. (ed.) *Research Highlights No.4: Social Work Departments as Organisations*, Aberdeen, social work department, Aberdeen University.

Hill Collins, P. (1990) *Black Feminist Thought – Knowledge, Consciousness and the Politics of Empowerment*, London, Unwin Hyman.

Holland, S. (2000) 'The assessment relationship: interactions between social workers and parents in child protection assessments', *British Journal of Social Work*, **30**: 149–63.

Holstein, J. and Miller, G. (1993) 'Social constructionism and social problems work' in Holstein, J. and Miller, G. (eds) *Reconsidering Social Constructionism*, New York, Aldine de Gruyter.

Hood, S. (1997) 'The purchaser/provider separation in child and family social work: Implications for service delivery and for the role of the social worker', *Child and Family Social Work*, **2**: 25–35.

Hooper, C.-A. (1987) 'Getting him off the hook', *Trouble and Strife*, **12**: 20–5.

Hooper, C.-A. (1992a) *Mothers Surviving Child Sexual Abuse*, London, Routledge.

Hooper, C.-A. (1992b) 'Child sexual abuse and the regulation of women: variations on a theme' in Smart, C. (ed.) *Regulating Womanhood: Historical Essays on Marriage, Motherhood and Sexuality*, London, Routledge.

Howe, D. (1992) 'Child abuse and the bureaucratisation of social work', *Sociological Review*, **40**(3): 491–508.

Howe, D. (1996) 'Surface and depth in social work practice' in Parton, N. (ed.) *Social Theory, Social Change and Social Work*, London, Routledge.

Howe, D., Sawbridge, P. and Hinings, D. (1992) *Half a Million Women: Mothers who Lose their Children by Adoption*, London, Penguin.

Howitt, D. (1992) *Child Abuse Errors: When Good Intentions Go Wrong*, London, Harvester Wheatsheaf.

Hugman, B. and Smith, D. (1995) 'Ethical issues in social work: an overview' in Hugman, B. and Smith, D. (eds) *Ethical Issues in Social Work*, London, Routledge.

Humphreys, C., Atkar, S. and Baldwin, N. (1999) 'Discrimination in child protection work: recurring themes in work with Asian families', *Child and Family Social Work*, **4**(4): 283–91.

Humphries, C. (1999) 'Avoidance and confrontation: social work practice in relation to domestic violence and child abuse', *Child and Family Social Work*, **4**: 77–87.

Jokinen, A., Juhila, K. and Pösö, T. (eds) (1999) *Constructing Social Work Practices*, Aldershot, Ashgate.

Jones, C. (1983) *State Social Work and the Working Class*, Basingstoke, Macmillan – now Palgrave Macmillan.

Jones, C. (2001) 'Voices from the front line: state social workers and New Labour', *British Journal of Social Work*, **31**(4): 547–62.

Jones, P. (2001) *Fuse*, Cardiff, Parthian Books.

Jordan, B. (1991) 'Competencies and values', *Social Work Education*, **10**: 5–11.

Jordan, B., with Jordan, C. (2000) *Social Work and the Third Way: Tough Love as Social Policy*, London, Sage.

Kähkönen, P. (1999) 'The assessment of parenting in the child welfare practice', *Children and Youth Services Review*, **21**(7): 581–603.

Kelly, L., Regan, L. and Burton, S. (1991) *An Exploratory Study of the Prevalence of Sexual Abuse in a Sample of 16–21 Year Olds*, Child and Woman Abuse Studies Unit, London, University of North London.

Kempe, C.H., Silverman, F.N., Steel, B.F., Droegemueller, W. and Silver, H.K. (1962) 'The battered child syndrome', *Journal of the American Medical Association*, **181**: 17–24.

Kemshall, H., Parton, N., Walsh, M. and Waterson, J. (1997) 'Concepts of risk in relation to organizational structure and functioning within the personal social services and probation', *Social Policy and Administration*, **31**(3): 213–32.

Kennedy, J. (1999) 'Class and the concept of difference: an empowering practice?' Paper at a conference of the British Association of Social Workers and University of Central Lancashire, Southport, March 22–25.

Kimmel, M. and Messner, M. (eds) (1998) *Men's Lives* (2nd edn) Boston, Allyn & Bacon.

King, M. and Piper, C. (1995) *How the Law Thinks About Children* (2nd edn) Aldershot, Arena.

King, M. and Trowell, J. (1992) *Children's Welfare and the Law: The Limits of Legal Intervention*, London, Sage.

Kitsuse, J.I. and Spector, M. (1973) 'The definition of social problems', *Social Problems*, **20**(4): 407–19.

Krane, J. and Davies, L. (2000) 'Mothering and child protection practice: rethinking risk assessment', *Child and Family Social Work*, **5**: 35–46.

La Fontaine, J.S. (1998) *Speak of the Devil. Tales of Satanic Abuse in Contemporary England*, Cambridge, Cambridge University Press.

Lambeth, London Borough of (1987) *Whose Child? The Report of the Public Enquiry into the Death of Tyra Henry*, London, London Borough of Lambeth.

Lawler, S. (1999) 'Children need but mothers only want: the power of needs talk' in Seymour, J. and Bagguley, P. (eds) *Relating Intimacies: Power and Resistance*, Basingstoke, Macmillan – now Palgrave Macmillan.

Lawrence, M. (1992) 'Women's psychology and feminist social work practice' in Langan, M. and Day, L. (eds) *Women, Oppression and Social Work. Issues in Anti-discriminatory Practice*, London, Routledge.

Leonard, P. (1978) *Social Work Practice Under Capitalism*, Basingstoke, Macmillan – now Palgrave Macmillan.

Lewis, G. (2000) *'Race', Gender, Social Welfare. Encounters in a Postcolonial Society*, Cambridge, Polity.

Lindsay, D. (1994) *The Welfare of Children*, New York, Oxford University Press.

Lipsky, M. (1980) *Street Level Bureaucracy*, New York, Russell Sage.

Little, M. (1997) 'The re-focusing of children's services' in Parton, N. (ed.) *Child Protection and Family Support*, London, Routledge.

Lupton, D. (1996) *Food, the Body and the Self*, London, Sage.

Lupton, D. and Barclay, L. (1997) *Constructing Fatherhood. Discourses and Experiences*, London, Sage.

Martin, J. (1983) 'Maternal and paternal abuse of children. Theoretical and research perspectives' in Finkelhor, D., Gelles, R.J., Hotaling, G.T. and Staus, M.A. (eds) *The Dark Side of Families. Current Family Violence Research*, Beverly Hills, Sage.

Maynard, M. (1985) 'The response of social workers to domestic violence', in Pahl, J. (ed.) *Private Violence and Public Policy*, London, Routledge & Kegan Paul.

McMahon, A. (1998) *Damned If You Do, Damned If You Don't. Working in Child Welfare*, Ashgate, Aldershot.

McMahon, A. (1999) *Taking Care of Men*, Cambridge, Cambridge University Press.

McVeigh, T. (2001) 'Children may die in care crisis', *The Observer*, 16 September, p. 1.

Mead, M. (1935) *Sex and Temperament in Three Primitive Societies*, New York, William Morrow.

Mellor, P.A. and Shilling, C. (1997) *Re-forming the Body: Religion, Community and Modernity*, London, Sage.

Messerschmidt, J. (2000) 'Becoming "real men": adolescent masculinity challenges and sexual violence', *Men and Masculinities*, **2**(3): 286–307.

Messner, M. (1997) *The Politics of Masculinity*, London, Sage.

Middleton, P. (1992) *The Inward Gaze. Masculinity and Subjectivity in Modern Culture*, London, Routledge.

Milner, J. (1993) 'A disappearing act: The differing career paths of fathers and mothers in child protection investigations', *Critical Social Policy*, **38**: 48–63.

Morgan, D. (1996a) *Family Connections. An Introduction to Family Studies*, Cambridge, Polity.

Morgan, D. (1996b) 'The gender of bureaucracy' in Hearn, J. and Collinson, D.L. (eds) *Men as Managers, Managers as Men*, London, Sage.

Morris, L. (1994) *Dangerous Classes*, London, Routledge.

Morrison, T. (1990) 'The emotional effects of child protection work on the worker', *Practice*, **4**(4): 253–71.

Mullender, A. (1996) *Rethinking Domestic Violence: the Social Work and Probation Response*, London, Routledge.

Mullender, A. (1997) 'Domestic violence and social work. The challenge to change', *Critical Social Policy*, **50**: 53–78.

Mullender, A. and Morley, R. (eds) (1994) *Children Living with Domestic Violence*, London, Whiting & Birch.

Munro, E. (1998) 'Improving social workers' knowledge base in child protection work', *British Journal of Social Work*, **28**: 89–105.

Murcott, A. (1982) 'On the social significance of the "cooked dinner" in South Wales', *Social Science Information*, **21**(4/5): 677–96.

Murray, C. (1990) *The Emerging British Underclass*, London, IEA Health and Welfare Unit.

Murray, T., Dingwall, R. and Eekelaar, J. (1983) 'Professionals in bureaucracies: solicitors in private practice and local government' in Dingwall, R. and Lewis, P. (eds) *The Sociology of the Professions*, Basingstoke, Macmillan – now Palgrave Macmillan.

Newburn, T. and Mair, G. (eds) (1996) *Working with Men*, Lyme Regis, Russell House.

Oakley, A. (1972) *Sex, Gender and Society*, London, Temple Smith.

Oakley, A. (1998) 'Science, gender and women's liberation: an argument against postmodernism', *Women's Studies International Forum*, **21**(2): 133–46.

Oakley, A. and Rigby, A.S. (1998) 'Are men good for the welfare of women and children' in Popay, J., Hearn, J. and Edwards, J. (eds) *Men, Gender Divisions and Welfare*, London, Routledge.

O'Brien, M. and Penna, S. (1998) *Theorising Welfare: Enlightenment and Modern Society*, London, Sage.

O'Hagan, K. (1997) 'The problem of engaging men in child protection', *British Journal of Social Work*, **27**: 25–42.

O'Hagan, K. and Dillenburger, C. (1995) *The Abuse of Women in Child Care Work*, Buckingham, Open University Press.

Otway, O. (1996) 'Social work with children and families: from child welfare to child protection' in Parton, N. (ed.) *Social Theory, Social Change and Social Work*, London, Routledge.

Parker, R. (1995) 'A brief history of child protection' in Farmer, E. and Owen, M. *Child Protection Practice: Private Risks and Public Remedies*, London, HMSO.

Parton, C. (1990) 'Women, gender oppression and child abuse' in The Violence Against Children Study Group (eds) *Taking Child Abuse Seriously*, London, Unwin Hyman.

Parton, C. and Parton, N. (1989) 'Women, the family and child protection', *Critical Social Policy*, **8**(3): 38–49.

Parton, N. (1991) *Governing the Family*, Basingstoke, Macmillan – now Palgrave Macmillan.

Parton, N. (1995) 'Neglect as child protection: the political context and the practical outcomes', *Children and Society*, **9**(1): 67–89.

Parton, N. (1996) 'Child protection, family support and social work: a critical appraisal of the Department of Health research studies in child protection', *Child and Family Social Work*, **1**: 3–11.

Parton, N. (1997) 'Child protection and family support. Current debates and future prospects' in Parton, N. (ed.) *Child Protection and Family Support. Tensions, Contradictions and Possibilities*, London, Routledge.

Parton, N. (1998) 'Risk, advanced liberalism and child welfare: the need to rediscover uncertainty and ambiguity', *British Journal of Social Work*, **28**: 5–27.

Parton, N. and O'Byrne, P. (2000) *Constructive Social Work*, Basingstoke, Macmillan – now Palgrave Macmillan.

Parton, N., Thorpe, D. and Wattam, C. (1997) *Child Protection: Risk and the Moral Order*, Basingstoke, Macmillan – now Palgrave Macmillan.

Parton, N. and Mathews, R. (2001) 'New directions in child protection and family support in Western Australia: a policy initiative to re-focus child welfare practice', *Child and Family Social Work*, **6**(2): 97–115.

Payne, M. (1991) *Modern Social Work Theory*, Basingstoke, Macmillan – now Palgrave Macmillan.

Payne, M. (1999) 'Social constructionism in social work and social action' in Jokinen, A., Juhila, K. and Pösö, T. (eds) *Constructing Social Work Practices*, Aldershot, Ashgate.

Pease, B. (1997) 'Teaching anti-patriarchal men's studies in social work', *Issues in Social Work Education*, **17**(1): 3–17.

Peile, C. (1998) 'Emotional and embodied knowledge: implications for critical practice', *Journal of Sociology and Social Welfare*, **25**(4): 39–59.

Pence, E. and Paymar, M. (1993) *Education Groups for Men who Batter: the Duluth Model*, New York, Springer.

Phillipson, J. (1992) *Practising Equality. Women, Men and Social Work*, London, CCETSW.

Philp, M. (1979) 'Notes on the form of knowledge in social work', *Sociological Review*, **27**: 83–111.

Pithouse, A. (1984) Social Work: The Social Organisation of an Invisible Trade, PhD thesis, University College, Cardiff.

Pithouse, A. (1987) *Social Work: The Social Organisation of an Invisible Trade*, Aldershot, Avebury.

Pithouse, A. (1998) *Social Work: The Social Organisation of an Invisible Trade* (2nd edn) Aldershot, Ashgate.

Pithouse, A. and Atkinson, P. (1988) 'Telling the case. Occupational narrative in a social work office' in Coupland, N. (ed.) *Styles of Discourse*, London, Croom Helm.

Pithouse, A. and Williamson, H. (1997) 'Introduction, apology and polemic' in Pithouse, A. and Williamson, H. (eds) *Engaging the User in Welfare Services*, Birmingham, Venture.

Polansky, N.A., Chalmers, M.A., Buttenwieser, E. and Williams, D.P. (1981) *Damaged Parents: An Anatomy of Child Neglect*, Chicago, University of Chicago Press.

Pollert, A. (1996) 'Gender and class revisited; or, the poverty of "patriarchy"', *Sociology*, **30**(4): 639–59.

Pringle, K. (1992) 'Child sexual abuse perpetrated by welfare personnel and the problem of men', *Critical Social Policy*, **36**: 4–19

Pringle, K. (1995) *Men, Masculinities and Social Welfare*, London, UCL Press.

Pringle, K. (1998a) *Children and Social Welfare in Europe*, Buckingham, Open University Press.

Pringle, K. (1998b) 'Current profeminist debates regarding men and social welfare: some national and transnational perspectives', *British Journal of Social Work*, **28**: 623–33.

Pritchard, M.J. (ed.) (1996) *Neglect: A Fifty Year Search for Answers*, London, The Bridge Child Care Consultancy Service/Islington Area Child Protection Committee.

Reid, W. and Zettergren, P. (1999) 'A perspective on empirical practice' in Shaw, I. and Lishman, J. (eds) *Evaluation and Social Work Practice*, London, Sage.

Rojek, C., Peacock, G. and Collins, S. (1988) *Social Work and Received Ideas*, London, Routledge.

Rose, N. (1987) 'Beyond the public/private division: law, power and the family', *Journal of Law and Society*, **14**(1): 61–76.

Ryan, M. (2000) *Working with Fathers*, Oxford, Radcliffe Medical Press.

Sands, R.G. and Nuccio, K. (1992) 'Postmodern feminist theory and social work', *Social Work*, **37**(6): 489–94.

Schön, D. (1991) *The Reflective Practitioner. How Professionals Think in Action*, Aldershot, Arena.

Scott, D. (1996) 'Parental experiences in cases of child sexual abuse: a qualitative study', *Child and Family Social Work*, **1**(2): 107–14.

Scott, D. (1998) 'A qualitative study of social work assessment in cases of alleged child abuse', *British Journal of Social Work*, **28**: 73–88.

Scott, S. (2001) *The Politics and Experience of Ritual Abuse: Beyond Disbelief*, Buckingham, Open University Press.

Scott, S., Jackson, S. and Backett-Milburn, K. (1998) 'Swings and roundabouts: risk anxiety and the everyday world of children', *Sociology*, **32**(4): 689–705.

Scourfield, J.B. (1998) 'Probation officers working with men', *British Journal of Social Work*, **28**(4): 581–99.

Scourfield, J.B. (1999) The Construction of Gender in Child Protection Social Work, PhD thesis, Cardiff, Cardiff University.

Scourfield, J.B. and Dobash, R.P. (1999) 'Programmes for violent men: recent developments in the UK', *Howard Journal of Criminal Justice*, **38**(2): 128–43.

Secretary of State for Social Services (1988) *Report of the Inquiry into Child Abuse in Cleveland*, London, HMSO.

Shaw, I. (1999) 'Evidence for practice' in Shaw, I. and Lishman, J. (eds) *Evaluation and Social Work Practice*, London, Sage.

Sheppard, M. (1995) 'Social work, social science and practice wisdom', *British Journal of Social Work*, **25**: 265–93.

Shilling, C. (1993) *The Body and Social Theory*, London, Sage.

Sibeon, R. (1990) 'Comments on the structure and forms of social work knowledge', *Social Work and Social Sciences Review*, **1**(1): 29–44.

Silverman, D. (1987) *Communication and Medical Practice*, London, Sage.

Skeggs, B. (1997) *Formations of Class and Gender. Becoming Respectable*, London, Sage.

Stainton Rogers, R. and Stainton Rogers, W. (1992) *Stories of Childhood. Shifting Agendas of Child Concern*, Hemel Hempstead, Harvester Wheatsheaf.

Stanko, E.A. (1990) *Everyday Violence: How Women and Men Experience Sexual and Physical Danger*, London, Pandora.

Stanley, N. (1997) 'Domestic violence and child abuse: developing social work practice', *Child and Family Social Work*, **2**: 135–45.

Stanworth, M. (1983) *Gender and Schooling: A Study of Sexual Divisions in the Classroom*, London, Hutchinson.

Steedman, C. (1982) *The Tidy House. Little Girls Writing*, London, Virago.

Stenson, K. (1993) 'Social work discourse and the social work interview', *Economy and Society*, **22**(1): 42–76.

Stevenson, O. (1998) *Neglected Children: Issue and Dilemmas*, Oxford, Blackwell Science.

Strauss, A. (1987) *Qualitative Analysis for Social Scientists*, Cambridge, Cambridge University Press.

Sullivan, M. (1996) 'Rozzie and Harriet? Gender and family patterns of lesbian co-parents', *Gender and Society*, **10**(6): 747–67.

Swift, K. (1995) *Manufacturing 'Bad Mothers'. A Critical Perspective on Child Neglect*, Toronto, University of Toronto Press.

Thoburn, J., Lewis, A. and Shemmings, D. (1995) *Paternalism or Partnership? Family Involvement in the Child Protection Process*, London, HMSO.

Thomas, N. (2001) Listening to children in Foley, P., Roche, J. and Tucker, S. (eds) *Children in Society: Contemporary Theory, Policy and Practice*, Basingstoke, Palgrave – now Palgrave Macmillan.

Thomas, N. and O'Kane, C. (1999) 'Children's participation in reviews and planning meetings when they are looked after in middle childhood', *Child and Family Social Work*, **4**(3): 221–30.

Thompson, N. (1997) *Anti-discriminatory Practice* (2nd edn) Basingstoke, Macmillan – now Palgrave Macmillan.

Tice, K.W. (1998) *Tales of Wayward Girls and Immoral Women. Case Records and the Professionalization of Social Work*, Chicago, University of Illinois Press.

Turner, B.S. (1996) *The Body and Society* (2nd edn) London, Sage.

Turney, D. (2000) 'The feminisation of neglect', *Child and Family Social Work*, 5(1): 47–56.

Twigg, J. (2000) 'Social policy and the body' in Lewis, G., Gewirtz, S. and Clarke, J. (eds) *Rethinking Social Policy*, London, Sage.

Twigg, J. and Atkin, K. (1994) *Carers Perceived: Policy and Practice in Informal Care*, Milton Keynes, Open University Press.

Waddington, P.A.J. (1999) 'Police (canteen) sub-culture: an appreciation', *British Journal of Criminology*, 39(2): 287–309.

Walby, S. (1989) 'Theorising patriarchy', *Sociology*, 23: 213–24.

Walby, S. (1990) *Theorising Patriarchy*, Oxford, Blackwell.

Walby, S. (1992) 'Post-post-modernism? Theorising social complexity' in Barrett, M. and Phillips, A. (eds) *Destabilizing Theory: Contemporary Feminist Debates*, Cambridge, Polity.

Walby, S. (1997) *Gender Transformations*, London, Routledge.

Waters, M. (1989) 'Patriarchy and viriarchy: an exploration and reconstruction of masculine domination', *Sociology*, 23(2): 193–211.

Watson, S. (2000) 'Foucault and the study of social policy' in Lewis, G., Gewirtz, S. and Clarke, J. (eds) *Rethinking Social Policy*, London, Sage.

Wattam, C. (1992) *Making a Case in Child Protection*, London, NSPCC/Longman.

Wattam, C. (1996) 'The social construction of child abuse for practical policy purposes – a review of Child Protection: Messages from Research', *Child and Family Law Quarterly*, 8(3): 189–200.

Waugh, P. (1998) 'Postmodernism and feminism' in Jackson, S. and Jones, J. (eds) *Contemporary Feminist Theories*, Edinburgh, Edinburgh University Press.

Weedon, C. (1997) *Feminist Practice and Poststructuralist Theory* (2nd edn) Oxford, Blackwell.

Weiner, G. (1994) *Feminisms in Education*, Buckingham, Open University Press.

White, S. (1996) 'Regulating mental health and motherhood in contemporary welfare services: anxious attachments or attachment anxiety?', *Critical Social Policy*, 46: 67–94.

White, S. (1997a) Performing Social Work: An Ethnographic Study of Talk and Text in a Metropolitan Social Services Department, Unpublished PhD, University of Salford.

White, S. (1997b) 'Exercising discursive power: forms of rhetoric and reasoning in social workers' case talk'. Paper presented at British Sociological Association Annual Conference 'Power and Resistance', University of York.

White, S. (1997c) 'Beyond retroduction? Hermeneutics, reflexivity and social work practice', *British Journal of Social Work*, 27(9): 739–53.

White, S. (1998a) 'Interdiscursivity and child welfare: the ascent and durability of psycho-legalism', *Sociological Review*, 46(2): 264–92.

White, S. (1998b) 'From realism to relativism and back (via the body) to pragmatism and common sense: An ethnographer's personal journey'. Paper presented to the British Sociological Association's Annual Conference, 'Making Sense of the Body: Theory, Research and Practice', University of Edinburgh.

White, V. (1995) 'Commonality and diversity in feminist social work', *British Journal of Social Work*, **25**: 143–56.

Williams, F. (1989) *Social Policy. A Critical Introduction*, Cambridge, Polity.

Williams, F. (1998) 'Troubled masculinities in social policy discourses: fatherhood' in Popay, J., Hearn, J. and Edwards, J. (eds) *Men, Gender Divisions and Welfare*, London, Routledge.

Wise, S. (1990) 'Becoming a feminist social worker' in Stanley, L. (ed.) *Feminist Praxis. Research, Theory and Epistemology in Feminist Sociology*, London, Routledge.

Wise, S. (1995) 'Feminist ethics in practice' in Hugman, R. and Smith, D. (eds) *Ethical Issues in Social Work*, London, Routledge.

Witkin, S. (1999) 'Constructing our future', *Social Work*, **44**(1): 5–8.

Witz, A. (1992) *Professions and Patriarchy*, London, Routledge.

Witz, A. and Savage, M. (1992) 'The gender of organisations' in Witz, A. and Savage, M. (eds) *Gender and Bureaucracy*, Oxford, Blackwell.

Wolock, I. and Horowitz, B. (1984) 'Child maltreatment as a social problem: the neglect of neglect', *Journal of Orthopsychiatry*, **54**: 595–602.

Worrall, A. (1990) *Offending Women. Female Law-breakers and the Criminal Justice System*, London, Routledge.

Wyre, R. (1990) *Women, Men and Rape*, Sevenoaks, Headway.

Young, A. (1996) *Imagining Crime*, London, Sage.

Zelizer, V.A. (1985) *Pricing the Priceless Child: the Changing Social Value of Children*, New York: Basic Books.

Index